Our Consul in Havana

Confidential and Classified Documents and Information Gathered by the American Consulate in Havana during the Days of the Cuban Wars of Independence 1868 - 1898

What did they know and How ?

From the Same Author:

Historia de la Química Industrial
Total Quality and Productivity Management
Performance Management
Strategic Planning
Management Development
Process Improvement Teams
Quality Strategies
Gestión de Futuro

Contramaestre
Baraguá
Poemas y Memorias de Cuba
Jimaguayú
Guáimaro
Freedom Embattled
Colonial Cuba
Republican Cuba
Exiled Cuba
Three Days in March
Raíces cubanas
Álbum de Cuba
Rescatando a Martí
Un Festin de Palabras
Damn the Revolution
Madame Secretary
La Gran Estafa
Las Memorias del Almirante Cervera
Matanzas en la Independencia de Cuba
Mis Diarios de Campaña - Máximo Gómez
Our Consul in Havana

COLECCION CUBA Y SUS JUECES

DEDICATION

For all of us
who had to leave Cuba

EDICIONES UNIVERSAL, Miami, Florida 2018

Fitzhugh Lee

MAJOR-GENERAL, U. S. A.

Born November 19th, 1835.

Who, as U. S. Consul-General at Havana, protected American interests in a brave and efficient manner, and was one of the last Americans to leave the City.

Designed and Engraved by
Central Bureau of Engraving, N. Y.

RAUL EDUARDO CHAO

Our Consul in Havana

CONFIDENTIAL AND CLASSIFIED DOCUMENTS
AND INFORMATION GATHERED BY THE AMERICAN
CONSULATE IN HAVANA DURING THE DAYS OF
THE CUBAN WARS OF INDEPENDENCE
1868 - 1898

Copyright © 2018 por **Raúl Eduardo Chao**.

First Edition by:

EDICIONES UNIVERSAL
P.O. Box 450353 (Shenandoah Station)
Miami, FL. 33245-0353. USA
Tel: (305) 642-3234 Fax: (305) 642-7978
email: ediciones@ediciones.com
http://www.ediciones.com
Since 1965

Library of Congress Catalog Card No.: 2018944761
ISBN-10: 1-59388-298-x
ISBN-13: 978-1-59388-298-3

Cover design: Luis García Fresquet

FRONT COVER:

Havana skyline in 1898

BACK COVER:

American military men in the Hispano-Cuban-War of 1898

All rights reserved.
No part of this book can be reproduced
or transmitted in any form or by any electronic
or mechanical means, including photocopiers, recorders
or computer systems, without the written permission
of the author, except in the case of brief citations
incorporated in critical articles or in
journals. For more information, write to
Ediciones Universal

Table of Contents

PREFACE	8
INTRODUCCION	18
IMAGES OF THE WAR OF 95 ENGRAVINGS FROM *LA ILUSTRACION ESPAÑOLA Y AMERICANA* IN THE ISSUES CORRESPONDING TO THE YEARS 1895 TO 1897.	43
CHRONOLOGICAL RECORD OF EVENTS DURING THE 1895 WAR OF CUBAN INDEPENDENCE AND SOME OF THE IMPORTANT THINGS THAT WERE HAPPENING IN THE REST OF THE WORLD FROM 1895 TO 1901	59
CONFIDENTIAL AND CLASSIFIED DOCUMENTS AND INFORMATION GATHERED BY THE AMERICAN CONSULATE IN HAVANA DURING THE DAYS OF THE CUBAN WARS OF INDEPENDENCE 1868 - 1898	80
POSTSCRIPT	328
INDEX	330
MAP OF HAVANA IN 1898	332
MAP OF CUBA IN 1898	333

Preface

AUTONOMY was instituted in Cuba on New Year's Day, 1898. Twelve months later to a day, Spanish sovereignty was surrendered to the United States. The brief existence of this Spanish colonial experiment of Autonomy has not received sufficient study by historians, yet it was the first attempt of Spain in four centuries to give Cuba, her last colony, a system of self-government.

The real inducement of autonomy for Cuba was the memories of the *Ten Year War* (1868-1878). On those years, the machete and the torch tried to obtain what peaceful agitation was not able to accomplish in the island of Cuba. The pact of *El Zanjón,* which brought that insurrection to an end, was agreed to by Spanish General Martínez Campos and Cuban Amy leader Máximo Gómez. It tried to erase, so to speak, the past and bring in solemn pledges for a happy future. It was based on promises to Cuba which would grant to the "*ever faithful island of Cuba*," distinct political rights. Radical changes were to be made in the organic laws and in the administrative system and Cubans were to be recognized as Spanish citizens and to share in the government of the island.

Nothing like that happened over the next 15 years.

On one hand, Spain apparently did carry out in great detail the letter of the pact of *El Zanjón*. The organic laws were changed. The restrictive statutes of printing, of public meetings, and of freedom of association and respect for Cuban institutions and society were modified and liberalized. A supposedly popularly elected basis of Cuban representation in the Cortes was provided, and the electoral law was passed in conformity with that provision. In the administrative system the statute changes were many. They were carried into effect to the extent of a nominal compliance with the new laws. Mediaeval absolutism yielded some of its cherished and hereditary privileges.

On the other hand, neither the spirit nor the letter of the legislation enacted in 1878 and in subsequent years, was real. They were presented as if one of the most prosperous provinces of the kingdom, which had been under a discriminating system of laws and administration, had finally succeeded in getting itself placed on the same plane as all other peninsular provinces. For a colony beyond the seas requiring a definite measure of independence there was no recognition. Any serious study of the statutes and the administrative reforms enacted by the Spanish Government after the peace of *El Zanjón* had arrived to an unquestionable conclusion: a Cuban native (a *criollo*) engaging in political activity after the *Zanjón* had the same chances of being accused under the charge of conspiracy than he would have been before the *Zanjón*; his right to a share in the local administration was an illusion.

A look at the legislation and the decrees of 1878 and subsequent years shows that in essence there was little softening of what had always been the cardinal principle of Spanish colonial approach: there was never other style than a military rule. The paths were sometimes twisted, the passages wound into labyrinths of *cédulas*, decrees, orders, edicts, circulars, and *bandos*. But in the end, they brought up the same result: from day one, the Governor General of Cuba had to exercise his military functions as Captain-General, and his success depended on keeping peace in the territory, at whatever cost. After 1878, Cuba had good, bad, and mediocre Captain-Generals. The educated and wealthy Cubans who for years organized themselves into political parties and urged administrative and economic changes upon Madrid, always reached the conclusion that no effort would find understanding among Spanish statesmen. Sooner or later, when their petitions were rejected in their entirety, they were compelled to cease asking favors. They first started the *Ten Year War*. After its failure they had to try once more with the insurrection of 1895. It was to be the last act in the uprising which began in 1868. The in between had simply been an interregnum, nothing more. Armed revolt was bound to resume.

It was known in the United States, in the winter months of 1894-95, that something was going to happen in Cuba. The Spanish authorities in the island were both blind and impotent. They knew that something was going on, yet they did not know where to look for the uprising. One day a small party of insurgents raised the banner of revolt at the hamlet of Ibarra, within the municipality of Unión de Reyes in Matanzas province. Four hundred miles away in the Villages of Baire and Jiguaní, in the province of Santiago de Cuba, small uprisings also were noted. At Baire the peaceable demand was made for the implantation of reforms. At Jiguaní the demand was for the removal of the local *ayuntamiento*, or municipal council, because of some alleged malfeasance. At Guantánamo there was an open revolt without a stated grievance. The movement at Ibarra was premature. The little band of insurgents was quickly dispersed. Some of the leaders were arrested and deported in chains to the penal settlements of Africa, among them a mulatto publicist by the name of Juan Gualberto Gómez. Small risings in the province of Santa Clara were also dispersed. But the alarm bell had been sounded and it was difficult to unring it. It was to chime through the next months and years. The night of February 23rd, 1895, the printing presses in Habana were kept whirling with the proclamation of the Governor General, Emilio Calleja, suspending the constitutional guarantees. This was followed by the official announcement that the provinces of Matanzas and Santiago de Cuba were in a state of war. Then, it was disclosed the existence of the *Cuban Revolutionary Party* with headquarters and branches in the United States, and with a net extended throughout the island. The island became cluttered with agencies of secret police. New York became a city inundated with Pinkerton cops in the service of Spain. All engaged in the business of discovering and apprehending the agents of a gigantic political conspiracy. The United States, with hundreds of its citizens living in Cuba and sizable investments in its economy could not remain disengaged. It sent to the island about one hundred quiet observers under the authority of a Consul that would reside in Havana.

What was happening in Cuba was not difficult to report. José Martí, dreamer, poet, and idealist, had visited Máximo Gómez in his retirement in Santo Domingo, and on behalf of the Cuban revolutionary societies had offered him the command of an insurgent army that was to come up from the *criollos* of Cuba and the exiles in the United States. Gómez gladly accepted the command. Antonio Maceo had also been recruited and was ready to help. The sympathizers in Cuba had been secreting arms, and were awaiting the call. Bartolomé Masó, a sugar planter in Manzanillo, who had been an insurgent colonel in the Ten Years War, was quickly in the field with armed followers. He had the respect of the Cubans and of the Spanish. Though he had been friendly to the Autonomist propaganda, he had refused to accept the presidency of the party, yet he was said to have taken up arms in order to compel Spain to yield autonomy without necessarily granting absolute independence. Minor engagements began to take place in Oriente, as Eastern Cuba was called, and within a month the insurrection was in full movement. Spain was sending troops across the ocean, and the leading Spaniards in Habana were calling for more vigorous action by the Government. The *criollos* were claiming responsibility for the insurrection, which meant independence. It was the outgrowth, as they had warned the loyal classes, of the insensate dreams and doctrines of the autonomists.

On July 13th was fought the first real battle of this War of 1895. It was at *Peralejo*, near Bayamo. Maceo and Jesus Rabí were known to be contemplating an attack on the Spanish garrison which occupied the city of Bayamo. The columns under Martínez Campos were advancing from Manzanillo. The Spanish troops, according to the statement of the officers, thought the insurgents under Maceo had no more than 200 men. The Spaniards afterwards said, claimed they had between 1,000 and 1,500. The Cubans descended upon advancing Spanish columns of equal number, attacking them in front and in the rear. General Juan Fidel Santocildes, a distinguished officer and a devoted friend of Campos, was killed at the head of his column. Many other officers were killed and wounded. General Campos himself narrowly escaped death. Maceo, by a strategic movement, turning his rear guard into a vanguard and changing the course, finally succeeding in leading his troops into Bayamo.

The laurels of the engagement were with both Maceo and Gómez and the insurgent cause gained prestige. General Campos, after strengthening the fortifications of Bayamo and increasing the garrison, succeeded in clearing the country in the immediate neighborhood of the insurgents, who confined their activity to the northern part of the province. He then returned to Manzanillo. Gómez made his conclusions and said in his address to the Cuban people that... «*Spain would never yield the island while it was worth possessing.*» He spent the next few years showing his troops how the island might be rendered "*not worth possessing.*"

From there on, nightly, the skies of Cuba were lit up by the blazing fires in cane fields everywhere. Tall columns of smoke in the center of wide, scorched plains were all that was left of the great sugar Centrales and sugar lands. Blackened walls were all that remained of country villas. In the villages and towns, ruins were all that remained of fine residences and substantial buildings. The destruction was not wanton. The insurgents never rioted. The devastation was in pursuance of Gómez' campaign against property. They did not seek to take human lives. They released Spanish prisoners when captured, and in their successful marches they were always merciful to the small garrisons that were reduced to rubble. In regular fighting they would have been over matched and in time their small numbers would have been exterminated. So they applied the most advanced principles of modern warfare by systematic and remorseless destruction of property. It was also said that one purpose of Gómez was to force the plantation workers to join the insurrection by taking away their means of livelihood. Such a course was not necessary. The plantation hands flocked to the insurrection voluntarily, almost spontaneously. Later General Weyler was also to inaugurate a campaign of property destruction and to dispute the mastery of the scorched and barren wastes with Gómez. But in the beginning it was the insurgents under Gómez and Maceo who made a trail of fire from Villa Clara to Pinar del Rio.

Martial law was proclaimed in the provinces of Habana and Pinar del Rio as a tardy New Year's greeting on January 2nd, 1896. The whole island was therefore officially recognized as in a state of siege. The military operations of the Spanish troops in the western regions were paralyzed. The vanguard of Gómez advanced to Marianao, within ten miles of Habana. The insurgents occupied Punta Brava, Hoyo Colorado, and other towns in the vicinity. Cane fields were burned, railroad stations destroyed, trains set on fire, tracks torn up, and bridges dynamited. The railroads running out of the cities ceased to operate. Havana was quavering and in turmoil. Though Spanish troops had been disembarking by tens of thousands, they felt themselves defenseless. Though its fortifications and defenses, properly garrisoned, could hold out, as was later boasted, against an invading army of American soldiers, the community recoiled before a few thousand poorly armed insurgents. Panic stalked its streets. The military authorities were overwhelmed with the pleas to protect the city and its people.

Havana had passed through the Ten Year War without hearing the echo of a musket discharge from the insurgents in Oriente. This was now different. The Spanish authorities decided to alert people by a cannon signal. It recalled the measures against English attacks one hundred and thirty-four years earlier. Gómez knew where to stop his demonstrations of power. He never had the purpose of entering Havana within the garrisoned outposts of the city. Yet he did enter the town of Bejucal, only fifteen miles south, burned many of its buildings, and spread terror to the great city northward. Two or three days later in Bejucal again he successfully combated and evaded the Spanish troops under Generals Linares and Suárez Valdés. Maceo and Gómez had divided their followers in pursuance of very specific plans. Maceo was pushing on to the west, not seeking but rather avoiding the Spanish troops at some places, and at others carefully falling upon them. Gómez, in the meantime, was terrorizing Habana; Maceo, on his own, entered the province of Pinar del Rio. He had a sharp skirmish at the town of Guanajay, near the north coast, with the Spanish troops under General Prats. He roamed freely through the rich tobacco regions of the Vuelta Abajo as he had done in the sugar lands of Santa Clara and Matanzas. Constantly the insurgent forces were augmented by small parties of recruits. Never before had Pinar del Rio been in either secret or open rebellion. Now it blazed with revolt. Maceo carried his standard to the extreme western end of the island. During the last week of January he entered the provincial capital town of Pinar del Rio and held it for a few hours. The following day he fought a pitched battle on the adjacent hills of *Taironas*, in which, notwithstanding the Spanish accounts in the Madrid papers, he could claim a victory. Maceo then turned and led his forces towards the eastern end of the province. On the 6th of February he attacked the railroad town of *Candelaria* and besieged it for twenty-six hours.

The glory of the full execution of the western invasion fell on Maceo, yet its conception was by the graying chief of two insurrections. Gómez planned it. The success of his plans nationalized the insurrection and broke the military power of Spain in Cuba.

The treatment of American citizens by the Spanish was obviously a concern of the US government. That was something else. Madrid treated Americans with a high hand until an untoward event brought this to a climax. General Fitzhugh Lee, of Virginia, as we already said, was selected by President Cleveland for the delicate position of Consul General in Havana. One avowed purpose in his selection was to enable the administration to have the benefit of the presence of an experienced military observer. It was publicly stated that he was only to report on the military situation, but in time it became known that he credited the insurgents with moral values that were not of the liking of Spanish authorities in Cuba. The General's reports often included a reiterated statement that Spain was making no real progress in subduing the insurrection. The themes of these communications were probably well known to Madrid and to the Spanish authorities in Habana.

General Blanco arrived from Madrid in the early days of November of 1895. His welcome was not warm and affectionate.

The partisans of Weyler, the Spanish classes, were angry. The autonomists were waiting further information before committing themselves to the new administration. They were now a very small group, but were very respectable. The mass of the Cuban *criollos* were distrustful or indifferent. The community had no faith. When not critical it was cynical. The public was bored. The *Diario de la Marina* reported that the presence in Havana of the celebrated bull-fighter Mazzantini, excited greater popular interest than the promise of autonomy.

When Spain first proposed an autonomous regime for Cuba, Gómez, Calixto García, and the other insurgent commanders made known positively that their demand for independence was unwavering and they would not consider autonomy. The insurgent army would not permit autonomy to be even discussed. It was held that to propose it was a violation of the Cuban constitution and merited the quick execution of the proponent. The Spanish authorities then began a campaign of bribery and persuasion. They were very persistent in seeking to disintegrate the insurrection at any cost. Every inducement was offered to the Cubans in arms to surrender. The list of *presentados* began to be followed with interest. But those in arms who presented themselves were unpromisingly few. The insurgents in the field simply began to allow and authorize the presentations of their sick. This enabled the men that could no longer fight for Cuban independence to die among friends and relatives rather than in the *manigua*. Only a few chiefs presented themselves; very few were above the rank of Colonel. Most of them were Cuban army men who had been deprived of their command or degraded by Gómez, and their voluntary presentation was an act of revenge. Very few *mambises* were tired and weary of the long struggle and decided to accept the promises of the Spanish Government.

All of Spain's proselytism to secure the adhesion of insurgents was made by paid messengers and emissaries, not by official envoys. Often they were relatives who were forced to undertake the mission under dreadful threats. Gómez often said that the reason Spain was willing to continue defending Cuba was "*nothing but the result of Castilian pride, an almost insuperable obstacle.*" In fact, from 1895 to 1898, no peace conference was ever asked, no truce was ever proposed to discuss the proposition of autonomy, and no willingness to talk was ever shown. Instead, the Spanish Army reduced itself to secret messengers, even when these emissaries were executed by the insurgents.

The Spanish government was at a loss in every respect during those years. The popular newspaper *La Discusión*, for instance, had been suppressed because of its insurgent leanings and denounced as an organ of radical autonomist tendencies. When the censorship ended the paper reappeared and as soon as it did, it began to call attention to gross abuses of the army and to demand their reform. Other papers of less character began to be sensational and personal in their criticisms of the government. One night a group of *Voluntarios* got drunk in a café and did not leave till after midnight. In the early hours of the morning they went in uniform to the office of *La Discusión* and wrecked it. Then they proceeded to the office of other papers and began to demolish them. The office of *The New York Journal* was on the Prado Avenue, opposite to Central Park, in the very heart of Havana. The *Voluntarios* completely wrecked it.

The rioting was never directed against Americans, but there were many concerns and natural fear among the citizens of the US. Under those conditions, the US decided to look more carefully at the situation in Cuba, particularly after Spain began to call for more recruits and fresh troops began to come by the thousands to Cuba.

It might be said that the last chapter of autonomy was written when the *Maine* was blown up, But there was an epilogue. Elections were held after an electoral census had been taken. Not many people showed up to deposit a ballot, and the authorities had to "*arrange*" the election results.

In the meantime, the eyes, intellect and ears of the United States were centered on the stout and robust head of Mr. Fitzhugh Lee, *Our Consul in Havana*. Working with Mr. Lee were US trained reporters that read daily all the papers published in every town in Cuba, roving correspondents that frequently visited places where both Spanish and Cuban troops were actively seeking each other, several employees in the staff of Captain General's commanding centers in Havana, as well as military observers with the troops led by Antonio Maceo, Máximo Gómez and Calixto García. No one was better informed about the 1895 war in Cuba that this old Confederate cavalry general who had seen his first actions at the *Battle of Bull Run* in 1861.

You cannot really understand what went on in Cuba from 1895 to 1898 unless you know what crossed the eye and the mind of Fitzhugh Lee. He had an encyclopedic memory, a 20/20 vision, instant recall, a huge mental archive, the best contacts, the most perfectly well trained and best nose and insight, and the fastest gun in the west.

On the left, **Fitzhugh Lee** as a Lieutenant of Cavalry during the *First Battle of Manasas* on July 21, 1861 in Prince William County, Virginia.

On the right, **Fitzhugh Lee** at the time of the inaugural parade of President Grover Cleveland in 1893. In April of 1896 he was to be appointed as US Consul in Havana. By 1898 he had reentered the US Army.

INTRODUCTION

WILLIAM HENRY FITZHUGH LEE (Arlington, Virginia, 1837-Alexandria 1905), the American Consul-General to Cuba in April of 1896, was often seeing on the streets of Havana in the spring of 1897. He had been appointed by President Cleveland the year before; trying to be undetected, he roamed the city's bars dressed as a gentleman farmer in white suits that stretched around his abundant personal profile. He always wore a Panamá hat topping his spherical head, and most always strapped a pistol on the left side his ample waist, no doubt ensuring a level security that every man had to muster if they were unable to speak Spanish with a Cuban accent.

A West Point graduate, Lee was remembered more for his sense of humor, his horsemanship, and for the respect commanded by a well known nephew of Confederate general Robert E. Lee. As far as we know, no one ever remember him for his scholarly ability; he graduated near the bottom of his class. The Havana of the times did not pose much of an intellectual challenge to American officers. In fact, Lee found plenty of time for private business ventures on the capital of the last Spanish colony in America. He intensely pursued many other interests other than those of the American government, most notably looking for investors to launch a streetcar line in Havana. It became his business obsession and a well cherished dream.

William Henry Fitzhugh Lee

He attempted to curry favors among high profile political appointees in the McKinley administration; he had moderate success, given his rather cumbersome, burdensome and heavy-handed approach to dealing with people. In one message to Washington after his McKinley's confirmation as Consul in Havana, he tried colloquially to assure Mr. President that he was trustworthy, insisting that he could be absolutely reliable and depended upon and that he was not prone to hasty decisions of any kind..

«*Mr. President,*» he wrote, «*I never get keyed up or befuddled.*»

The note was not well received in the falsely sophisticated hall of Washington, D.C.

US President **William McKinley**

Yet this flamboyant rogue -trying to play at diplomat- had an extraordinary good ear and has reasoned a profound analysis of the situation in Cuba. The President's staff had reached the conclusion that, for the most part, the striving Mr. Lee had been and currently, in 1896, was dead-right on the situation in Cuba. The uprising launched when José Martí and Máximo Gómez landed their small boat on a Cuban beach in 1895, he wrote in a memo to Mr. McKinley, was spinning out of control. Non-combatant civilians were dying by the hundreds in Oriente province and American businessmen, as well as their financial interests on the island, were getting caught in the cross fire.

Cuba in 1896 was simply an island of barely 1.5 million people; as it was, it became virtually all that remained of Spain's once magnificent empire in the Americas. Rich in exotic woods, cattle and agricultural assets -it was the world's largest producer of sugar- the four-hundred-year-old «*always faithful island of Cuba,*» was a passionate possession in the hearts of all Spaniards. Cuba was, for the Spanish masses in the peninsula and in the island, the last but also the best part of an empire that constituted a reward from God; they could never forget that the landing of Cristobal Colón in Cuba, as legend had it, was a prize granted by God himself for liberating the Iberian Peninsula from Islam in the fifteenth century.

> «Cuba, as it was written by the best poets, theologians and even the non-believers in Spain, -was the velvety best of the fabric of Spain; it was an integral part of its history, its glory, and the grandeur of Spain.»

Yet this idea of Cuba as an «*ever faithful isle*» did not very well fit with reality. As recently as 1868-1878, Cuban patriots seeking independence had battled the Spanish before ending with surrender to exhaustion and promises of reforms. Convinced that Spain had never delivered on its pledges, they were trying again in 1880 and 1895. Rebel military leader Máximo Gómez y Báez, employed a strategy to destroy Cuba's economy to the point that the Spanish wouldn't want it. By turning Cuba into an *«an economic catastrophe, a financial desert,»* Gómez figured he could both bleed the Spanish of the resources to prosecute the war and raise doubts about whether it was worth the effort. His battalions, a volunteer's group of 30,000 or so machete-wielding and Springfield firing peasants, crisscrossed a hundred times the island laying waste to anything of value, houses, factories, burning cane fields and sugar mills, dynamiting railroad roads and trestles, decimating cattle herds, burning towns and cutting telegraph wires. He dictated that all sugar plantations, the backbone of the Spanish colonial economy, had to be leveled and the men who worked on them given the choice of joining the Cuban army or be shot as traitors. Harsh though his tactics were, Máximo Gómez succeeded in his most important objectives. Sugar production plunged and, with it, all of Cuba's economic fortunes. In 1894, the value of the sugar crop had commanded at least $62.1 million. In 1895, the first year of the uprising, it declined to $45.4

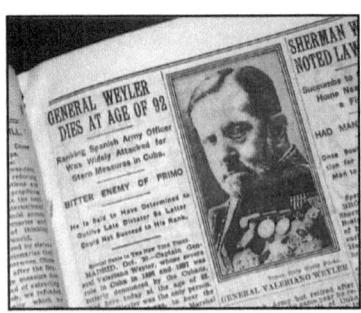

General Valeriano Weyler

million, and in 1896 it plunged to $13 million. There were no prospects for this to be reversed as long as the old man from the Dominican Republic was in charge.

The Spanish Crown, Lee noted with some trepidation, responded to the rebellion in February 1896 by assigning its most ruthless commander to the island: Valeriano Weyler Nicolau, a Spaniard of German ancestry. He was a soldier's soldier who didn't fuss much about his looks, his petit size, his high toned talk, his weakling appearance; he was a novel trait among the peacocks of the Spanish officer corps. He slept in a hammock on campaigns and ate enlisted men's rations of bread, sardines, and red wine. Refusing to smoke or drink liquor, he never participated in celebrations, seldom smiled, never entertained anyone with light talk, and always looked fit and youthful, with short hair, muttonchops, a mustache and little short arms.

The Spanish Royal Family, **King Alfonso XIII** with his mother (Regent María Cristina) and his sisters in 1897.

But it was Weyler's cold heart that early and forever made him famous. A veteran of Madrid's colonial wars, he had earned a fearsome reputation as *"el carnicero,"* the butcher, for his ruthless disregard for human life. In an article that appeared on February 23, 1896, *The New York Journal* reached deep into its sack of wicked adjectives to describe him as a...

> «*...fiendish despot*» who was «*pitiless and a brute, as well as an exterminator of men, women and children as if they were cockroaches.*»

A history professor at *New York University* wrote on *The New York Times:*

> «*There was nothing to prevent his carnal, beast-like brain from running riot with itself in inventing tortures and infamies*

of bloody debauchery.»

Weyler didn't disappoint his military mentors, the Crown or the Havana Spanish Volunteers when he revealed his strategy for crushing the rebellion. Recognizing that he couldn't keep up with the rebels' hit-and-run strategies, he decided to cut off their network of support among the peasants. In a massive relocation program infamously known as *La Reconcentración*, Weyler swept the countryside of every man, woman, and child his troops could find, relocating some four hundred to six hundred thousand people to encampments where they could be watched. It was the start of the infamous *Concentration Camps* that, many years later, Nazis would made infamous during World War II.

Without jobs, with very little to eat, and in some cases without a place to sleep, the uprooted "*guajiros*" (peasants) were plunged into a hellish existence of deprivation and cruelty by Weyler and his troops. Emaciated and sick, thousands wandered the dirty cobblestone streets of Cuban cities begging for scraps and fighting over morsels of food like animals, their children's stomachs bloated from bacteria, worms and malnutrition, their teenage daughters offering glances, sometimes furtive, sometimes odious at Spanish soldiers, hoping to have a final opportunity to malign them or to earn some quick money for their families.

Weyler's soldiers gathering **reconcentrados** in 1895 Cuba

Those "*guajiros*" who hid in the countryside, a much larger number than those who found their fate in the towns and cities, met an even shoddier fate. Spanish scouts patrolled the arid, rocky hills, poisoning water supplies and shipping off anyone they found illegally living outside the camps to a notorious penal colony at Ceuta in Africa. Estimates of the death toll vary widely, but even by conservative accounts, the carnage

Joseph Pulitzer's **New York World**

was horrific -most scholars have estimated that around four hundred thousand had died by 1898.

The remorseless and merciless Weyler dismissed their plight as «*the price of doing business.*» With a smiling face he told a New York reporter:

«*How do they want me to wage war?; with bishops, pastorals and presents of sweeties and baby candies?*»

Trapped between the rebels and the Spanish army, Cuban peasants didn't stand a chance. «*On the whole,*» said a Mr. Truffin, the Russian Consul in Havana,

«*it looks as if the two sides, equally aloof from the desire to make concessions, have sworn to lay waste to each other at the expense of this unfortunate country.*»

The rebellion would normally have been of little significance to most people in the continent, including Americans. Colonial wars had been waged for decades all over the globe with non-involved people taking little notice. Yet this uprising offered a fascinating concoction of political systems, economic theory, and even religion.

William Hearst's **New York Journal**

Equally important, people from New York and Washington to Key West could track its ghastly developments almost daily from their breakfast tables. It just so happened that the two greatest newspaper moguls of the times had decided to use Cuba as their battleground for sales, popularity, advertisements and media supremacy. They became known as the yellow journalists. William Randolph Hearst and Joseph Pulitzer: their own inventive reporters could not have scripted a more compelling pair of rivals. For starters, the two came from opposite ends of the economic spectrum. Hearst, the son of a salty California millionaire and U.S. senator, had been given the struggling *San Francisco Chronicle* almost as a new and unusual plaything, a venture to run for himself, since his father had no time and couldn't figure out what to do with a newspaper, much less what to with it daily. The young Hearst quickly displayed an ability for publishing and within months rescued the paper and began to enjoy a fresh challenge; he headed east in 1895 with a fat check from his mommy and a smoldering ambition to make himself the eastern shore most influential and richest newspaper publisher. He could not settle for less than a true tycoon. A year later, he purchased the almost defunct *New York Morning Journal* and hired star reporters such as Stephen Crane and Julian Hawthorne to boost circulation. He never returned to the West Coast and lived in New York like a popular and much sought media mogul.

Joseph **Pulitzer** (left) and William Randolph **Hearst** (right)

Pulitzer, on the other hand, was a self-made man, the archetypal American success story. A destitute Hungarian adventurer. He showed up in New York happy for the opportunity to ear $500 fighting in the Union Army. By mere chance, he took a chance trying to make it as a reporter on a German-language newspaper if he moved to St. Louis. In a few years he returned to the Iron Babel and climbed to the upper strata of American media as publisher of *The New York World*, even though he almost never set foot in the newsroom, suffering from near blindness and a hypersensitivity to dust, ink, cellulose and any sort of noise.

But, aside from their child and young years, Hearst and Pulitzer had much in common. Both welcomed any and many fights with bare-knuckled street gangsters; both were determined -no, more than that, obsessed- to give the people what they wanted, scandal, gossip, titillation, hearsay and

> "the kind of journalism that never let the facts and simple truth get in the way of a good story."

The unfolding events in Cuba in the mid 1890s provided all the inspiration they needed to promote their papers. To this day, students at Columbia's Journalism School snicker at one oft-repeated but unconfirmed barter between Hearst and then famous artist Frederic Remington: the master draftsman telegrammed his boss from Havana to tell him all was quiet on the island and «*there is no war here.*» Hearst supposedly replied,

> «Never mind; please remain there. You send me the facts and your drawings and I'll provide the war.»

From there on, the reporters and artists of Hearst's *Journal* - and by the way, also Pulitzer's *World*- would embellished every unimportant nugget of a story and turn it into a fascinating account that was sure to make it on the front page.

Pulitzer, for instance, began to pay attention to the Cuban Army female combatants; they became a godsend gift, providing an excuse to combine sex and violence in page-turning tales. They were his

> «... beautiful Amazons, unafraid to charge with Remington rifles, sticks and even machetes, at great speed, high on their horses against "pelandrines" in the Spanish troops.»

Pulitzer and his journalists -as well as Hearst- let their imaginations and the hyperbole run amok. *The World*, in particular, officially asked their journalists to

> «... if necessary, engage in as many episodes as possible of mass assault against non-eventual truths... act as single individuals engaged in a period of creative observation, if need be with exaggeration, to the point that could be increasingly viewed by others as psychopathological behavior...»

Following these directions, *The World* reported on April 5, 1896:

> «Nothing more dreadful has ever been conceived by mortal man than the behavior of the women who fight in Cuba. Most of them are beautiful, judged by ordinary standards....In battle they show no mercy; they slash, hack, hew with their machetes, and

scream and shout in such a way as to alarm any male opponents, and yet, when the fight is over, they are as tender to their foes as to their friends.»

That so many Cubans and Americans felt strongly about Cuba was hardly a surprise when seen through the prism of history and opportunity. Presidents, businessmen and even the religious men and women had long fantasized about bringing Cuba into the Union, casting a desirous eye towards the star of the Caribbean as early as the 1820s. Thomas Jefferson wrote in 1823:

«I have always looked on Cuba as the most interesting addition which could ever be made to our system of states,»

John Quincy Adams chimed in that it was...

«... scarcely possible to resist the conviction that the annexation of Cuba ... will be indispensable to the continuance and integrity of the Union itself.»

President Polk even tried to buy Cuba for $100 million in 1848, an offer rejected by a Spanish minister, who said

«I'd rather see the island sink than sell it.»

It was under those circumstances that Fitzhugh Lee landed with his mission in Havana. On one hand, were it up to the US Congress, Cubans could have done everything they wanted long ago. Any politician with even the faintest measure of the public's pulse could see that American sympathy for the insurgents was widely and deeply felt. With an enthusiasm not often associated with legislators, both Houses of Congress produced torrents of resolutions expressing support for the insurgents, calling for the US to grant them belligerent status first and then supporting with all their resources, including the military, their struggle for independence from Spain.

US President **Grover Cleveland**.

On the other hand, Cubans needed the support of President Cleveland, and his assistance was proving very harder to obtain. He had never been convinced that the Cuban revolutionaries were ready to govern. He though that deep down Cubans in the *manigua* were just a fanatical group composed of former black slaves and some uncomplicated peasant stock, and not the supposed movement of urbane patriots whose public image was falsely created by Hearst and Pulitzer. Far from being similar to members of America's Continental Army, to which they were often compared, soldiers of the rebellious forces in Cuba were not the type to carefully read a newspaper's political section or debate the issues at the local bar or town hall. Nor were they well organized. The insurgents had written a Constitution and referred to their elected leaders as a *Junta Patriótica*, but did not possess enough power to occupy so much as a single building in a meager town. It was unclear if the Cuban Army at War was in tune with the movement's political leaders. Fitzhugh Lee was convinced that the single voice of military leader Máximo Gómez, which was not even Cuban-born, dominated the cause of the *insurrectos*. He knew Gómez did not have to check with anyone his statements, his commands to the army, the locations to attack, or any other aspect of *"his"* War of Independence.

If the Cubans prevailed over Spain, Cleveland believed, their victory would bring chaos to Cuba and possibly create a power vacuum that a European nation such as Germany would eagerly fill, Monroe doctrine or not. Cleveland had made up his mind:

«as long as he was in the White House, all the congressional resolutions in the world were completely useless. The US would not help create a hornet's nest as a few miles from its shores.»

Then McKinley replaced Cleveland at the US presidency and the rules of the game changed drastically. As he assumed his tenure at the White House, unexpected swirls of public opinion, the decades old history of American wishes to expand into the Caribbean, and national security concerns began to make McKinley's head spin. To him, Cuba had nothing to offer but risks, with little prospects of returns. Quietly, he began to hope the whole Cuban thing would somehow magically disappear. On March 3, 1897, the night before his inauguration as the 25th President of the United States, William McKinley met with soon-to-be ex-President Cleveland; McKinley confided that he felt conflicted over whether Americans were duty-bound to intervene in the revolution that was gaining strength in Cuba. Cleveland later said:

> «He feared the horrors of war, and was intensely saddened by the prospective episode of loss of life, destruction of property, and the blows dealt at the higher morality and the terrible responsibility thrust upon him,»

Preparing to leave, the two shook hands and McKinley added,

> «Mr. President, if I can go out of office, at the end of my term, with the knowledge that I have done what lay in my power to avert this terrible calamity ... I shall be the happiest man in the world.»

For McKinley, there was more than an element of truth his dreams of professional bliss.

McKinley's Oath of Office, March 4, 1897; **Pres. Cleveland** second from right.

McKinley was essentially a good man, not prone to be alarmed or rushed to his daily duties. Each day, he found time to read a tower of newspapers that might include five or six of the New York dailies, a couple of the Washington and Chicago papers, and half a dozen from other cities, all in addition to regularly reading the *Canton Repository* from his home-town. After lunch, he would sometimes pause to cheer as the office staff played baseball on the south lawn. A pet parrot provided a musical accompaniment to his days when the two would take turns whistling *"Yankee Doodle Dandy."* Evenings were usually quiet affairs, spent at home with his wife Ida or a small gathering of close friends. Weather permitting, he often slipped out for a stroll down Pennsylvania or Connecticut avenues. By today's standards, these sojourns were unthinkably casual affairs. The leader of the nation would simply pack up a newspaper, pull on his dark frock coat, and stride out the front door of the executive mansion in his quick-paced, erect manner, nosing at store windows for gifts for Ida, and, if he wandered too far from home, taking a streetcar back. Other times McKinley would ride in a carriage with Ida or some White House guests and explore Washington; his favorite routes being the "Soldiers' Home" ground, the National Park, and Arlington. Children quickly learned his habits and would wait on the sidewalk, shouting *"Hello, Mr. President!"* as he passed. He would happily respond with a friendly wave, *"How do you do, guys?"* or *"How do you do, girls?"* Workmen would remove their caps.

Edna Wallace, the singer who popularized **Yankee Doodle** in 1895

One facet of McKinley's presidential life was the fact that he left the White House largely unattended, and maintenance under budgeted. Trampled under the feet of an unchecked multitude of visitors, including curious folks who simply wandered in off the street, the carpets were worn and frayed along the edge. Cracked paint was all over, specially on the ceilings. Wallpaper hung tattered. Stair banisters were more ornament than safety devices. Floors were so weak and noisy that even during small parties, employees had to rush to the basement to affix and support some deafening beams and bricks. Both the structure and the layout were in desperate need of repairs. The state dining room was so small that tables had to be set up in the halls. A slightly more than usual amount of food if there was a party had to be prepared

The Office of the Chief of Staff of the **White House** in 1895

in the basement, inevitably arriving cold to the tables. Velour curtains at sixty cents a yard were hung in the entrance hall to hide an acquired collection of secondhand racks and boxes to store visitor's things. McKinley found out that the White House budget was so small that he had to pay the salaries for some of his staff out of his own pocket, including forty dollars a month for a decent cook.

Under those conditions, McKinley could not escape the demands that Cuba was exerting on his mind and humor during his entire presidency. Incessantly, new problems about Cuba were closing in upon him; one of the most bothersome was the predicaments of American business on the island of Cuba. In May 1897, some three hundred prominent American bankers, merchants, manufacturers, steamships owners and many others who did business in or out of Cuba signed and sent him a letter pleading for his help. The group believed the Cuban revolution had already "*seriously injured*" their businesses, which were "*more and more threatened with total annihilation.*" It was true that Americans invested in Cuba never reached the top of the lists of America's businessmen, they were not even a worthy number in importance. But America's president, in "*the age of prosperity*" could not nonchalantly take the worries of American businessmen anywhere.

Yet there was more than a dire need to have the Consul in Havana keep track of a lot of Cubans, Cuban insurgents and American investors in Cuba, past and future. It was said that over 100 agents kept Fitzhugh Lee -as well as other American Consuls in Matanzas, Santiago and other Cuban cities- informed about the whereabouts of all units of Cuban insurgents and kept their ears close to Spain's Captain General from in-

US Consul in Havana from 1874 to 1894 (on and off)
Ramón O. Williams

side his own offices. It was also generally believe in Washington that some of Lee's informants came from the ranks of the insurgents, including the staff of Máximo Gómez himself. It was even speculated that Gómez knew that and only kept for himself and his close associates the most delicate of his strategies and plans.

When it came to American businesses, Cuba had, in fact, for years been a popular destination for American companies. A New York-based firm ran the largest sugar property in the world in Cuba, the sixty-thousand-acre *Constancia Plantation*. An American company printed most of the money used on the island, and quite a few cork companies and tobacco plantations operated under American control. The *Bethlehem Steel Corporation* had established the *Juragua Iron Company, Ltd.*, and the *Ponupo Manganese Company* near Santiago. Three American iron and manganese companies claimed to have investments totaling $6 million of purely American capital. As early as 1882, one of Lee's predecessors, US Havana Consul Ramón O. Williams [1] was able to write:

William J. Calhoun

«*De facto, Cuba is already inside the commercial union of the United States.*»

The petitioners did not know exactly what was the president supposed to do and would only ask that he seek an «*honorable reconciliation between the parties in conflict.*» As much as they worried about their Cuban investments and longed for new markets, the specter of war was something that none could bring themselves to contemplate.

---

[1] On the breaking out of the Cuban insurrection in 1895, Mr. Williams had to defend, under the treaties between the two governments, many Cubans who had obtained naturalization papers in the United States and had taken part in the insurrection, and having, in consequence, been considered *persona non grata* by the Captain-General of Cuba (Callejas), and the Madrid government, and also for reasons of self-respect, he obtained a leave of absence to go to Washington, where he signified his intention to President Cleveland to resign at once. But he returned to Havana, at the request of the President, for a short time, intending to forward his resignation from there.

Constancia Plantation, largest sugar property in the world in 1894. Sixty thousand acres, property of an American investment syndicate. It was located 12 miles NW from Cienfuegos, Cuba.

From the well-padded seats of their carriages to the snooty elegance of their clubs, industrialists sang the chorus in almost perfect harmony.

The last thing American balance sheets needed was for their country to be exchanging cannon fire with a European power. Not now, not as US prosperity was just starting to return. In 1897, sales of everything from buggy whips to Cracker Jack snacks began to rebound from the depths of the depression that had begun four years before. The terrible bout of deflation that had so ravaged farmers was subsiding. After three years of waiting and of false starts, the groundswell of business had at last begun to rise with a steadiness which left little doubt that an era of prosperity was around the corner. McKinley, as he had promised from his front porch, was delivering prosperity to an extent that had everyone lost for words. Under those conditions, a military showdown with Spain threatened everything. War would rattle consumer confidence, which was so important to boosting demand. Foreign trade might be disrupted. Corporate investment could be shelved. The recession could come back. McKinley was far from being just seated in the chair where he conducted most of his work, at the head of the polished, heavy table in the cabinet room adjoining his office, squirming over the Cuban dilemma that taunted him.

Studying newspapers for hours on end, he studied in detail the sharply incompatible New York editorials on what he should do about Cuba. Drawing long breaths from his ever present cigar, filling the room with its pungent smoke, he would listen intently as quite a few visitors from Cuba pleaded for his help in dealing with the insurgents. Every now and then, quite irritated, he would arise from his seat and walk across the Oriental carpet to spin the large globe in the corner of his office, stopping it when his fingers found the small outline of this beautiful island just off Florida. Always deliberate, always careful, always cautious, McKinley finally decided he needed more information that he was getting from the 100 men working for his Consul Fitzhugh Lee, whom, by the way, he hardly knew in person. Somebody he trusted had to go to Cuba to corroborate Lee's firsthand accounts of the events in that island that seemed so perilous to the United States. He knew two such men. William J. Calhoun and Charles G. Dawes; they spent four weeks that spring traveling throughout the island conducting interviews, studying the land, furiously taking notes, and apparently suffering terribly from the mosquitoes, the climate and the cruel suspicions by everyone in Cuba. Describing their journey to reporters waiting at the base of Wall Street for their return on the steamship *Saratoga*, Calhoun and Dawes complained that the rain in Cuba came down so hard that he once had to take a carriage to cross a street that had flooded in less than ten minutes. What they found about the uprising shocked both of them. In a private conversation with McKinley on June 22, 1897, they related how Weyler had laid waste to the country.

> «*Every house has been burned, most banana and guava trees have been cut down, almost all cane fields have been destroyed with fire, everything that could serve as food has been destroyed.... The country was wrapped in the stillness of death and the silence of desolation.*»

Unfortunately for the Cuban insurrects, they asserted a view that was at odds with American public opinion.

«It would be neither wise nor feasible to recognize as combatants the rebels that seek Cuban independence.»

The only one who benefited from their report was Fitzhugh Lee. Calhoun and Dawes confirmed Lee's reports that the rebels in Cuba were poorly educated and disorganized, wholly unsuited to democratic government. Exactly Lee's words. Nearly all the affluent segments of society, be they Spanish or Cuban, preferred annexation by the United States over a government dominated by the insurgents. Like former President Cleveland, Calhoun and Dawes feared

Charles G. Dawes.

that the most likely outcome of a rebel victory over the Spanish seemed to be instability and chaos. Moreover, Spain was a failed state and its defeat would invite another European power to take charge; the US should not provide a free pass to Germany or England into an island that could almost be seen from the Florida

shores. It was a frightening thought: American commerce, one day traveling distance from Cuba, would be required to pass directly under the noses of the returning British or under the barrels of the Kaiser's guns. From that day on, McKinley trusted Fitzhugh Lee as much as if his words were taken verbatim from the Holy Book itself.

In the days immediately thereafter, McKinley drafted and sent a letter to Madrid. Destiny had it that it would not reach the Spanish Prime Minister hands.

On the quiet Sunday of August 8, 1897, Spanish Prime Minister *Antoni*o Cánovas del Castillo and his wife were enjoying a relaxing afternoon and recuperating from his *"labors of State"* at Santa Agueda, a fashionable summer resort and spa notable for its baths, between San Sebastián, the summer residence of the Spanish Courts and Vittoria, the capital of the province of Alava, about 30 miles south of Bilbao. The respite was a welcome escape for Cánovas, who was sick of American whining about Cuba and would soon have to meet the new American minister to Madrid, sixty-two-year-old Civil War veteran Stewart Woodford, who was carrying McKinley's letter. In Cánovas mind,

«*Cuba is a Spanish business and no one else's, and I am in no mood to take advice from anybody about how to deal with it, especially upstart Americans who had recently fought a brutal Civil War.*»

His own methods were no more harsh, he believed, than those of the Union army that had laid waste to the Confederate South. What's more, Cánovas knew that the Spanish public opinion stood solidly behind him. So hostile were the Spanish to American interference that the State Department had warned Woodford and his nervous wife to postpone their arrival in Madrid until after the end of the bullfighting season, when presumably «*the well known unchristian Spanish bloodlust would have been quenched.*» Cánovas was midly enthusiastic about Woodford's visit, yet plans were made for the Spanish military and the police to take up positions on board Woodford's train to protect it as it traveled through the country and to closely guard the train station when he arrived to deliver McKinley's message.

No doubt feeling relaxed after a morning of treatments and an enjoyable lunch, Cánovas was lingering in the spa's gallery when he noticed a young man approaching. As he neared, the stranger reached inside his coat and withdrew a revolver. In quick succession, three shots echoed throughout the building. The prime minister received one of these shots on his forefront, crumbled to the ground, blood oozing at the feet of his terrified wife. He died two hours later. The assassin was an Italian by the name of Michele Angiolillo, the newspapers reported, and he had killed the Spanish leader in the name of anarchy. In the gilded halls of European capitals, monarchs and heads of state nervously gulped and wondered who would be next.

Antonio Cánovas del Castillo,
Prime Minister of Spain

In Washington, newspaper headlines elicited a somewhat different reaction. More than one guilty smile crept across the face of State Department staffers as they realized their incredible good fortune.

Ten days after, on September 18th, 1897, President McKinley with his Assistant Secretary of the Navy Theodore Roosevelt seated next to him, drove his carriage out of the White House grounds into the streets of Washington. Roosevelt believed that the United States was on an inevitable collision course with Spain and had strong opinions on what the president should do in case of war. As they bounced over the cobblestones, he argued that the United States should be ready to quickly dispatch an expeditionary force to Cuba and that a flying squadron of ships be formed to harass the coast of Spain. And there was one more thing.

Thedore Roosevelt, US Assistant Secretary of the Navy

«*Our Asiatic squadron should blockade, and if possible, take Manila,*» he insisted.

McKinley listened to Roosevelt politely, but refused to consider any objective other than averting war. Although he could have approved and lent credence to Roosevelt's plan with a wave of his hand, McKinley kept his peace and let the experts play their war games. The same day the Spanish summer capital of San Sebastian, perched above the turquoise waters of the Bay of Biscay, was just stirring to life when U.S. envoy Woodford stepped into his coach and directed the driver to take him to the offices of the foreign ministry. Arriving a few minutes later, at 5 p.m., he put on his most amiable face and proceeded to explain McKinley's hopes for Cuba.

«*The United States had the right to involve itself on Cuba. Both economic and humanitarian concerns compel us to do so. Correspondence I have received from Washington says... the chronic condition of trouble... causes disturbances in the social and political condition of our people... a continuous irritation within our own border injuriously affects the normal functions of business, and tends to delay the condition of prosperity to which our country is entitled...»*

Yet McKinley had decided, for the time being at least, that he would let the Spanish sort out their uppity colony on their own. There would be no official American demand for Cuban independence. Spain, Woodford said, should offer proposals to end the war that were

«... honorable to herself and just to her Cuban colony and to mankind... the United States will not tell the Spanish how to end the fighting... we must insist, however, that Spain establishes a durable peace on the island as early as November 1st... »

Had Cánovas still been alive, this would probably have elicited an extemporaneous tirade. Who were the Americans to be giving his government timetables? But the Spanish listened with polite interest. Práxedes Mateo Sagasta, Spain's new prime minister, was a liberal who, as McKinley's luck would have it, had months before championed a kinder, gentler approach to dealing with Cuba. Within weeks, Sagasta's cabinet was well on its way toward implementing the reforms that McKinley had requested. The murderous Weyler was ordered back to Spain. Political prisoners, among them a number of Americans, were freed from Cuban jails. And while Spain would retain control of military and foreign affairs, it would grant Cuba a level of autonomy that it had never seen before.

Práxedes Mateo Sagasta, Prime Minister of Spain

Spain's acquiescence marked a diplomatic triumph for McKinley. He appeared to have averted a war with Spain and established a level of authority on the island that would safeguard American business interests. In his message to Congress on December 6, 1897, McKinley wrote that Spain should be given

«...a reasonable chance to realize her expectations and to prove the efficacy of the new order of things to which she stands irrevocably committed.»

In dusty rebel camps around Cuba that autumn, revolutionaries studied the proposal that Sagasta and McKinley had agreed upon. With some sense of victory, they could smile at news that Weyler was being sent home. Yet a close reading of the proposal revealed unacceptable provisions. It stated, for example, that the upper house of a new Cuban parliament would be made up of men mostly appointed by Spain's governor-general to the island. The governor also would retain the power to veto legislation and dissolve parliament whenever he saw fit. In short, under this definition of autonomy, Cuba would remain firmly under Spanish rule. Máximo Gómez declared that he would die fighting for independence rather than accept this offer from Spain. Anyone who openly favored autonomy would be subject to court-martial and sentenced to death. One tobacco planter in the Santa Clara Province told Stephen Bonsal of *The New York Herald*,

«The only way for Spain to retain her sovereignty over these islands is to exterminate -butcher if you like- every man, woman, and child upon it who is infected with the contagion and dreams of 'Cuba libre.'»

Stephen Bonsal, War Correspondent in Havana

Throughout the later part of the year, rallies and meetings were held all over the island denouncing Madrid's autonomist plan. In December, a statement purporting to represent the views of men holding 80 percent of Cuba's wealth was circulated demanding a change in policy. On *The Washington Post* an anonymous journalist wrote in December that the *peninsulares* feared that autonomy «would be the death knell of civilized society in Cuba.»

None were more upset than the Spanish soldiers based in Cuba, many of whom had not been paid in months and were held together only by their faith in Weyler. The bitter ex-commander could do little to soothe their worries. As his bags were being loaded on a steamship for the trip back to Spain on October 31, 1897, he told well-wishers gathered on the dock that Sagasta didn't have the guts to defend Spain's interests.

> «*I had expected my release from the time of the death of Prime Minister Cánovas, not believing that any political leader would be strong enough to sustain me when the United States and the rebels were together constantly demanding that Spain should come to a settlement.*»

Unwilling to defend an autonomist government without Weyler leading them, scores of officers quit. Those who remained spent the Christmas holidays sipping wine, smoking cigars, and plotting against Weyler's replacement, General Ramon Blanco, all the while cursing the interfering Americans.

The morning of January 12, 1898, Fitzhugh Lee awoke in his room at the *Hotel Inglaterra* to a disturbance in the streets outside his window. From the narrow alleys and streets below echoed the sound of breaking glass and chants: «*Death to Blanco and death to autonomy*» and «*Viva Weyler.*» An article in *El Reconcentrado* that morning infuriated Spanish troops stationed in the city. It leveled a stinging attack on a subordinate of their hero Weyler. Mobs of riotous Spaniards, most of them soldiers, surged toward the city's central park in numbers that would eventually reach an estimated five thousand. Renegade troops ignored the commands of their superiors. One cavalry commander, ordered to charge into the swelling crowd, asked his superior officer,

> «*Whom shall I charge, Loyal Spaniards for shouting Long Live Spain, and Long live the Spanish Generals'?*»

Madrid Mobs protesting the firing of Weyler

This was exactly the sort of lawlessness that Lee had most feared and warned against with increasing passion since November. Unchecked, renegade soldiers might easily attack American citizens or their factories and plantations. Throughout the day, Lee dispatched frenzied, terse notes to Washington that seemed only to raise more questions than they answered. Early that afternoon he wrote:

> «Mobs, led by Spanish officers, attacked today the offices of the four newspapers advocating autonomy. Rioting at this hour, 1 P.M. continues. Much excitement, which may develop into serious disturbances.... No rioting at present, but rumors of it are abundant. Palace heavily guarded. Consulate also protected by armed men.»

The next day, January 13, 1898, Lee wrote:

> «Today all is quiet, but business had been suspended and the city is heavily guarded. I have heard protesters shout the day before that they should march on the U.S. consulate. Presence of ships may be necessary later, but not now. Uncertainty exists whether Blanco can control the situation. If demonstrated he cannot maintain order, preserve life, and keep the peace, or if Americans and their interests are in danger, ships must be sent, and to that end should be prepared to move promptly. Excitement and uncertainty predominates everywhere. No one has lifted a finger against a single American in Havana, yet my confidential reports should shocked Washington.»

Enrique Dupuy de Lôme

Events in Cuba seemed to fulfill the worst expectations of the US State Department's foremost experts on Spanish affairs. Americans had been skeptical of Sagasta's plan to begin with, and after Lee's communications a heavy traffic messages began to go back and forth to Havana. At the center of this was Fitzhugh Lee, to whom McKinley candidly referred to as «Our Consul in Havana.»

This book recalls the history of those years in which US and Spain faced each other in countless maneuvers to control power in Cuba. Warships were requested, communications were cut off and opened back on, American naval commanders of the European and Asiatic fleets were asked to retain all seamen whose enlistments were to expire soon, Cervera's powerful Spanish fleet was at points unknown while US squadrons in the Gulf of Mexico were ready to enter into action in a matter of hours, knowing that an emergency could arise at any moment. The New York newspapers fueled a sense of panic with characteristic swagger. *The New York World* wrote:

The ABC of Madrid in 1897

«The riots in Havana mean revolution.»

Not to be outdone, Pulitzer's *World* warned of danger to all Americans, both those residing in Cuba and hundreds of thousands living under the American flag. The *Journal* told its readers that the riots were aimed at Americans and predicted American military intervention within days. The news from Spain were inconsistent and incoherent. The *ABC* in Madrid reported on January 16, 1898 that Spanish ambassador to Washington Enrique Dupuy de Lôme said:

«... the Government and Cabinet, although officially they have said nothing to me, seem to have lost all faith in Spain's success, and, to some extent, to have lost their peace of mind.»

Dupuy de Lôme, the man that had yet to insult President McKinley in a letter that was intercepted and made public by Cuban operatives, was surprisingly best informed than he even thought. De Lôme was a suave, debonair and worldly professional career diplomat yet he was considered imperious and insufferable by Americans and even by his own colleagues, who believed he labored under delusions of grandeur. To some friends he had confided his thought on America: a country too new for the world to trust its durability, far too rough around the edges, too driven by the citizens with the lowest common denominator, a country that could not to be considered Spain's equal. He would add:

> «Spain represents Europe; it is a timeless monarchy and a centuries old sophisticated civilization. The US, on the other hand, is part of the New World, a yet to mature Republic, weighted under the lineage of a former rebellious colony.»

All throughout the next five years, Fitzhugh Lee became the essential contact to the bureaucrats at the *State, War, and Navy Building* next door to the White House at 17th Street and Pennsylvania Avenue.[2] Unbeknownst to him, a test of his nerves and knowledge was about to come his way with a rude awakening. McKinley had decided to send a warship, the USS *Maine*, to Havana on what the Spanish would be told was a courtesy call. Yet courtesy had very little to do with it. Lee immediately knew it: the ship's visit had a double-sided intention. Beneath the surface, America was interested in having a ship in Havana because «*some means of protection should be on hand.*» Spanish authorities in Havana became very annoyed by the spectacle of a brash Yankee warship anchored outside their bedroom windows. Lee suggested that the United States hold off for a few days. «*With this visit, you are placing a lighted candle on top of an open cask of gunpowder,*» he wrote to his friends in Washington.

SOME OF THE INFORMATION, CHARACTERIZATIONS AND SPECIFICS IN THIS INTRODUCTION WERE BASED ON BOOKS AND ARTICLES BY *SCOTT MILLER*, *J.N.LARNED*, *MARK I. HAYWES*, *STEPHEN BONSAL*, *CHARLES M. PEPPER* AND OTHERS IN *THE NEW YORK TIMES*, *THE NEW YORK WORLD* AND THE *NEW YORK JOURNAL*, AS WELL AS THE NEWSPAPERS *LA LUCHA* OF HAVANA AND THE *ABC* OF MADRID. THE AUTHOR OWES A GREAT DEAL TO THE GENEROUS ASSISTANCE OF *ROBIN HARVEY*, OF THE *US LIBRARY OF CONGRESS* FOR HER HELP IN FACILITATING ACCESS TO US HAVANA CONSULAR ARCHIVES.

---

[2] This massive gray structure, which took seventeen years to construct, had been designed in the style of the French Second Empire. Yet, built from granite and cast iron, it most closely resembled nothing more elegant than an imposing gray pile of rocks.

IMAGES OF THE WAR OF 95

ENGRAVINGS FROM *LA ILUTRACION ESPAÑOLA Y AMERICANA* IN THE ISSUES CORRESPONDING TO THE YEARS 1895, 1896 AND 1897.

The **Alfonso XIII Cruiser** in a dry dock in Ferrol, Galicia; several of the ships of the **Spanish Transatlantic Company** that carried Spanish soldiers to Cuba; **Spanish soldiers** arriving at Santiago de Cuba.

Friends of **Don Salvador Cisneros Betancourt**, Marquis of Santa Lucia; Spanish troops resting at **Ingenio Mi Rosa**, near Rincón, in Havana, January 11, 1895; Cuban troops in Tampa getting aboard the **Laurada** steamer.

El Jagüey coffee plantation, in Guantánamo; the General Headquarters of **Máximo Gómez** in the outskirts of Havana; **General Ríus Rivera** and his escort.

Calixto García camp near Guáimaro; an insurgent fleeing the Spanish troops; **blood hospital** of the Cubans near Bayamo; **observation post** of the Cubans near the Sierra Maestra, Oriente; **General Rozas** camp near Guáimaro.

El vapor filibustero *Dauntless*.

El vapor filibustero *Three Friends*.

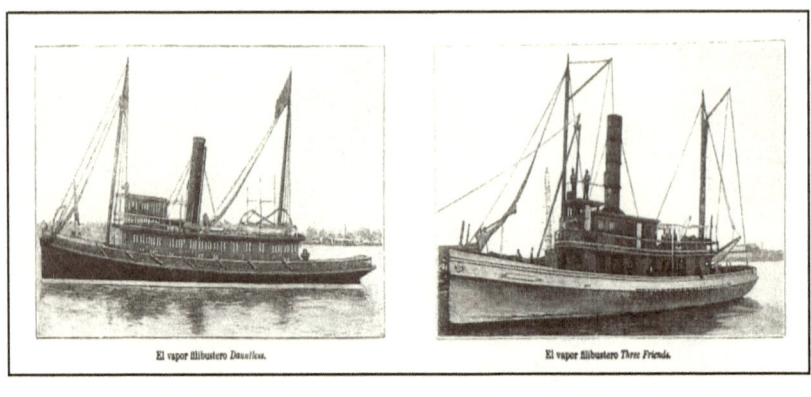

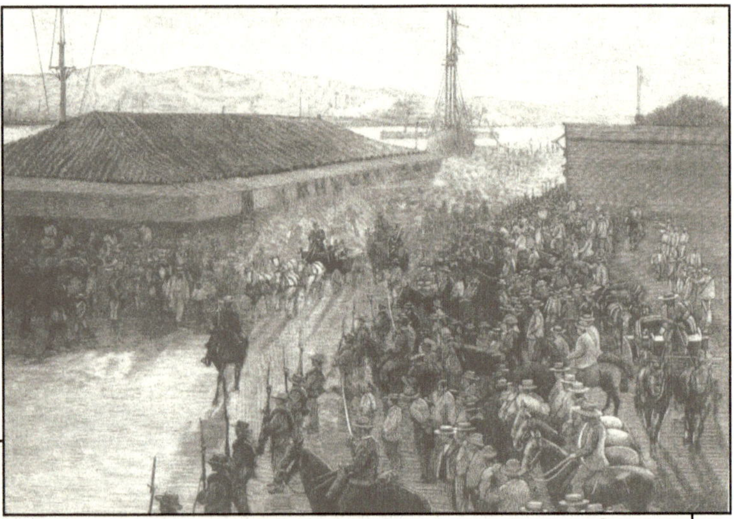

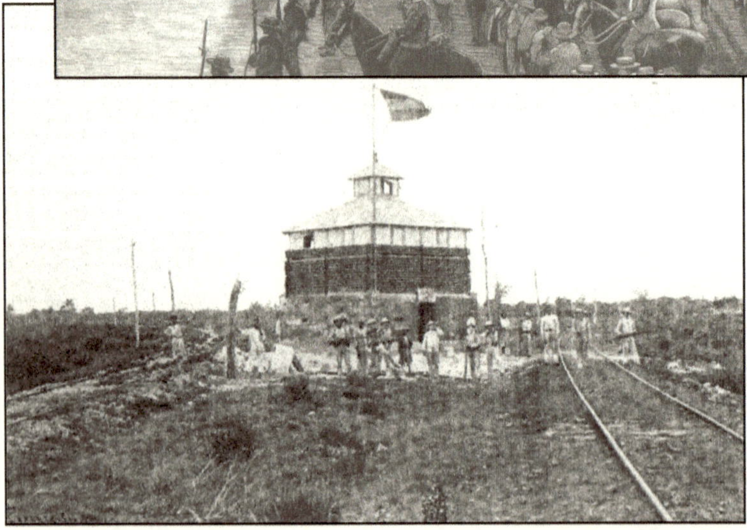

Two Cuban expeditionary vapors: the **Dauntless** and the **Three Friends**; entrance of **General Martínez Campos** in Santiago de Cuba on April 16, 1895; the Spanish fort of the **Compañía de Ferrocarriles de Cárdenas y Júcaro.**

General **Máximo Gómez** in his tent; the inauguration of the statue of **Francisco de Albear** in Havana; Soldiers under the Spanish General **Suárez Inclán** resting in Bramales, Pinar del Rio.

One of the most dramatic images of Cuba, published in **La Ilustración Española y Americana** on May 30, 1895 and reproduced in many European and North American magazines, among them **Scientific American**. A gigantic **Jagüey** tree born among the remains of the machinery in the 1868 ruins of the **Central La Demajagua**.

A view of the Parish Church of **San Felipe, in Quivicán**, founded in a hamlet built by the **Havana Railway Company**, as it was surrounded by Spanish troops; the **Parish Church of Artemisa** in Pinar del Rio; the docks and warehouses of the **port of Manzanillo**.

Scenes from the *Júcaro to Morón* Military Trocha

The **Morro of Santiago de Cuba** (fortress) seen from the entrance to the bay; the **Manzanillo Plaza de Armas**; the port of **Baracoa, near Duaba**, where Maceo landed on April 1, 1895 with his brother José, Flor Crombet and 21 other members of a patriotic expedition.

Destruction of the railways on the route from **Cifuentes to Santa Clara** by Cuban troops.

Bridge over the **Yayabo river** in Sancti Spíritus; the ruins of the town of **Punta Brava**; Spanish soldiers in Dos Caminos, near **Santa Catalina del Guaso**, Guantánamo, where the Spanish forces of the *Simancas Battalion* were defeated in a 9-hour struggle by the Cuban troops under **General Jesús Miró**.

Transfer of **Cuban prisoners** in the outskirts of Camagüey.

Spanish soldiers in the **Jatibonico river**; train derailed by the insurgents in the outskirts of **Cienfuegos**; Cuban troops lurking in the outskirts of **Santiago de Cuba**.

Excmo. Sr. D. Julio de Apezteguía y Tarafa,
Jefe del Partido Unión Constitucional de Cuba.

Excmo. Sr. D. Ramón Herrera y Gutiérrez,
Jefe del Partido Reformista de Cuba.
(De fotografía de Cohner, de la Habana.)

Excmo. Sr. D. José M. Gálvez y Alfonso,
Jefe del Partido Autonomista de Cuba.
(De fotografía de los Sres. Maceo, hermanos, de la Habana.)

THE LEADERSHIP OF THE POLITICAL PARTIES IN CUBA DURING THE WAR OF 95:

Julio de Apezteguía, Leader of the Pro-Spanish *Constitutional Union Party*;
Ramón Herrera y Gutiérrez, Leader of the *Reformists*;
José María Gálvez, Leader of the *Autonomists*.

CHRONOLOGICAL RECORD OF EVENTS DURING THE 1895 WAR OF CUBAN INDEPENDENCE AND SOME OF THE IMPORTANT THINGS THAT WERE HAPPENING IN THE REST OF THE WORLD FROM 1895 TO 1901

1895

January
25. Death of Lord Randolph Churchill.
February
24. Renewal of insurrection in Cuba against Spanish rule.
March
17. Bloody battle in the streets of Lima, Peru, ending in the overthrow of the usurping government of Caceres.
May
1. Proclamation by the British South Africa Company giving the name "*Rhodesia*" to its territories.
8. Re-hearing granted by the Supreme Court of the United States on cases testing constitutionality of the income tax.
20. Final decision of the Supreme Court of the United States against the constitutionality of the income tax.
23. Consolidation of the Astor and Lenox libraries with the "Tilden Trust," to form the New York Public Library.
July
20. Pressing dispatch of Mr. Olney, United States Secretary of State, to the American Ambassador to Great Britain, on the question of the Venezuela boundary, asserting the Monroe Doctrine.
August
1. Massacre of English and American missionaries at Hua Sang in China

September
16-18. Adoption of a constitution and organization of a republican government by the Cuban insurgents.
28. Death of Louis Pasteur, the father of bacteriology.
30. Attack by Turkish police in Constantinople on Armenians who had gathered to present their grievances to the Sultan.
October
8-9. Massacre of Armenians at Trebizond by a Turkish mob.
November
8. Discovery of the X rays by Professor Röntgen.
26. Reply of Lord Salisbury, for the British government, to the despatch of Mr. Olney, on the Venezuela question.
27. Death of Alexandre Dumas, the younger.
December
17. Message of President Cleveland to the Congress of the United States on the boundary dispute between Great Britain and Venezuela.
18-20. Passage by the two branches of the Congress of the United States of an act authorizing the President to appoint a commission to ascertain the true boundary of Venezuela.
20. Special Message of President Cleveland to the Congress of the United States on the financial situation of the country.

1896.

January
1. Appointment of an United States Commission to investigate the divisional line between Venezuela and British Guiana.
8. Death of Paul Verlaine, French poet.
February
6. Death of Jean Auguste Barre, French sculptor.
10. Arrival of General Valeriano Weyler at Havana as Governor and Captain-General of Cuba.
16. Promulgation of Weyler's concentration order in Cuba.
March
1. Defeat of the Italians by the Abyssinians at Adowa.
30. Resumption of the authority of the Pope over the Coptic Church, and re-establishment of the Catholic patriarchate of Alexandria.
31. Reopening of the military and naval service of the United States to persons who had held commissions in the Confederate army or navy during the civil war.
April
6. Revival of Olympic games at Athens.

Some of the Important World Events in 1895-96 after Cubans started their Independence War

May 1, 1895. Proclamation by the British South Africa Company giving the name *"Rhodesia"* to its territories.

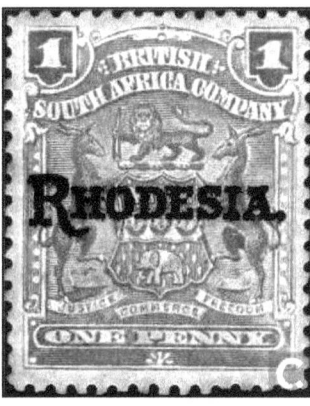

September 28, 1895. Death of Louis Pasteur, the father of bacteriology.

November 27, 1895. Death of Alexandre Dumas, the younger, author of *La Dame aux Camélias*

April 6, 1896, *Panathenaic Stadium,* home of the athletic events of the renewal of Olympic Games in Athens.

8. Highest latitude reached by Dr. Nansen, within 261 statute miles of the north pole.
24. Promulgation of amendments to the Constitution of the Republic of México.

May
1. Opening of German industrial exposition at Berlin.—Assassination of the Shah of Persia.— Promulgation of additional amendments to the Mexican Constitution.
11. The bill to consolidate New York, Brooklyn, and neighboring cities, in the "*Greater New York*," made law by the Governor's signature.
19. Promulgation of the law of public education in Mexico, establishing a national system.
24. Outbreak of Turks against the Christians in Canea, Crete.
26. Coronation of the Russian Tzar, Nicholas II; suffocation of nearly 3,000 people at the feasting.
27. The city of St. Louis struck by a hurricane.
27-28. Meeting of the national convention of the Prohibition Party, at Pittsburgh, to nominate candidates for President and Vice President of the United States.

June
16-18. Meeeting, at St. Louis, of the Republican National Convention, and nomination of William McKinley and Garret A. Hobart for President and Vice President of the United States.
26. Resignation of Cecil J. Rhodes from the board of directors of the British South Africa Company.
28. Re-election of President Porfirio Díaz, of Mexico, for a fifth term.

July
1. Abolition of inter-state taxes in Mexico.—Death of Mrs. Harriet Beecher Stowe.
20. Death of Charles Dickens, eldest son of the novelist.
23. Death of Mary Dickens, eldest daughter of Charles Dickens.

August.
Discovery of the Klondike gold fields.
1. Death of Rt. Hon. Sir William R. Grove, jurist and man of science.
26-28. Attack of Armenians on the Ottoman Bank at Constantinople; horrible massacre of Armenians by the Turks.

September
15. Publication in the Paris "*Eclair*" of the fact that Captain Alfred Dreyfus (degraded and imprisoned in 1894 for alleged betrayal of military secrets to a foreign power) was convicted on the evidence of a document shown secretly to the court martial, and unknown to the prisoner and his counsel.
29. Official announcement of bubonic plague at Bombay.

Some of the Important World Events in 1896 after Cubans started their Independence War

May 1, 1896. Assassination of the Shah of Persia, **Nassr-Eddin**,

May 26, 1896. Coronation of the Russian Tzar, **Nicholas II**; suffocation of nearly 3,000 people at the feasting.

June 28, 1896. Re-election of President **Porfirio Díaz**, of Mexico, for a fifth term.

November 16, 1896. First **transmission of electric power** from Niagara Falls to Buffalo.

December 10, 1896. Death of **Alfred Nobel**, Swedish engineer and founder of a great fund for annually rewarding benefactors of humanity.

October
20-22. Celebration of the one hundred and fiftieth anniversary of the founding of The College of New Jersey, which then formally assumed the name of *Princeton University*.
26. Peace made between the government of Italy and King Menelek, of Abyssinia.
November
3. Presidential election in the United States.
9. Announcement by Lord Salisbury of the settlement of the Venezuela question between Great Britain and the United States.
16. First transmission of electric power from Niagara Falls to Buffalo.
December
7. Death of Antonio Maceo, leader of Cuban insurgents, killed in a skirmish with the Spaniards.
10. Death of Alfred Nobel, Swedish engineer and founder of a great fund for annually rewarding benefactors of humanity.
11. Political suffrage extended to women in Idaho by an amendment of the Constitution.

1897

February
2. Signing, at Washington, of the treaty of arbitration between Great Britain and Venezuela.
7. Union of Crete with Greece proclaimed by insurgent Christians at Halepa.
9. The taking of the first general census of the Russian Empire.
11. Announcement by the government of Greece to the Powers that it had determined to intervene by force in behalf of the Christians of Crete.
14. Landing of a Greek expedition of 2,000 men in Crete, under Colonel Vassos.
15. Landing of a mixed force at Canea, Crete, by the Powers of the "*European Concert*," to protect the town; proclamation by the Greek commander, Colonel Vassos, that he had occupied the island in the name of the King of the Greeks.
17. Attack by the Greeks on the Turkish forces at Canea.
March
2. Veto of Immigration Bill by President Cleveland.—Joint note by the Powers of the "*Concert*" to Greece and Turkey, declaring that Crete cannot be annexed to Greece, but that the island will be endowed by the Powers with an autonomous administration.

Some of the Important World Events in 1897 after Cubans started their Independence War

March 8, 1897. Inauguration of **William McKinley** in the office of President of the United States

April 3, 1897. Death of Johannes Brahms, German composer

May 4, 1897. Fire in a charity bazaar at Paris which was horribly destructive of life

June 20-22, 1897. Celebration in London of the sixtieth anniversary -the "*Diamond Jubilee*- of the accession of **Queen Victoria** to the throne of the United Kingdom.

August 8, 1897. Assassination of **Cánovas del Castillo**, Prime Minister of Spain.

8. Inauguration of William McKinley in the office of President of the United States,
21. "*Pacific blockade*" of the coast of Crete established by the Powers of the European Concert.
April
Unprecedented floods along the Mississippi river.
3. Death of Johannes Brahms, German composer.
6. Edict of the Sultan of Zanzibar terminating the legal status of slavery.
9. Incursion of irregular Greek troops into Turkish territory.
17. Turkish declaration of a state of war with Greece; beginning of hostilities between regular troops, at Milouna Pass.
22-24. Retreat of the Greek army in panic rout from Tyrnavo.
27. Resignation of the Greek Ministry of M. Delyannis.
30. Repulse by the Greeks of a Turkish attack on positions near Velestino.
May
4. Fire in a charity bazaar at Paris which was horribly destructive of life.—The "*Greater New York*" charter becomes law.
20. Arrangement of an armistice between the Turks and the Greeks.
June
1. Census taken in Egypt.
10. Effect given to a new constitution for the state of Delaware, establishing an educational qualification of the suffrage.
16. Transmission to Congress of a new treaty for the annexation of the Hawaiian Islands to the United States.
20-22. Celebration in London of the sixtieth anniversary —the "*Diamond Jubilee*"— of the accession of Queen Victoria to the throne of the United Kingdom.
August
8. Assassination of Cánovas del Castillo, Prime Minister of Spain.
25. Assassination of President Borda, of Uruguay.
12. Ending of a great strike of coal miners in the United States, which began in July.
18. Signing of a preliminary treaty of peace between Turkey and Greece.
October
6. The Philippine Islands swept by a typhoon, destroying over 6,000 lives. Death of Sir John Gilbert, English artist.
19. Death of George Mortimer Pullman, American inventor.
November
2. Election of the first Mayor of "*Greater New York.*"
10. Adoption of plans for a building for the New York Public Library.

15. Commandant Esterhazy denounced to the French Minister of War, by M. Mathieu Dreyfus, as the author of the "*bordereau*" on which Captain Alfred Dreyfus was secretly convicted.
16. The Dreyfus case brought into the French Chamber of Deputies by a question to the Minister of War.
19. Great fire in London, beginning in Aldersgate and spreading over six acres, destroying property estimated at £2,000,000 in value.
25. Promulgation by royal decree at Madrid of a constitution establishing self-government in Cuba and Puerto Rico.
14. Signing of the treaty of Biac-na-bato, between the Spaniards and the insurgent Filipinos.

1898.

January
12. Acquittal of Commandant Esterhazy, after a farcical pretense of trial by a military tribunal, on the charge of being the author of the "*bordereau*" ascribed to Dreyfus.
13. Publication in Paris of a letter (*J'Accuse*) by M. Zola, denouncing the conduct of the courts martial in the cases of Dreyfus and Esterhazy.
24. Declaration by Count von Bulow, in the German Reichstag, that no relations or connections of any kind had ever existed between Captain Dreyfus and any German agents.
25. Friendly visit of the United States battle ship "*Maine*" to Havana, Cuba.

February
7-15. Prosecution of M. Zola for defamation of certain military officers; his scandalous trial and conviction.
14. Destruction of the United States battle ship *"Maine,"* by an explosion, in the harbor of Havana, Cuba.

March
1. Retirement of General Crespo from the Presidency of Venezuela; succession of General Andrade to the office.
16. Death of Aubrey Beardsley, English artist.
17. Speech of Senator Proctor, of Vermont, in the United States Senate, describing the condition of the reconcentrados in Cuba, as he saw them during a recent visit to the island.
21. Report of the United States naval court of inquiry on the destruction of the battle ship *"Maine."*
22. Report of Spanish naval board of inquiry on the destruction of the United States battle ship *"Maine."*
27. Proposal by the government of the United States to that of Spain of an armistice and negotiation of peace with the insurgents in Cuba.
28. Message of the President of the United States to Congress on the destruction of the battleship *"Maine."*

Some of the Important World Events in 1898 after Cubans started their Independence War

Images, top to bottom, left to right

January 13, 1898. Publication in Paris of a letter *J'Accuse*, by **M. Zola**, denouncing the conduct of the Court Martial in the case of Dreyfus.

April 29, 1898. Proclamation of neutrality by the Portuguese government, which required the Spanish fleet under **Admiral Cervera** to "*depart from the Cape Verde islands.*"

May 1, 1898. *Destruction of the Spanish squadron in Manila Bay* by the American squadron under Commodore Dewey.

July 31, 1898. Death of Prince Otto von Bismarck, at the age of 83.

November 17, 1898. Death of Baron Ferdinand James de Rothschild.

31. Reply of the Spanish government to the proposals of the United States, for an armistice and negotiation with the Cuban insurgents

April

2. Quashing of the sentence pronounced on M. Zola, upon his appeal to the *Court of Cassation.*

10. Passage of bill through the German Reichstag to greatly increase the German Navy.

11. Special Message of the President of the United States to Congress on the relations of the country to Spain, consequent on affairs in Cuba.

13. Adoption by the United States House of Representatives of a joint resolution authorizing and directing the President to "*intervene at once to stop the war in Cuba.*"

16. Adoption by the United States Senate of a joint resolution not only directing intervention to stop the war in Cuba, but recognizing the insurgent government of *"the Republic of Cuba."*

17. Arrangement of the disagreement between the two branches of the United States Congress respecting the recognition of *"the Republic of Cuba,"* and passage of a joint resolution to intervene for the stopping of the war in the island.

20. Passports asked for and received by the Spanish Minister at Washington.

21. Appointment of Rear-Admiral Sampson to the command of the U. S. naval force on the Atlantic station.

22. Proclamation by the President of the United States declaring a blockade of certain Cuban ports.

23. Proclamation by the President of the United States calling for 125,000 volunteers.

25. Formal declaration of war with Spain by the Congress of the United States, with authority given to the President to call out the land and naval forces of the nation.

29. Proclamation of neutrality by the Portuguese government, which required the Spanish fleet under Admiral Cervera to "*depart from the Cape Verde islands.*"

May

1. Destruction of the Spanish squadron in Manila Bay by the American squadron under Commodore Dewey.

9. Serious fighting in Milan, ending bread riots in that city and elsewhere in northern Italy.

12. Attack on the Spanish forts at San Juan, Puerto Rico, by Admiral Sampson, then searching for Cervera's fleet.

19. Death of Mr. Gladstone.

25. Proclamation by the President of the United States calling for 75,000 additional volunteers.
28. Public funeral of Mr. Gladstone; burial in Westminster Abbey.
29. Blockade of the Spanish squadron under Rear-Admiral Cervera, in the harbor of Santiago de Cuba, by the American flying squadron under Commodore Schley.
30. Agreement between Great Britain, Canada and the United States, creating a Common Market.

June
1. Arrival of Admiral Sampson and his fleet off the entrance to the harbor of Santiago de Cuba, to perfect the blockade of the Spanish squadron.
3. Sinking of the collier *"Merrimac"* in the channel of the harbor-entrance at Santiago de Cuba, by Assistant Naval Constructor Hobson, U. S. N.
6. Bombardment of Spanish forts at Santiago de Cuba by the American blockading fleet.
7-10. Possession of the lower bay at Guantánamo, near Santiago de Cuba, taken by vessels of the American navy, and a marine battalion landed.
14. Sailing, from Tampa, Florida, of the military expedition under General Shafter for the capture of Santiago de Cuba.
15. Adoption by the House of Representatives of a joint resolution to provide for annexing the Hawaiian Islands to the United States.
16. Second bombardment of forts at Santiago de Cuba by the American blockading fleet.
20. Arrival, off Guantanamo, of the expedition under General Shafter.
21. Capture and occupation of the island of Guam by the USS Charleston.
22-24. Landing of General Shafter's army at Daiquiri and Siboney.
24. First engagement between American and Spanish troops in Cuba, at *"Las Guásimas."*

July.
1. Assault by the American forces, at San Juan Hill and El Caney, on the Spanish lines defending Santiago.
2-3. Continued fighting on the lines around Santiago de Cuba.
3. Demand of General Shafter for the surrender of Santiago, under the threat of bombardment; truce arranged by foreign consuls and negotiations for surrender opened.—Destruction of the Spanish fleet of Admiral Cervera on its attempting to escape from the blockaded port of Santiago de Cuba.
6. Destruction of the Spanish cruiser *"Alfonso XII,"* when attempting to escape from the harbor of Havana.—Adoption by the U. S. Senate of the joint resolution to provide for the annexation of the Hawaiian Islands.—

Exchange of Lieutenant Hobson and his fellow captives for prisoners taken from the Spanish forces.

7. Declaration of M. Cavaignac, Minister of War, in the Chamber of Deputies, of his absolute certainty of the guilt of Captain Dreyfus.—**Death of Francisco Javier Cisneros, Cuban patriot.**

10. Termination of truce at Santiago; resumption of hostilities; bombardment of the city by the US Navy.

12. Outbreak of yellow fever in the military hospital at Siboney.—Arrival of General Miles at Santiago with reinforcements for General Shafter.

13. Interview of General Miles and General Shafter with General Toral, the Spanish commander at Santiago.

14. Agreement by General Toral to surrender the city of Santiago and the entire district of eastern Cuba with 24,000 Spanish troops.

16. Signing of the terms of the Spanish surrender at Santiago.

18. Opening of second trial of M. Zola, at Versailles.

25. Landing, at Guánica, of the expedition of United States troops, under General Miles, for the conquest of Puerto Rico.

26. Overtures for peace addressed by the Spanish government to that of the United States through the French Minister at Washington.

31. Death of Prince Otto von Bismarck, at the age of 83.

August

3. Urgent message from General Shafter to the U. S. War Department, asking for the instant withdrawal of his forces from Santiago, on account of the deadly ravages of yellow fever, typhoid and dysentery.

4. Orders given for the removal of the American army from Santiago de Cuba to Montauk Point, Long Island.

7. Acceptance by Spain of the terms of peace offered by the United States.

12. Ceremony, at Honolulu, of the transfer of sovereignty over the Hawaiian Islands to the United States. Signing of the protocol of terms for the negotiation of peace between the United States and Spain; proclamation by the President of the United States suspending hostilities.

21. Friendly letter of Spanish soldiers at Santiago, Cuba, before departing for Spain, to their late enemies, the American soldiers.

24. Proposal by the Tzar of Russia of a conference of governments to discuss the means of stopping the progressive increase of military and naval armaments and promote the peace of the world.

25. Transfer of command at Santiago from General Shafter to General Lawton.

31. Termination of the minority of Queen Wilhelmina, of the Kingdom of the Netherlands, and of the regency of her mother, Queen Emma.

Suicide of Colonel Henry, of the Intelligence Department of the French Army, after confessing that he had forged one of the documents on which M. Cavaignac based his certainty of the guilt of Captain Dreyfus.

September
4. Resignation of M. Cavaignac from the French cabinet, because of his opposition to a revision of the Dreyfus case.
10. Assassination of Elizabeth, Empress of Austria and Queen of Hungary.
14. Death of Samuel Eliot, American historian.
29. Government of a Philippine Republic organized at Malolos; a National Congress convened, and Aguinaldo declared President.
30. Mob attack on foreigners near Peking.

October.
Discovery of the Cape Nome mining region in Alaska.
1. Call by foreign representatives at Peking for guards of marines to protect their legations.— **Meeting of Spanish and American commissioners at Paris to negotiate a Treaty of Peace.**
25. Decision of the *Court of Cassation* requiring a supplementary investigation of the case of Captain Dreyfus.

November
1. Establishment of the Constitution of the United States of Central America.
15. Order by the *Court of Cassation* that Dreyfus be notified by telegraph of the pending revision of his trial.
25. Dissolution of the United States of Central America by the secession of Salvador.
6. General Guy V. Henry appointed Military Governor of Puerto Rico.
10. Signing, at Paris, of the Treaty of Peace between the United States and Spain.
11. Death of General Calixto García, Cuban military leader.
13. Appointment of General Brooke as commander and military governor of Cuba, by direction of the President of the United States
17. Death of Baron Ferdinand James de Rothschild.
22. Death of Sebastian Bach Mills, composer and pianist.

1899

January
1. Formal relinquishment of the sovereignty of Spain over the island of Cuba, by ceremonies performed at Havana.
4. The Treaty of Peace between the United States and Spain sent to the United States Senate by the President.

Some of the Important World Events in 1899 after the time Cubans fought alongside the US Army in the pursue of their Independence

Images, top to bottom, left to right

May 25, 1899. Death of Emilio Castelar, Spanish orator and statesman.

June 12, 1899. Death of Johann Strauss, Austrian composer.

July 7, 1899. Destructive hurricane in Puerto Rico named after *San Ciriaco*

August 11, 1899. Death of Cornelius Vanderbilt, millionaire.

September 12, 1899. First act in the British-Boer war, in South Africa; Boer invasion of Natal and of Cape Colony.

11. Second communication of the Tzar of Russia to other governments on the subject of an International Conference for the promotion of peace.
22. Encyclical letter of Pope Leo XIII. condemning certain opinions called Americanism.
February
6. Ratification by the United States Senate of the Treaty of Peace with Spain.
12. Sale of the Caroline and the Marianne or Ladrone Islands (excepting Guam) by Spain to Germany. —Death of Henry Jones ("Cavendish").
16. Sudden death of Francois Felix Faure, President of the French Republic.
23. Funeral of the late President Faure, at Paris; attempted revolutionary rising by the "League of Patriots," and others.
28. Defeat and resignation of the Spanish Ministry of Sagasta, on the question of the signing of the Treaty of Peace with the United States.
March.
3. Creation of commission to examine and report on all possible routes for an inter-oceanic canal, under the control and ownership of the United States.
11. The signing of the treaty of peace with the United States by the Queen of Spain, on her own responsibility.
18. Modification of the plan of the Bureau of the American Republics, at a conference of the representatives of the American nations.
May
8. General George W. Davis appointed Military Governor of Puerto Rico.
11. Papal proclamation of the "*Jubilee of the Holy Year 1900.*"
25. Death of Emilio Castelar, Spanish orator and statesman.
29. Order by President McKinley seriously modifying the civil service rules.
June
2. Confession of Commandant Esterhazy, a refugee in England, that he wrote the *"bordereau"* ascribed to Captain Dreyfus.
3. Decision of the *Court of Cassation*, quashing and annulling, in certain particulars, the judgment of condemnation pronounced against Captain Dreyfus in 1894 and ordering a new trial by court martial, to be held at Rennes.
12. Death of Johann Strauss, Austrian composer.
18. Death of Horatio Alger, American writer of stories for boys.
20. Assassination of General Heureaux, President of the Dominican Republic.
July
7. Destructive hurricane in Puerto Rico.—Opening of the new trial of Captain Dreyfus by court martial at Rennes.—A terrific hurricane in the West Indies; loss of life estimated at 5,000.

13. Russian imperial order declaring Talienwan a free port.
14. Attempt, at Rennes, to assassinate M. Labori, one of the counsel for Captain Dreyfus.
20. Rioting in Paris; barricading of M. Guerinand other members of the "Anti-Semitic League" in their headquarters, to defy arrest.

August
9. Verdict of "guilty," pronounced against Dreyfus by five of the seven members of the Rennes court martial.
11. Death of Cornelius Vanderbilt, millionaire.
12. Impassioned protest by M. Zola against the Rennes verdict.
19. Pardon of Captain Dreyfus by President Loubet.

October.
International Commercial Congress and National Export Exposition at Philadelphia.

September
3. Fall of eleven columns of the great temple at Karnak, Egypt.
9. Ultimatum of the South African Republic to Great Britain.
10. Reply of the British government to the Boer ultimatum.—Contract of the Maritime Canal Company of Nicaragua declared forfeited by the Nicaraguan government.
12. First act in the British-Boer war, in South Africa ; Boer invasion of Natal and of Cape Colony.
16. Census of Cuba and Puerto Rico, taken under the direction of the War Department of the United States. —Agreement between Great Britain and the United States upon a "*modus vivendi*" pending the settlement of the Alaska boundary.
28. Death of Ottmar Mergenthaler, inventor of the linotype printing process.

December
6. Appointment of General Leonard Wood to the military command and governorship of Cuba.

1900.

January
1. Abolition of Roman Law and introduction of the Civil Code throughout Germany.—Reelection of President Porfirio Díaz, of Mexico, for a sixth term.
15. Letting of contract for building the Rapid Transit Tunnel in New York.

Some of the Important World Events in 1900 after Cubans fought alongside the US Army in the pursue of their Independence

Images, top to bottom, left to right

June 1-3, 1900. Fruitless peace parley between **British and Boer** military commanders.

June 13, 1900. Massacre of native Christians and burning of foreign buildings by "**Boxers**" **in Peking.**

June 29, 1900. Assassination of **King Humbert, of Italy**.

August 14, 1900. Rescue of the **besieged Legations at Peking**; entrance of the allied forces into the city.

October 22, 1900. Death of **John Sherman**, American statesman.

February
5. Signing at Washington of the *Hay-Pauncefote Treaty* between the United States and Great Britain, to facilitate the construction of an inter-oceanic canal.
April.
2. Visit of Queen Victoria to Ireland. —Death of Frederick E. Church, American landscape painter.
30. Approval of an Act of the Congress of the United States "to provide a government for the *"Territory of Hawaii."*
June
1-3. Fruitless peace parley between British and Boer military commanders.
5. Occupation of Pretoria, the capital of the South African Republic, by the British forces.—
6. Approval by the President of the United States of an act providing for the civil government of Alaska.
12-15. Second fruitless discussion of terms of peace between the British and Boer military leaders.
16. Election of municipal officers throughout the island of Cuba, under an election law promulgated by the military governor in the previous April.
7. Passage by the British Parliament of the Act to constitute the Commonwealth of Australia.
29. Assassination of King Humbert, of Italy.
August
14. Rescue of the besieged Legations at Peking; entrance of the allied forces into the city.
15. Forcing of the gates of the *"Forbidden City,"* at Peking, and expulsion of Chinese troops, by the American forces, under General Chaffee.
25. Death of Friedrich Wilhelm Nietzsche, German philosopher.
28. March of the allied army through the "*Forbidden City*," at Peking.
September
8. Letter of President McKinley, accepting his re-nomination for a second term as President of the United States.
15. General election in Cuba of delegates to a convention for framing a Constitution.
22. Gigantic banquet in Paris to 23,000 representatives of the municipalities of France, in celebration of the centenary of the proclamation of the first French republic.
October
22. Death of John Sherman, American statesman.
November
4. Rejection by popular vote in Switzerland of proposals for proportional representation.

5. Meeting of Cuban constitutional convention at Havana.
December
3. Meeting and organization of the first Legislative Assembly in Puerto Rico.
12. Celebration of the centennial anniversary of the removal of the capital of the United States from Philadelphia to Washington.
31. Fall of two stones at Stonehenge.

1901.

January
18. Encyclical letter of Pope Leo XIII. concerning Social and Christian Democracy.
22. Death of Queen Victoria.
24. Formal proclamation of the accession of King Edward VII. to the throne of the United Kingdom of Great Britain and Ireland.
25. Death of Baron Wilhelm von Rothschild, financier.
27. Death of Giuseppe Verdi, Italian composer.

February
1-4. Ceremonies of the funeral of Queen Victoria.
2. Act to increase the regular army of the United States to 100,000 men approved by the President.
12. Death of Don Ramón de Campoamor, Spanish poet, philosopher and statesman.
27. Adoption by the U. S. Senate of the Platt Amendment to the Army Appropriation Bill, defining the conditions under which the President may *leave the government and control of the island of Cuba to its people.*"

March
1. Concurrence of the U. S. House of Representatives in the "Spooner Amendment" and the Platt Amendment of the Senate to the Army Appropriation Bill.
2. Official announcement of the terms of the formation of the United States Steel Corporation.
4. Inauguration of William McKinley for a second term as President of the United States.
12. Offer, by Mr. Andrew Carnegie, of US$ 85,200,000 for the establishing of branches of the New York Public Library.
20. Passage of a new election law by the Legislature of Maryland, to exclude the illiterate from the suffrage.
23. Capture of the Philippine leader, Aguinaldo, by stratagem.

April

2. An oath of allegiance to the government of the United States taken by Aguinaldo.

19. Address to his countrymen issued by Aguinaldo, counseling submission to the sovereignty of the United States.

Some of the Important World Events in 1901 after Cubans fought alongside the US Army in the pursue of their Independence

Images, top to bottom, left to right

January 27, 1901. Death of Giuseppe Verdi, Italian composer.

February 1-4, 1901. Ceremonies of the funeral of Queen Victoria.

March 12, 1901. Offer, by Mr. Andrew Carnegie, of US$ 85,200,000 for the establishing of branches of the New York Public Library.

Confidential and Classified Documents and Information Gathered by the American Consulate in Havana during the Days of the Cuban Wars of Independence 1868 - 1898

El Palacio de Armona, on No. 2 Lamparilla Street, location of the American Consulate in Havana in the years after the Cuban War of Independence in 1895. Office of Mr. Fitzhugh Lee, US Consul General.

Spain could not continue to support Valeriano Weyler after the international public opinion had severely condemned the Reconcentration Policies of Weyler. One of the Spanish Generals with Cuban experience and a well deserved reputation as a conciliatory figure and the know-how and peacemaking skills was Ramón Blanco Erenas. This led the government of Práxedes Mateo Sagasta to send him to Cuba, where he replaced the decidedly inflammatory Valeriano Weyler as Captain General of the island. By the second half of 1897, Weyler had relocated more than 300,000 Cubans into *"Reconcentration Camps,"* where he failed to provide for them adequately. Consequently, these areas became cesspools of hunger and disease, where many hundreds of thousands died.

Blanco was asked to reverse Weyler's harsh Spanish policy against the Cubans while at the same time carry out the late plan of Cuban autonomy and defend the island after the outbreak of the Third Cuban War of Independence.

On October 8, 1897, Ramón Blanco Erenas was appointed as Captain General of Cuba. He arrived on October 31 to take office, and on November 14, he repealed the sections that established the criminal reconcentration dictated by Weyler.

Six days earlier, on November 7, the American Consul in Havana had transmitted to Washington the entire text of Blanco's proclamation to the people of Cuba.

> GENERAL GOVERNMENT OF THE ISLAND OF CUBA.
> **PROCLAMATION.**
> Don Ramón y Erenas, Marquis of Pena Plata, governor-general, captain-general, and general in chief of the army of this island.
>
> Decided to afford the protection due by the Government to the country people concentrated in the towns, I have procured, by all means within the reach of the authority, to better the condition to which the rural population of this island has been reduced, more than by the direct effort of the war measures previously adopted, as a natural consequence of a violent and unjust insurrection, which, having imposed itself on this country, made itself felt from the first moment as an attempt against the national sovereignty and as a work of devastation of the country, but especially as the result of extreme passions let loose against the majority of the Cuban population, honest, active, and loyal, con-

tended with the progress of its increasing culture, satisfied with the prosperity attained by its arts, its agriculture, industry, and commerce, proud of its race and nationality, and which after having undergone without disturbance the transformation from the work of slaves to that of freemen, offered to the world, as a special case of history, one of the most beautiful triumphs of liberty, united with the cause of order, was resolved to preserve in the noble purpose of obtaining through the evolution of ideas and by the peaceful struggles of law the consecration of its aspirations within the Spanish sovereignty.

To that purpose I have directed all the efforts which I have deemed opportune and pertinent, from ordering in a decided and conclusive manner that the reconcentrados be furnished with a daily ration and that the sick in the hospitals be duly attended, to ordering by a recent decree (bando) the reorganization of agricultural and industrial labors, as well as its normalization, to the end that without obstacles nor difficulties the poor people, specially, should be able to find means of subsistence, mitigation for their economic situation, and a possible remedy for their misfortunes.

The work of absolutely suspending the concentration and of remedying immediately the evils derived there from not being possible, unless it should be pretended that a crowd, composed largely of women and children, be launched into the fields, exposed, therefore, to suffer even greater evils than that which they may experience by remaining in the towns and which would surely give rise to as serious censures as the concentration measures have caused, it becomes necessary to proceed in this matter with the foresight, good sense, and tact imposed by events and which the authority cannot ignore.

In view of these considerations and having resolved to make the causes of this evil disappear as far as possible, prudently, and for the benefit of all, until obtaining the complete reestablishment of the normality in the life of the rural population

I have decided to order as follows :

First. All reconcentrados possessing farms, as owners, lessees, or in partnership, and who possess elements and resources to help themselves, can again establish themselves in same and commence to work, for which they shall count with the protection and aid assured to them by the last instructions regarding the reorganization of agricultural and industrial labors. To this end, they shall obtain from the proper civil or military authority the piece of land where they are to establish themselves, a permit bearing the name of the individuals composing the family, the names of the persons accompanying them, number and kind of animals which they may keep, agricultural and other implements which they may need, and the kind of labor they will undertake; and they shall at the same time prove how they will obtain the implements, clothes, and effects which they may need from the moment of their establishment.

Second. Those not comprised in such case, but who attend to the industrial and agricultural labors, as artisans and laborers, can do so, provided they reside in the farm or plantation where they work, that they pass the night within the fortified place of said farm or plantation, and that they always carry with them their proper personal documents.

Third. To this end the sugar estates, cane fields (colonias de caña), tobacco plantations, coffee plantations, and other farms or plantations of importance properly defended shall be considered as centers of labor, and their owners are authorized to have in them the necessary employees and laborers —the present reconcentrados as well as persons who having invoked pardon have complied with the formalities of surrender. Special care should be adopted that the proper hygienic measures are carried out which may guarantee the health of the laboring population.

Fourth. In all cases to which the preceding paragraphs refer to, are the owners, lessees, or partners of the farms or plantations obliged to build centers of defense of the zones of cultivation which they comprehend, and in the exterior circuit of which shall be established, in compliance with orders from the general staff of the army, the basis of operations of the columns in charge of fighting the rebels and of defending such centers whenever necessary. To this end the owners, lessees, and partners of farms or plantations are authorized to carry arms for their defense, and the employees and laborers are authorized to carry revolver and machete for the defense of the zone which guarantees the elements of life to their person and their families' subsistence—after obtaining due permission from the local authorities in accordance with the owners of the farms or plantations.

Fifth. The families and persons now concentrated who will not be able to enjoy the benefits which those comprised in the foregoing cases may obtain, either because they have no piece of land, or because they have no resources with which to establish themselves in same, or because they are unable to work, shall remain in the towns under the direct protection of the boards for the protection of the reconcentrados which shall be constituted with Government funds and with the aid o public charity.

Sixth. These boards shall be immediately organized in the capitals of the provinces by the civil governors, by the alcaldes (mayors) in the municipal districts, and by the deputies from the city governments (ayuntamientos) in the towns,

and they shall act under the direction and presidency of the said civil authorities, who for the purpose of constituting said boards shall associate themselves as follows :

(1) To the military commandants, who are already instructed by the general staff of their obligation to ration the reconcentrados;

> (2) to the parish priests, whom the ecclesiastic authority shall inform them of the cooperation they shall tender to such humane purposes;
>
> (3) to the municipal physicians, to whom pertains the medical aid of those who may need it; and
>
> (4) to the proprietors, merchants, traders, and agriculturists whom the presidents may designate.
>
> **Seventh**. The protection afforded by these boards shall extend under the same conditions, not only to the reconcentrados, but to persons coming from the rebel camp and who have invoked pardon, while they lack means of subsistence.
>
> **Eighth**. These boards shall report their works every fifteen days to their respective presidents or to their superiors, who in turn shall report to the secretary's office of the General Government of the island.
>
> **Ninth**. The civil and military authorities in charge of the execution of these provisions shall see that they are strictly complied with, under their responsibility.
>
> **RAMÓN BLANCO.**
> Havana, 13 November, 1897.

Upon receiving Lee's communiqué in Washington, William Rufus Day, US Assistant Secretary of State during McKinley's' first presidency, asked for a detailed account of affairs in Cuba.

William Rufus Day, a graduate of the University of Michigan in 1870, was one of the more distinguished jurists in the US government. He eventually succeeded John Sherman, the Secretary of State, after disagreements between Sherman and McKinley.

Day had been instrumental in securing from Congress a US$50,000 appropriation on May 24, for the relief of American citizens residing in Cuba. On November 23, 1897 and November 27, Lee wrote two extensive messages to Mr. Day, informing him of the position of the Cuban Independent Army as well as the terrors of Weyler's Concentration Camps.

Letter of Mr. Lee to Mr. Day.
[No. 710.] *United States Consulate-General,*
Havana, November 23, 1897.

Sir: I have the honor to briefly submit a statement of what appears to be the present condition of affairs in this island.

First. The insurgents will not accept autonomy.

Second. A large majority of the Spanish subjects who have commercial and business interests and own property here will not accept autonomy, but prefer annexation to the United States rather than an independent republic or genuine autonomy under the Spanish flag.

Third. The Spanish authorities are sincere in doing all in their power to encourage, protect, and promote the grinding of sugar. The grinding season commences in December.

Fourth. The insurgents' leaders have given instructions to prevent grinding wherever it can be done, because by diminishing the export of sugar the Spanish Government revenues are decreased. It will be very difficult for the Spanish authorities to prevent cane burning, because one man at night can start a fire which will burn hundreds of acres, just as a single individual could ignite a prairie by throwing a match into the dry grass.

Fifth. I am confident that General Blanco, and Pando, his chief of staff, as well as Dr. Congosto, the secretary general, with all of whom I have had conversations, are perfectly conscientious in their desire to relieve the distress of those suffering from the effects of Weyler's reconcentration order, but unfortunately they have not the means to carry out such benevolent purposes.

I have read letters stating that charitable persons in the United States will send clothing, food, and some money to these unfortunate people, and I have arranged with the Ward Line of steamers to provide free transportation from New York. I hope to secure the permission of the Spanish authorities here for such things to be entered free of duty. I am told, however, that they must come consigned to the bishop of Havana. The sufferings of the Reconcentrado class have been terrible beyond description, but in Havana less than in other places on the island; yet Dr. Brunner, acting United States sanitary inspector here, informed me this morning that the death rate of the reconcentrados in this city was about 50 per

cent in other places of the island, and when it is remembered that there have been several hundred thousands of these noncombatants, or pacíficos, mainly women and children, who are concentrated under General Weyler's order, some idea can be formed of the mortality among them.

In this city matters are assuming better shape. Under charitable committees large numbers of them have been gathered together in houses, and are now fed and cared for by private subscriptions. I visited them yesterday and found their condition comparatively good, and there will be a daily improvement among them, though the lives of all cannot be saved. I witnessed many terrible scenes and saw some die while I was present. I am told General Blanco will give $100,000 to the relief fund.

I am, etc.,
FITZHUGH LEE,
Consul General.

Letter of Mr. Lee to Mr. Day.
[No. 712.] *United States Consulate-General,*
Havana, November 27, 1897.

Sir: One of two gentlemen who visited the reconcentrados after they were concentrated in los fosos (the ditches) in this city handed me to-day the enclosed paper. The names of these two gentlemen are not signed to it for obvious reasons.

I personally know the gentleman who brought the communication, and know that he stands high in this community as a man of integrity and character.

The number of reconcentrados here, as I had the honor to report already, have always been less than elsewhere. I am able to say now that they will be taken care of and fed by committees of charitably disposed persons.

The ayuntamiento (city government) of Havana has ordered an additional tax of 5 per cent to be levied upon real estate in this city. I am informed that this sum has already reached the amount of $80,000, and that it is to be devoted exclusively to the relief of the reconcentrados.

The $100,000 reported in a former dispatch as being given by the Governor-General, is in Spanish silver, and is to be applied to the reconcentrados over the whole island.

I am, etc.,
FITZHUGH LEE,
Consul General.

[Enclosure with dispatch No. 712.]

Sir: The public rumor of the horrible state in which the reconcentrados of the municipal council of Havana were found in the fosos haying reached us, we resolved to pay a visit there, and we will relate to you what we saw with our own eyes:

Four hundred and sixty women and children thrown on the ground, heaped pell-mell as animals, some in a dying condition, others sick and others dead, without the slightest cleanliness, nor the least help, not even to give water to the thirsty, with neither religious or social help, each one dying wherever chance laid them, and for this limited number of reconcentrados the deaths ranged between forty and fifty daily, giving relatively ten days of life for each person, with great joy to the authorities who seconded fatidically the politics of General Weyler to exterminate the Cuban people, for these unhappy creatures received food only after having been for eight days in the Fosos, if during this time they could feed themselves with the bad food that the dying refused.

On this first visit we were present at the death of an old man who died through thirst. When we arrived he begged us, for God's sake, to give him a drink. We looked for it and gave it to him, and fifteen minutes afterwards he breathed his last, not having had even a drink of water for three clays before. Among the many deaths we witnessed there was one scene impossible to forget. There is still alive the only living witness, a young girl of 18 years, whom we found seemingly life less on the ground; on her right-hand side was the body of a young mother, cold and rigid, but with her young child still alive clinging to her dead breast; on her left-hand side was also the corpse of a dead woman holding her son in a dead embrace; a little farther on a poor, dying woman having in her arms a daughter of fourteen, crazy with pain, who after five or six days also died in spite of the care she received.

In one corner a poor woman was dying, surrounded by her children, who contemplated her in silence, without a lament or shedding a tear, they themselves being real specters of hunger, emaciated in a horrible manner. This poor woman augments the catalogue already large of the victims of the reconcentration in the fosos.

The relation of the pictures of misery and horror which we have witnessed would be never ending were we to narrate them all.

It is difficult and almost impossible to express by writing the general aspect of the inmates of the fosos, because it is entirely beyond the line of what civilized humanity is accustomed to see; therefore no language can describe it.

The circumstances which the municipal authorities could reunite there are the following: Complete accumulation of bodies dead and alive, so that it was impossible to take one step without walking over them; the greatest want of cleanliness, want of light, air, and water; the food lacking in quality and quantity what was necessary to sustain life, thus sooner putting an end to these already broken-down systems; complete absence of medical assistance; and what is more terrible than all, no consolation whatever, religious or moral.

If any young girl came in any way nice looking, she was infallibly condemned to the most abominable of traffics.

At the sight of such horrible pictures the two gentlemen who went there resolved in spite of the ferocious Weyler, who was still Captain-General of the island, to omit nothing to remedy a deed so dishonorable to humanity, and so contrary to all Christianity. They did not fail to find persons animated with like sentiments, who, putting aside all fear of the present situation, organized a private committee with the exclusive end of aiding materially and morally the reconcentrados. This neither has been nor is at present an easy task. The great number of the poor and scarcity of means make us encounter constant conflicts.

This conflict is more terrible with the official elements and in a special manner with the mayor of the city and the civil authorities, who try by all means to annihilate this good work. The result of the collections are very insignificant if we bear in mind the thousands of people who suffer from the reconcentrations; but it serves for some consolation to see that in Havana some 159 children and 84 women are well cared for in the asylum erected in Cadiz street, No. 82, and 93 women and children are equally well located in a large saloon erected for them in the second story of the fosos, with good food and proper medical assistance, as also everything indispensable to civilized life.

According to the information which we have been able to acquire since August until the present day, 1,700 persons have entered the Fosos proceeding from Jaruco, Campo Florido, Guanabo, and Tapaste, in the province of Havana. Of these, only 243 are living now and are to be found in Cadiz street—82 in the saloon already mentioned and 61 in the Quinta del Rey and the Hospital Mercedes, the whole amounting to about 397. and of these a great many will die on account of the great sufferings and hunger they have gone through.

From all this we deduct that the number of deaths among the reconcentrados has amounted to 77%.

Remains of a mass-burrial in Jovellanos, Matanzas, 1896

As Spain was favoring Autonomy for Cuba in 1897 and the US was helping the insurgents, rebel leaders engaged in extensive propaganda to get the U.S. to intervene, as shown in this cartoon in an American magazine. Columbia (the **American people**) reaches out to help oppressed **Cuba** in 1897 while **Uncle Sam** (the U.S. government) is blind to the crisis and will not use its powerful guns to help. Image taken from ***Judge Magazine***, February 6, 1897.

On November 25th, 1897, the ***Autonomy Statute of Cuba*** received formal approval with a Royal Decree from Sagasta's liberal government. The Decree aimed to resolve the issue of Cubans requesting commercial and political self-reliance as well as to end the war started in 1895. The self-determination of the Island had a great impact in the US press. Many newspapers showed their approval or disagreement over the Decree, all of them showing clearly their political or ideological tendencies. This cartoon published in **Puck** shows the Autonomous position: **defend us from the evil of the separatists**.

Fitzhugh Lee, as American Consul in Havana, used to spend a good two hours daily in his office reading the most important newspapers published with emphasis in Cuban affairs. This daily task involved going through **El Diario de la Marina**, **La Lucha**, **El Avisador Comercial**, **El Siglo**, **La Discusión** (in Havana), **The Times of Cuba** (in Santiago) and **Patria** (New York). One of the articles in La Lucha is Transcribed here.

These sources available to Mr. Lee included also important documents issued by the leaders of the insurrectos in Cuba, like Mayor General Mayía Rodríguez, one of whose dispatches Mr. Lee sent to Mr. Day on November 23, 1879.

> *MR. LEE SPEAKS.*
> From the newspaper *La Lucha*, of Havana, November 15, 1897.
>
> With the arrival of the consul-general of the United States of America in this island, Mr. Fitzhugh Lee, and because of the rumors published by the press of his country regarding the attitude which the said consular representative would assume, as well as because of the report published by some Madrid paper relative to a banquet given by the New York filibusters to Mr. Lee, everything connected with the latter has again obtained a certain importance.
>
> Yesterday, by the American steamer *Segurança*, Mr. Lee arrived from the leave of absence granted to him by his Government. Desirous of greeting Mr. Lee and of learning the position he would adopt in connection with the new policy which the Supreme Government intends to pursue in this island, we commissioned one of our reporters to interview the distinguished consul-general.
>
> At dinner hour, in the *Hotel Inglaterra*, where he stops, we approached his table and met him in company with the esteemed vice-consul, Mr. Joseph A. Springer. After exchanging courtesies we inquired, in the first place, for his family. He told us that Mrs. and Miss Lee had remained in Virginia, one of his sons in the Military Academy of West Point, and the other one, Fitz, who accompanied him before, had a position with a railroad company.
>
> Regarding the passage from New York to Havana he told us that he had left the former port last Wednesday, and that on
> Thursday the wind blew so hard that the *Segurança*, notwithstanding her excellent conditions, rolled so much that the gen-

eral fell in his stateroom, causing himself a slight wound on the forehead.

«What instructions have you received from the President?»

«I have received no special instructions of any kind,» he answered. «My functions in the future shall be the same as those of the past; namely, to protect the property and lives of the American citizens in this island, and to encourage the development of the commercial interests of both countries. Nothing further.»

With respect to the banquet which, according to a cablegram from New York, published by *La Lucha* on Saturday, had been given to him in New York by the Cuban filibusters, Mr. Lee told us that he had not attended any banquet there, and consequently made no speech ; that he only remained in New York two or three days before leaving for this city, during which period he attended lunches offered to him by personal friends, with no political character whatever.

He says such a telegram is untrue, and he does not know the reason which may have inspired the author of same.

We inquired from Mr. Lee regarding the effect which the first measures of General Blanco have produced in the United States, and he told us that they had been received favorably, as would be all tending to make less sensible the horrors of the war. «In my country...» he added, «...peace is desired. The last words I heard from President McKinley were: "My sincere wish is that peace be not disturbed."»

«Aside from official circles,» we inquired, «how does the American people think in regard to autonomy, about to be established in Cuba?»

«Outside of official circles,» he answered, «not much is known about autonomy, and the popular classes rarely speak of it. Besides, until the new regime does not commence to act it cannot be judged, and then they will see how it is received by the Cubans.»

We did not wish to occupy any longer the attention of the amiable Mr. Lee, and we took leave of him, thanking him for the deference he has always shown to *La Lucha*.

Letter of Mr. Lee to Mr. Day.
[No. 709] *United States Consulate-General,*
Havana, November 23, 1897.

Sir: Someone handed me yesterday the enclosed paper, of which I accompany a translation, and which purports to be signed by the insurgent chief in command of the Havana province.

I am, etc.,

FITZHUGH LEE,
Consul-General.

William Rufus Day, Assistant Secretary of State in the first McKinley Cabinet, to whom most of the dispatches from Consul Lee were addressed.

[Enclosure with Dispatch No. 709.]
WESTERN MILITARY DEPARTMENT.

To the inhabitants of Cuba:

Upon the initiation of the winter campaign by General Blanco, after the failure of the bloodthirsty Weyler, I wish to remind you of our firm resolution to continue fighting until the attainment of absolute independence.

Our principles are well defined. We wish to have a republic where all its inhabitants shall enjoy equal rights and live in fraternity. We do not hate the Spaniard.

Our conduct toward the Spanish wounded and prisoners prove it. Remember "*La Larga*," "*El Senado*," "*Ramón de las Yaguas*," "*Guáimaro*," and "*Victoria de las Tunas*" in Oriente and Camagüey, and "*Lomitas*" in Las Villas, as well as "*Viñales*" and "*Ojo de Agua*" in Pinar del Rio. Our wounded have, nevertheless, been mutilated, our prisoners shot, and the peaceful inhabitants, even women and children, murdered without pity, as if the Spanish representative, sent to Cuba by the unfortunate Cánovas del Castillo, had proposed to exterminate the inhabitants of this country.

Spaniards, we only consider as enemies those who combat against us. Cubans, do your duty and the end of the struggle will be abbreviated, and the horrors and ruins suffered by our country will terminate.

Long live the Cuban Republic!

J. M. Rodríguez *(aka Mayía Rodríguez)*
November 10, 1897,
Major-General, Chief of the Western Department.

Mayor General *José María Rodríguez* (Mayía), Chief of the Western Department of the Cuban Independence Army in the War of 1895

Early in December of 1897, an additional problem became important in the mind of Fitzhugh Lee. There were continuous rumors across Cuba of efforts by the Spanish authorities, and possibly by some Cubans loyal to Spain, to induce the population to take action against the Americans living in Cuba. The issue had a historical significance.

The United States served as a refuge for many Cubans fleeing in the aftermath of the 1868 war, and Washington allowed revolutionaries like José Martí, the founder of el *Partido Revolucionario Cubano* (the Cuban Revolutionary party), to collect war funds and organize a second revolution in places like New York City, Key West, Tampa and Philadelphia. The United States was seen by Spain a pivotal component for the Cuban struggle for independence from Spain. Madrid was afraid that in a few years they could see Cuban freedom fighters battling the Spanish army, and perhaps joining forces with the United States, who already had extensive commercial and cultural ties with the Cubans. These issues had generated resentment and a negative sentiment toward the United States from the Cubans loyal to Spain as well as from the Spanish government and its people.

To clarify this issues and to keep Mr. Day up to date on the rumors, Lee sent a ciphered telegram to Washington and confirmed it with a telex confidential message on December 3:

Letter of Mr. Lee to Mr. Day.

[No. 717] *United States Consulate-General,*
Havana, December 3, 1897.

Sir: Referring to my cipher telegram of the 1st instant, which I beg to confirm, reading as follows:

ASSISTANT SECRETARY OF STATE, ETC. :

Inform the Department that he has learned from the United States consul at Matanzas of an extensive and dangerous conspiracy, under the ex-governor of the province, directed against Americans, action against them to lie contingent upon movement of the United States Government in favor of independence to Cuba.

I have the honor to state that rumors have been more or less frequent regarding the riotous intentions of some of the dissatisfied elements toward citizens of the United States dwelling here and in other parts of the island. Any riotous demonstrations here must come from the Spanish noncombatants or from the volunteer forces. I do not think there is any danger from the former, many of whom seem to be in favor of annexation, rather than for real autonomy or for an independent Cuban Republic. And I am inclined to think if General Blanco can manage the volunteers as yesterday he said he could, the trouble from that source is diminishing. The origin of the mobs in this city in the past has always been located in the ranks of the volunteers, who alone have organization and arms.

The Governor and Captain-General is now investigating the Matanzas rumors and will, I am sure, deal promptly with any conspirators found there.

The Weyler police have all been changed and the officers of the volunteers, too, when the Government here has reason to doubt their loyalty.

In consequence of all this, and the assurances of the governmental authorities that American life and property will, if necessary, be protected by them at a moment's notice, I have declined to make an application for the presence of one or more war ships in this harbor, and have advised those of our people who have wives and children here not to send them away, at least for the present, because such proceedings would not, in my opinion, be justifiable at this time, from the stand point of personal security.

I still think that two war ships at least should be at Key West, prepared to move here at short notice, and that more of them should be sent to Dry Tortugas, and a coal station be established there. Such proceedings would seem to be in line with that prudence and foresight necessary to afford safety to the Americans residing on the island, and to their properties, both of which, I

> have every reason to know, are objects of the greatest concern to our Government.
> I am, etc.,
> *Fitzhugh Lee,*
> Consul General.

Additionally, Mr. Lee sent Mr. Day a newspaper cutout from page 8 of the Semi-weekly *The Express*, published in Terre Haute, Indiana on November 2, 1897. The article refers to an interview of former Prime Minister ***José Canalejas Méndez*** by a local newsman upon his arrival to New York:

> **New York, Oct. 30.**—Among the passengers who arrived in this city this morning on the steamship *La Touraine* from Havre was Senor, one of the leading Spanish statesmen, who came to the United States en route for Cuba. Senor Canalejas was met at the pier by Senor Fialdasano, the Spanish-Consul in this city.
> The greatest importance is attached to Senor Canalejas' trip. The Spanish statesmen govern their colonies from Madrid, and are not in the habit of visiting them. Senor Canalejas is the first Spaniard of real political standing who has undertaken the task of finding out for himself what makes the inhabitants of Cuba rebellious, and so his decision to go to that island gave rise to much comment among his colleagues. He has held the portfolios of public works, justice and finance. He Is one of the most eloquent speakers in the Spanish Cortes, and figures among the more prominent lawyers in Madrid. He is the proprietor of the *Heraldo de Madrid*, the leading evening paper in the Spanish capital. He was a political friend of Sagasta, the Spanish Premier, until about three months ago, when he withdrew from the Liberal Party because Sagasta endorsed the program of the Cuban home rulers. He then announced his intention of going to Cuba to study the situation in order to be able to inform Spain as to the exact conditions there and the best method of dealing with them.
> Senor Canalejas said this morning:.
> «*Before proceeding to Cuba I shall visit several important cities in the United States, and if I have time I shall also go to Canada. My intention is to investigate the actual feeling of American, people as regards the Cuban problem. We have been told in Spain so many things concerning the United States that, feeling that many of them were utterly absurd, I wish to find out the truth. With this aim in view I shall interview such public men here as will best inform me of be situation. At the same time I shall see certain Cubans of real prominence with whose views, however, opposed to mine, I should like to become acquainted. I*

> *am not blindly partisan, and do not will to be led into error after taking the trouble to make this voyage.»*
> "How is it," was asked, "that you object to colonial home rule, and yet you boast of liberal democratic principles?"
> *«I do not object to autonomy from an abstract point of view. How could I? In my opinion Cuba has not been duly prepared for self-government. I agree that she is entitled to every reasonable liberty, but she is still in her infancy, and needs the tutelage of a strong nation.»*
> "It has been said that you have seriously considered Silvela's hints concerning the advisability of abandoning Cuba, and that you really purpose going there to acquire that authority over all the other Spanish politicians, with which a personal inspection of the island alone could invest you, and thus be able to come put in behalf of evacuation when you return to Spain. Is this true?"
> *«I have no comment to make in that regard,»*
> ...was Señor José Canalejas response.

> **Editor's Note:** ***Francisco Silvela y Le Vielleuze*** was a Spanish politician who became the Prime Minister of Spain on May 3, 1899, succeeding Práxedes Mateo Sagasta. He served in this capacity until October 22, 1900.

The newspaper article from *The Express* was followed by Lee with several comments having to do with Canalejas' visit to Cuba:

> ***Letter of Mr. Lee to Mr. Day.***
> [No. 718] *United States Consulate-General,*
> Havana, December 3, 1897.
> Sir: I have the honor to state that a representative of a Madrid paper here says that:
> Canalejas has said, upon his return from the Vuelta Abajo, or Pinar del Rio province, after the recent combat there between the Spanish generals Bernal and Hernández de Velasco, in command of 2,300 men, and two pieces of artillery, and Cuban forces under Pedro Díaz, that although the Spanish troops have displayed once more their usual valor in the said fight, and the enemy must have suffered heavy losses, yet the province of Pinar del Rio is not pacified, and that there are numerous rebel forces still there.
> That out of about 14,000 Spanish regular troops in that province, only about 3,000 or 4,000 are able to operate, the balance being sick at the hospitals, garrisoning towns, and other

> wise distributed. That he believes autonomy premature, and inclines himself to the adoption of energetic military action for the purpose of finally pacifying said province. That he does not believe in altering facts and news. That the truth, no matter how painful and bitter it may be, must be known in the peninsula, where public opinion and the press has been deceived regarding the annihilation of the war and the so-called pacification of the western provinces, among which that of Pinar del Rio has been included.
>
> *La Lucha* to-day publishes that Canalejas has said " that the economic condition of the Pinar del Rio province is deplorable, there being 40,000 reconcentrados absolutely destitute, 15,000 of which are children, most of whom are orphans; that they are unequally distributed throughout "the different towns in the province, there being only 460 at the capital, city of Pinar del Rio, while in small towns like Consolación and Candelaria there are over 4,000. The municipalities cannot incur any expense, because the taxes cannot be collected, because most of the taxpayers, if not all, have been ruined by the war."
>
> I am, etc.,
> FITZHUGH LEE,
> Cónsul General.

A Few days later, in a letter from Mr. Lee to Mr. Day, the Consul-General informs the Assistant Secretary of State that measures for the relief of the reconcentrados are not sufficiently energetic to be effective, and that he is advised by the Governor-General that authority to admit articles of food and clothing from the United States to Cuban ports free of duty rested with the authorities at Madrid.

> *Letter of Mr. Lee to Mr. Bay.*
> [No. 723] *United States Consulate-General,*
> Havana, December 7, 1897.
> Sir:
>
> I see no effects of the governmental distribution to the reconcentrados. I am informed that only $12,500, in Spanish silver, had been dedicated to the Havana province out of the $100,000 said to have been set aside for the purpose of relieving them on the island, and that reports from all parts of the province show that 50 per cent have already died and that many of those left will die. Most of these are women and children. I do not believe the Government here is really able to relieve the distress and sufferings of these people.

I am informed an order has been issued in some parts of the island suspending the distribution of rations to reconcentrados. The condition of these people is simply terrible.

I enclose herewith an official copy of the comparative mortality in Havana for the six months ending November 30. It will be perceived that there has been a great increase in the death rate, and without adequate means in the future to prevent it the mortality will increase.

I hear of much suffering in the Spanish hospitals for want of food and among the Spanish soldiers. I hear, also, that the Spanish merchants in some parts of the island are placing their establishments in the names of foreigners in order to avoid their provisions being purchased on credit by the military administration, and that the Spanish army is suffering much from sickness and famine, and that a great deal of money is needed at once to relieve their condition. In some parts of the island, I am told, there is scarcely any food for soldiers or citizens, and that even cats are used for food purposes, selling at 30 cents apiece.

It is a fair inference therefore to draw from the existing conditions, that it is not possible for the Governor General of this island to relieve the present situation with the means at his disposal.

I am, etc.,
FITZHUGH LEE,
Consul-General.

Washington became increasingly insistent that Mr. Lee keep them informed of the status of the concept of Autonomy in the minds of the Cuban population and its leaders, as well as the support such concept would have among Spanish leaders.

[Confidential.]
Letter of Mr. Lee to Mr. Bay.
[No. 726] *United States Consulate-General,*
Havana, December 13, 1897. (Received December 18.)
Sir: I have the honor to make the following report:

The contest for and against autonomy is most unequal. For it, there are five or six of the head officers at the palace, and twenty or thirty other persons here in the city.

Against it, first, are the insurgents, with or without arms, and the Cuban noncombatants; second, the great mass of the Spaniards, bearing or nonbearing arms—the latter desiring, if there must be a change, annexation to the United States.

> Indeed, there is the greatest apathy concerning autonomy in any form. No one asks what it will be, or when, or how it will come.
>
> I do not see how it could be even put into operation by force, because, as long as the insurgents decline to accept it, so long, the Spanish authorities say, the war must continue.
>
> I am obliged to say, too, that the Government of this island has not been able to relieve from starvation the Cuban population driven from their homes by the Weyler edict, and no longer attempts to do so.
>
> I am, etc.,
> FITZHUGH LEE,
> Consul General.

The subject of *reconcentrados*, however, was never far from the concerns of Washington officials.

> **Letter of Mr. Lee to Mr. Day,**
> [No. 727] United States Consulate-General,
> Havana, December 14, 1897.
>
> Sir: I have the honor to report that I have received information that in the province of Havana reports show that there have been 101,000 "*reconcentrados*," and that out of that 52,000 have died. 32,000 of the said 101,000 were children. This excludes the city of Havana and seven other towns from which reports have not yet been made up. It is thought that the total number of reconcentrados in Havana province will amount to 150,000, nearly all women and children, and that the death rate among their whole number from starvation alone will be over 50 per cent.
>
> For the above number of reconcentrados $12,500, Spanish silver, was set aside out of the $100,000 appropriated for the purpose of relieving all the reconcentrados on the island. Seventy-five thousand of the 150,000 may be still living, so if every dollar appropriated of the $12,500 reaches them the distribution will average about 17 cents to a person, which, of course, will be rapidly exhausted, and as I can hear of no further succor being afforded, it is easy to perceive what little practical relief has taken place in the condition of those poor people.
>
> I am, etc.,
> FITZHUGH LEE.

The Cuban conflict had aroused a great interest in the Spanish public opinion. As events rushed towards a war, the press was particularly intent on informing, and also forming, a public opinion favorable to autonomy rather than colonial status or independence for Cuba.

The campaign of war in Cuba, the arrival of Weyler to the Peninsula after his dismissal, the attitude of the United States in the crisis and the terms of autonomy were issues that monopolized the spaces of the newspapers in the days before and immediately after the approval of the autonomic regime for the island. On November 27, two days after his signature, the new Cuban Autonomy Constitution was published in the official paper *La Gaceta*. Washington observed that step with increasing interest as it was vital to receive fresh news from their Consul in Cuba at the earliest possible time.

Letter of Mr. Lee to Mr. Day.
[No. 732] *United States Consulate-General,*
Havana, December 28, 1897.

Sir: I have the honor to report that I have been informed by the authorities here that they are now engaged in forming an autonomist cabinet and arranging for the members to take the required oath on the 1st January next, and also for an election to take place thirty days thereafter.

My present information is that most of the Spaniards will refrain from voting, and nearly all of the (Cubans.

The feeling in Havana, and I hear in other parts of the island, is strong against it—the Cubans desiring an independent republic and the Spaniards preferring annexation to the United States rather than autonomy. On the night of the 24th instant there seems to have been a concerted plan over the island to testify the disapprobation of the people to the proposed autonomist plans of the Spanish Government.

It culminated in this city about 2 o'clock in the morning of the 25th, in the principal square of Havana, where a mob assembled with cries of " Death to autonomy!" and to General Blanco, and shouting " Viva Weyler!" These men came to the square with stones in their pockets, and some of them armed with weapons.

They made a demonstration, too, against the office of the Diario de la Marina, a paper published in this town favoring autonomy, but were dispersed by the military police and soldiers.

I am, etc.,
Fitzhugh Lee.

The fact that the autonomy issue was important did not distract Washington from its commitment to assist the people of Cuba with the recovery from Weyler's atrocities. The inquiries about Spain's political plans alternated with requests of information about the needs to be fulfilled in Cuba.

> *Letter of Mr. Lee to Mr. Day.*
> [No. 733] *United States Consulate General,*
> Havana, December 28, 1897.
> Sir : I have the honor to acknowledge receipt of the following telegrams:
>
> Washington, December 24.
> Lee, Consul-General, Havana:
> The following was given to the public, in pursuance of an arrangement this day made with the Spanish minister to that effect:
> «*By direction of the President, the public is informed that in deference to the earnest desire of the Government to contribute by effective action toward the relief of the suffering people in the Island of Cuba, arrangements have been perfected, by which charitable contributions in money or kind can be sent to the island by the benevolently disposed people of the United States. Money, provisions, clothing, medicines, and the like articles of prime necessity can be forwarded to General Fitzhugh Lee, the consul-general of the United States at Havana, and all articles now dutiable by law so consigned will be admitted into Cuba free of duty.*
> *The consul-general has been instructed to cooperate with the local authorities and the charitable boards for the distribution of such relief among the destitute and needy people of Cuba. The President is confident that the people of the United States, who have on many occasions in the past responded most generously to the cry for bread from people stricken by famine or sore calamity, and who have beheld no less generous action on the part of foreign communities, when their own country men have suffered from fire and flood, will heed the appeal for aid that comes from the destitute at their threshold, and especially at this season of good will and rejoicing, give of their abundance to this humane end. —John Sherman.*»
> Please cooperate with the local authorities to this end.
> DAY.
>
> LEE, *Consul-General, Havana:*
> Wire immediately character of supplies most needed for Cuban relief. Will money be of more service than food, clothing, etc.? DAY.

The *New York Journal's* publisher, William Randolph Hearst, had sent Julian Hawthorne, the son of novelist Nathaniel Hawthorne and one of his best reporters, to Cuba where he filed dispatches that aroused American sympathy for the Cuban people and fomented pro-war sentiment. On February 4 Hawthorne met with Fitzhugh Lee in his offices and shared with him a report he was sending his paper. Lee included a copy on his next dispatch from Havana. It was published both in *The New York Journal* and in the *Chicago Tribune* on February 14, 1897.

> «Cuba is an earthly paradise, and the climate the most exquisite and caressing that man has ever known. There is no richer soil in the world. Nature has withheld nothing that could make man happy or serve to render him prosperous. The Eden that is Cuba has been transformed it into a hell by a man named Weyler. Not in this age, certainly, has a crime been perpetrated more revolting to humanity than Weyler committed when he forced the women and children of the patriots in the Cuban army to come within the Spanish lines and then deliberately starved them there. His ostensible purpose was to weaken the heart of resistance by attacking its tenderest point, but his real aim was the literal extinction of the Cuban race, and he has so far succeeded that out of the million and a half inhabitants of this island when the war began, 600,000 at least, by far the most of them women and children, have been destroyed, either by direct murder or by the slower and more agonizing torture of famine and of disease caused by famine. The Cuban soldiers fighting to save their country have not been met and defeated in the field. They have been barbarously robbed of their mothers, wives, sisters, and offspring. When and if their independence is won they will have no families to return to.
>
> Weyler's policy did not succeed in breaking their iron spirit of resistance to tyranny, but in other respects it has been only too successful. More than a third of the population is dead. Hundreds more are dying daily in Havana and its environs alone; dying with accompaniments of misery and suffering almost inconceivable, wholly indescribable. They fall dead in the streets; they do it before your eyes, as you stand in the wretched pens where they are huddled together. They die with an agony of body which is equated only by the hopeless anguish and forlornness of their minds. Until lately, when an attempt to relieve some of them was made in America, they die unpitied and uncared for.
>
> It was thought and often asserted that Blanco would reverse the policy of Weyler. Today those who are well informed shake their heads and say that the improvement is in profession only. Substantially the same things are done now as before. Moreover, Blanco could hardly relieve the situation were he so dis-

posed. Most of the mischief has been already accomplished. The survivors are dying, and were they permitted to go back to what were their homes, and supposing them to have strength to do it, still death would await them. Their fields and houses have been ravaged and burned, and the roving bands of guerrillas would slaughter them without mercy. All this seems incredible, or at least exaggerated, but it is all true and within the truth.»

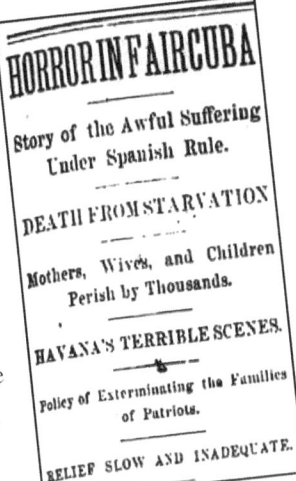

The headline of Hawthorne's article about hunger in Cuba on **The New York Journal**.

Julian Hawthorne

Cuban families reconcentrated in Cienfuegos, Cuba.

Images from Hawthorne's article about hunger in Cuba on **The New York Journal**.

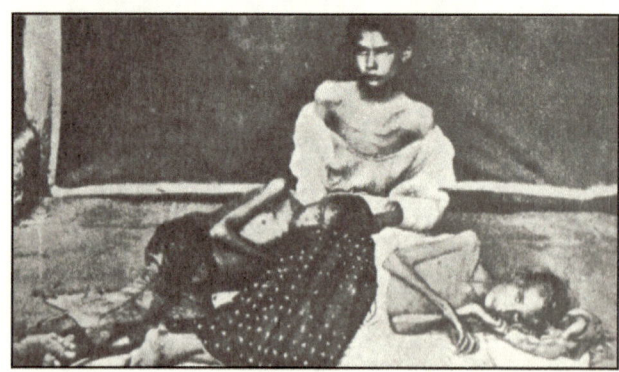

A communiqué from Consul Lee to Assistant Secretary of State May in early January of 1898 provided more details on the extent of the humanitarian crisis in Cuba after the actions of Weyler's reconcentration policies:

> *Letter of Mr. Lee to Mr. Bay.*
> [No. 742] *United States Consulate-General,*
> Havana, January 8, 1898.
>
> Sir: I have the honor to state, as a matter of public interest, that the *"reconcentrado order"* of General Weyler, formerly Governor-General of this island, transferred about 400,000 self-supporting people, principally women and children, into a multitude, to be sustained by the contributions of others or die of starvation or of fevers, resulting from a low physical condition, and being massed in large bodies, without change of clothing and without food.
> Their houses were burned, their fields and plant beds destroyed, and their live stock driven away or killed.
> I estimate that probably 1,200,000 of the rural population in the provinces of Pinar del Rio, Havana, Matanzas, and Santa Clara have died of starvation or from resultant causes, and the deaths of whole families almost simultaneously or within a few days of each other, and of mothers praying for their children to be relieved of their horrible sufferings by death, are not the least of the many pitiable scenes which were ever present. In the provinces of Puerto Principe and Santiago de Cuba, where the *"reconcentrado order"* could not be enforced, the great mass of the people are self-sustaining.
> A daily average of 10 cents' worth of food to 200,000 people would be an expenditure of $20,000 per day, and of course the most humane efforts upon the part of our citizens cannot hope to accomplish such a gigantic relief, and a great portion of these people will have to be abandoned to their fate.
> I am, etc.,
> FITZHUGH LEE.

It was followed by a translation of an article published in the *Diario de la Marina* on January 13, 1898.

> *Letter of Mr. Lee to Mr. Day.*
> [No. 744] *United States Consulate-General,*
> Havana, January 13, 1898.
>
> Sir: I have the honor to enclose a translation of an editorial published in the *Diario de la Marina* of today.
> I am, etc.,
> FITZHUGH LEE.

[Translation.—From the *Diario de la Marina*, of Havana, January 13, 1898.]

Perdónalos, Señor. (Forgive them, for they do not know what they are doing) .

They came against the Diario. They cried out against it. They stoned it. And the *separatists* looked on with joy. And the *laborantes* (abettors of the rebellion), of all well known, could not restrain their rejoicing.

It was natural ; what a great victory for them !

What was not accomplished by Maceo, nor Quintín Banderas, nor Máximo Gómez, was accomplished yesterday by an unconscious mob; carrying disorder, carrying riot, carrying anarchy into the heart of Havana.

And the foreign consuls witnessed the shameful spectacle from the balconies of the *Hotel Inglaterra* ! What shame!

Down with the Diario de la Marina ! Death to the Diario de la Marina !

And Máximo Gómez alive! And Calixto García alive ! And the assassins of the martyr Ruiz also alive ! Poor Spain !

What a difference between yesterday and to-day: Yesterday, your sons, liberals and reactionaries, fell in the streets of Madrid, righting together the common enemy, against the oppressors of Europe, against the invincible hosts of the great Napoleón.

To-day the bravery and the patriotism and the heroism consist in shouting, in out raging, and in knifing, if possible,, defenseless journalists, against whom the action of the laws of the State and in the last extreme, the laws of honor, are sufficient in any civilized country.

But what pains us the most is not this; what our hearts lament at present is not the sentiment of the honorable profession outraged; no. It is the Spanish sentiment; it is the patriotism which boils in our veins with more heat; with a hundred times more enthusiasm than in that of those braves, that in a mob, and in an anonymous manner, have pretended to offend us, without understanding, unfortunates, that what they have trampled on, that what they have dragged through the mud, has been the majesty of the law, the principle of authority, and the honor of the country.

What will say the representatives of foreign powers who witnessed the shameful spectacle of yesterday ? What effect will this great scandal cause in the United States, where they watch our discords, where they await our errors, where they count on our folly to take possession of the apple which they have been waiting for one hundred years to ripen and thereby fall in their hands?

This, this is what pains us; this, this is what shames us; this, this is what frightens us, and not the personal danger which we may risk; if with our blood and with the sacrifice of our lives we could avoid the consequences that for our beloved country we

> foresee and feel as a fatal result of the sad spectacle which happened in the streets of Havana yesterday, the shedding of our blood and the sacrifice of our blood we would consider as well employed.
>
> "This is the greatest victory which up to the present has been gained for the independence of Cuba by Máximo Gómez," was said to us by an invalid chief of the army, a veteran in the past insurrection and of the African war, who came to the *Diario de la Marina* as soon as he received notice of the uprising.
>
> Yes, a victory for Máximo Gómez and a day of rejoicing for the enemies of Spain.
>
> This is what signifies, before all and above all, the seditious tumult of yesterday.

After a request from the Department of States asking Lee to secure solid data that could be presented to Congress, Lee proceeded to send to Washington information gathered on the fields having to do with population numbers and the effects of Weyler's policies.

> ***Letter to Mr. Lee to Mr. Day.***
> [No. 746] *United States Consulate General,*
> Havana, January 13, 1898.
>
> Sir: I have the honor to transmit herewith some statistics sent me about the mortality in the town of Santa Clara, the capital of Santa Clara province, situated about 33 miles south of Sagua, which numbers some 14,000 inhabitants. It will be noticed that there were 5,489 deaths in that town in the seven years previous to 1897, which included 1,417 in one year, from an epidemic of yellow fever, while in 1897, owing to the concentration order, there were 6,981; the concentration order went into effect in February.
>
> In that year, 1897, the month's death rate for January was 78, but in February, the first month of reconcentration, there were 114, and there has been a gradual increase since, as you will see, until in December, 1897, the number of deaths was 1,011. I refer to this as a specimen of the mortality on this island in consequence of the "Reconcentrado order" of the late Captain and Governor General, Weyler.
>
> I am, etc.,
> *FITZHUGH LEE,*
> Consul General

> Enclosure in No. 746
> **STATISTICS OP DEATH RATE IN SANTA CLARA.**
> (A town of 14,000 inhabitants.)
>
> 1890 578   1896 (epidemic of yellow fever
> 1891 720   among army and Cubans) 1,417
> 1892 596   TOTAL: 5,489
> 1893 619
> 1894 687   1897 (no epidemic)   6,981
> 1895 872
>   (1,492 more than in seven previous years.)
>
> Concentration order in February, 1897- Monthly death rate.
> January   78   August   645
> February (concentration) 114   September 630
> March   333   October   884
> April   524   November 1,037
> Mav   539   December 1,011
> June   531
> July   655   TOTAL: 6,981
>
> Sample month, December, 1897.
> Number of Number of deaths and of patients.
>
> Civil Hospital   143 of 170
> Military Hospital   23 of 700
> San Lazarus Hospital   2 of 10
> Buried in poor carts   228
> Buried by family   553
> Prison   2
> TOTAL   951

The situation in Cuba, aside from the effects of Weyler's policies, was turning into a serious security concern for American citizens as well as other civilians living in the capital city of Havana. Lee continued to maintain the US Department of State aware of these events:

> **Letter of Mr. Lee to Mr. Day.**
> [No. 747] *United States Consulate-General,*
> Havana, January 15, 1898.
>
>   Sir:: I have the honor to confirm the following cipher telegrams to you:

Havana, January 18.
Spanish officers with a mob at their heels make an attack upon four autonomist newspapers. The rioting continued until 1:00 pm

Havana, January 1S.
Apprehend serious disturbances as consequence of intense prevailing excitement. Antiautonomists began trouble, confining their attacks to autonomists. Rioting ceased, but many rumors. Consulate-general and palace heavily guarded.

Havana, January 13.
Reports condition of affairs quiet. City under guard. Mobs yesterday cried, Death to autonomy and Blanco, and long live Weyler. The conflict is between Spanish factions. Some of the rioters proposed going to United States consulate. Ships not needed now, but may be later.

Havana, January 13.
Spanish officers and mob attacked three newspaper offices, not four (as reported yesterday). Soldiers joined the mob when sent to defend the newspapers, and outside the palace shouted death to Blanco and autonomy. If Americans are in danger ships should be ready to move promptly for Havana. Uncertainty and excitement widespread.

Havana, January 14.
A few casualties. Disorder last night and this morning and crowds shouting death to Blanco and autonomy. Fears nothing very grave at present. Havana. (Noon. All quiet.)

Havana, January 15.
Quiet prevails.

I have also the honor to acknowledge the receipt of the following cipher telegram, received yesterday from you:

Washington, January 14.
Lee, Consul-General, Havana:
(Instructs him to maintain frequent communication with United States squadron in Key West as to state of affairs at Havana. He should also frequently advise the Department of the situation.)

I am, etc., *FITZHUGH LEE.*

Letter of Mr. Lee to Mr. Hay.
[Confidential.]
[No. 749] *United States Consulate-General,*
Havana, January 18, 1898. (Received January 22.)

Sir: The recent disorders in this city are to be primarily attributed to a group of Spanish officers who were incensed at articles appearing in three of the newspapers of Havana, *El Reconcentrado, La Discusión,* and *El Diario de la Marina.* The first was very pronounced against General Weyler and his methods, *La Discusión* had been suppressed by Weyler, but its

> publication was permitted to be resumed by Blanco, and the last had been an ultra Spanish organ, but had been converted by the present authorities to autonomy.
>
> It is probable that the Spanish officers were first provoked by the denunciations of Weyler in the columns of one of these papers and determined to stop it, and afterwards, being supported by the mob, turned the demonstration into an anti-autonomistic affair.
>
> I send today an analysis of the autonomistic plan. The intense opposition to it on the part of the Spaniards arises from the fact that the first appointment of officers to put into form its provisions were made generally outside of their party in order to show the Cubans in arms that autonomy was instituted for their benefit and protection.
>
> The intelligent Spaniards see no prosperity in the future, but rather other wars and more confusion in the same old attempts to make the waters of commerce flow in unnatural channels. The lower Spanish classes have nothing in mind when autonomy is mentioned except Cuban local rule; hence their opposition.
>
> I am, etc.,
> *FITZHUGH LEE,*
> Consul-General.
> P. S.—The paper referred to will go by the next steamer.

On November 25th, 1897, the Autonomy Statute of Cuba had received formal approval with a Royal Decree from Sagasta's liberal government. The Decree was aimed at resolving the issue of Cubans requesting commercial and political self-reliance as well as to end the war started in 1895. Once it was carefully translated, Fitzhugh Lee lost no time sending his analysis of the Decree to Washington as an enclosure with **Dispatch 754**.

> ***Letter of Mr. Lee to Mr. Day.***
> [No. 754] *United States Consulate-General,*
> Havana, January 21, 1898. (Received January 25.)
>
> Sir: I have the honor to transmit herewith a document containing *"Observations regarding the decree which established on the Island of Cuba the autonomic regime,"* and two copies of the *Havana Gazette* containing the decree referred to.
> I am, etc.,
> *FITZHUGH LEE,*
> Consul- General.

[Enclosure No. I, with dispatch No. 754. [**Translation**.]

OBSERVATIONS REGARDING THE DECREE WHICH ESTABLISHES ON THE ISLAND OF CUBA THE AUTONOMIC REGIME.

1. Article 3 grants to the insular chambers, together with the Governor-General, the power to legislate regarding colonial affairs "in the form and terms designated by law." What law? Those decreed By the Cortes at Madrid? It appears so, because the provisions of a general character emanating from the said Cortes shall receive the name of laws, while the colonial legislative provisions shall be called statutes. And if the Cortes of the Kingdom is the one to fix the form and terms of the colonial resolutions, it has a powerful arm in its hands and can annul the action of the insular chambers.

2. The insular representation is composed of two bodies, with the same authority—the chamber of representatives and the council of administration. Article 4 provides that the chamber is formed by popular election; but that concession, which at first seems extensive, when examined in its relations with the other powers given to the insular representation, is practically deficient. No colonial resolution can be in force unless it has been approved by the chamber and the council. The council, as we shall see later, from the nature of its composition, will be controlled by the Government in such a manner that the representatives of the people to the chamber will always find themselves in the power of the Government in some way. They will not be able to do anything, because if the council does not approve, or should modify the decision of the other house—the chamber—the latter's decisions will have no effect. The veto granted by article 43 will not be required.

3. The council of administration is composed of 25 members; 17 are appointed directly by the Government; the remaining 18 are elected by popular vote. To be elected a member of said council it is necessary to be a Spaniard (Spanish subject), 35 years of age, and possessing an income of $4,000 for two years previous to election. The formation of the council will be therefore controlled by the Government, because the Government will appoint unconditionally the 17 members, and it will be very easy for the Government to find one or more votes among those owing their election to the people, the more so as the conditions required to be a councilor are favorable to those near the Government. In order to pass any measure the presence of a majority of those composing this legislative body is required. It will be very difficult to have all the 18 members elected by the people vote as a unit, and the absence of one or two will be sufficient to give the governmental members control of the body, or the vote be a tie. If the members elected should stand together on any measure objectionable to the Government, they could be sent to their homes by the Governor-General, and he can instruct or direct the election of others more accommodating. On the other hand, the members by governmental appointment cannot be removed—their offices or positions cease with their lives. The Governor-General cannot remove them. And to this end they will be carefully selected as faithful instruments of the Government, in whose hands the whole autonomistic machine will be placed. It is known that in Canada all senators are appointed by the Government; but it should be remembered that the Governor-General appoints them, with the advice and consent of its counselors or ministers, and that these counselors are elected by the parliament, and the parliament by the people, the result is, that in Canada the senators are representatives of the people, while here in Cuba the Government can control them.

4. As if the authority to veto was not sufficient (art. 43) and the power did not exist to suspend, close the sessions, and adjourn both bodies, or either of them, by the decree of the Governor-General, article 30 grants more authority or power to present [prevent ?] or annul the freedom or liberty of the discussions of the colonial parliament, when, in the opinion of the Governor-General, the national interests will be affected by a colonial statute. The bill in question cannot even be discussed unless previously authorized by the central government, and it is a limitation or restriction which has no precedent in any known autonomistic legislation. It is improper because the restriction arises before the debates show the character of the measure to be discussed. It reveals, besides, a mistrust or want of confidence of the mere discussion of the subject. A Governor-General may decree that all bills or colonial statutes may be, in his opinion, contrary to the national interest, and that nothing should be discussed in the local legislative bodies without the previous consent of the Madrid Government. All guaranties are for the Madrid power; there are none for the colony, except the one named in article 43, which fixes the limit within which the Madrid Government has to decide regarding the right of a veto which a colonial statute may have received from the Governor-General.

5. Article 36 grants exclusive power to the Cortes of the Kingdom to determine the expenses of sovereignty which the colony has to pay and the necessary receipts to cover them, for the Cortes can alter them at pleasure. Therefore the colony has no direct vote in a matter of so great importance. It may be said that she is allowed to appoint her deputies to the Cortes of the Kingdom, and that through them the colony can be heard. But the colony's voice will be lost, because their number would be insignificant before the remaining deputies of the nation. And it may happen that the expenses of sovereignty, put by the Cortes on the colony, absorb all of its receipts, because neither of the two houses (chambers) can deliberate regarding the colonial budget without having first voted to pay the expenses of sovereignty.

6. Article 37 speaks of treaties of commerce which may affect Cuba, and states that the Madrid Government shall make them, aided by the delegates of the colonial government. And, further, that when the treaties are approved by the Cortes of the Kingdom they will be published as general laws, and as such will be respected in the insular territory, but it is left doubtful whether they would be laws in Cuba if the colonial delegates should reject them. If the Madrid Government is not to rule in such a case it should be so stated. And if it is a law notwithstanding the colonial opposition, why is the concurrence of the colony asked? The case referred to in article 38 does not decide it, because it only refers to those treaties in the negotiation of which the insular government has had nothing to do.

7. Article 40 gives in a very ingenious manner a method of deciding the differences arising from privileged articles of commerce, in comparison to similar foreign articles, and in reference to the extension of such a privilege, within the maximum limit of 35 per cent differential duty. When the two governments making the treaty do not agree, a committee is formed of the same number of Cuban and peninsular deputies. These deputies appoint their president ; if they do not agree, the eldest in age presides. And the president has the casting vote. Let us suppose the Cuban deputies to be very patriotic, which is, by the way, supposing a great deal, but as they will never be more patriotic than the peninsular delegates, it will result that they will not agree, and then the eldest will decide. As there are a large number of peninsular deputies and a very small number of insular deputies to select from, care will be taken that some aged peninsular deputy be appointed on said committee, and he would be the one to decide. The matter would have been simplified by stating that the eldest peninsular deputy would be the one to make the lists, as such will be the result.

8. Article 40 also refers to the schedules of the merchandise, which will appear in the privileged lists. The decree only says that they shall be made by mutual con sent (meaning Cuban and Peninsular deputies). It does not make any reference to the case when there is no mutual consent, which makes us suppose that the same procedure recommended in the other lists will be observed. The eldest Peninsular deputy will therefore make the said schedules.

9. The Governor-General has the power to suspend the constitutional guarantees, apply legislation of public order *(Ley de Orden Público)*, and adopt any measures he may deem fit to maintain peace, etc. This power the Governor-General can exercise at will, without any limitation, because he is not obliged to hear the opinion of the council of secretaries (ministry), and thus the whole political system of the country lies with the Governor-General. The latter can therefore find any pretext for courts martial, the application of the code of military justice, and all that series of proclamations and orders which have caused so much harm, and which rob the citizen of all guarantees and protection.

10. The distribution of the public debt of Cuba remains completely in the hands and subject to the decision of the Cortes of the Kingdom, which will try to assign to Cuba as much of it as it can, so that Spain will pay the smallest part. Beyond all this, even, the fact remains and makes useless, while it exists, all orderly and pacific development of the autonomic regime, and this fact is the existence of the volunteers in arms. The political party in power is unarmed, has no force of its own, while the Spanish radical (intransigent) party, which is in the opposition, is armed, having on its side the armed volunteers. Under such conditions there can be no genuine autonomic government, because the opposition can ride over, whenever it pleases, the authority of the local government, and of which we had a very recent example, and it can have it repeated whenever the radical Spanish (intransigent) party so desire.

Letter of Mr. Lee to Mr. Day.
[No. 756] *United States Consulate General,*
Havana, January 22, 1898.

Sir: I have the honor to acknowledge receipt of the following telegrams from you:

Washington, January 17.

Instructs consul general to report concerning rumor that the landing of supplies from the *Vigilancia* for the Cuban sufferers was being obstructed by customs authorities, and to prevent such delays, if likely to occur.

And I beg to confirm the following telegrams to you :

Havana, January 15. (All quiet.)

Havana, January 16. All quiet.

Havana, January 17. (Reports supplies by Carcho a week since delivered to-day. Regulations and recent rioting causes of delay. Apprehends no difficulty as to landing supplies and reports arrival to-day of *Vigilancia.*)

Havana, January 18. All tranquil.

At the end of January of 1898, a communiqué of extraordinary importance was sent by Consul Lee to Mr. Day in Washington. Given the nature of this information, the letter was given the outmost of security, without any knowledge by other employees of the consulate except for Mr. Lee. The dispatched read like this.

Letter of Mr. Lee to Mr. Day.
[No. 758] *United States Consulate General,*
Havana, January 30, 1898.

Sir: I have the honor to enclose herewith a statement given to me by one of our informants close to the insurgents in Havana whose word has always been faithfully truthful. According to him, the enclosed letter from the Spanish Ambassador to the US Enrique Dupuy de Lôme to Don José Canalejas, the Foreign Minister of Spain, was intercepted from the mail by Cuban revolutionaries and will soon be released to the Hearst press for publication in the *New York Journal.* The letter criticizes American President William McKinley by calling him weak and concerned only with gaining the favor of the crowd.

Senor Dupuy de Lôme has a large diplomatic experience, having represented Spain in London, Paris, Berlin and Brussels. The letter will be sent to the Cuban Junta in New York for the purpose of publication and the original will be sent to US Secretary of State William R. Day. I have met with our Consuls Barker of Sagua, McGarr of Cienfuegos and Brice of Matanzas and we are all of the opinion that once the letter is published, the news of the insults will fill newspapers across the country, and the story will become a true international scandal.

I am, etc.,
FITZHUGH LEE,
Consul General.

[Enclosure in No. 758] **[Translation]**

LEGACION DE ESPAÑA.
WASHINGTON.
His Excellency Don José Canalejas.

My distinguished and dear friend:
You have no reason to ask my excuses for not having written to me, I ought also to have written to you but I have put off doing so because overwhelmed with work and *nous sommes quittes [NR: we are even).*

The situation here remains the same. Everything depends on the political and military outcome in Cuba. The prologue of all this, in this second stage (phase) of the war, will end the day when the colonial cabinet shall be appointed and we shall be relieved in the eyes of this country of a part of the responsibility for what is happening in Cuba while the Cubans, whom these people think so immaculate, will have to assume it.

Until then, nothing can be clearly seen, and I regard it as a waste of time and progress, by a wrong road, to be sending emissaries to the rebel camp, or to negotiate with the autonomists who have as yet no legal standing, or to try to ascertain the intentions and plans of this government. The (Cuban) refugees will keep on returning one by one and as they do so will make their way into the sheep-fold, while the leaders in the field will gradually come back. Neither the one nor the other class had the courage to leave in a body and they will not be brave enough to return in a body.

The Message has been a disillusionment to the insurgents who expected something different; but I regard it as bad (for us).

Besides the ingrained and inevitable bluntness (*NR: grosería*) with which is repeated all that the press and public opinion in Spain have said about Weyler, it once more shows what McKinley is, weak and a bidder for the admiration of the crowd besides being a would-be politician (*NR: politicastro*) who tries to leave a door open behind himself while keeping on good terms with the jingoes of his party.

Nevertheless, whether the practical results of it (the Message) are to be injurious and adverse depends only upon ourselves.

I am entirely of your opinions; without a military end of the matter nothing will be accomplished in Cuba, and without a military and political settlement there will always be the danger of encouragement being given to the insurgents, by a part of the public opinion if not by the government.

I do not think sufficient attention has been paid to the part England is playing.

Nearly all the newspaper rabble that swarms in your hotels are Englishmen, and while writing for the *Journal* they are also correspondents of the most influential journals and reviews of London. It has been so ever since this thing began.

As I look at it, England's only object is that the Americans should amuse themselves with us and leave her alone, and if there should be a war, that would the better stave off the conflict which she dreads but which will never come about.

It would be very advantageous to take up, even if only for effect, the question of commercial relations and to have a man of some prominence sent hither, in order that I may make use of him here to carry on a propaganda among the Senators and others in opposition to the Junta and to try to win over the refugees.

So, Amblard is coming. I think he devotes himself too much to petty politics, and we have got to do something very big or we shall fail.

Adela returns your greeting, and we all trust that next year you may be a messenger of peace and take it as a Christmas gift to poor Spain.

Ever your attached friend and servant,
ENRIQUE DUPUY DE LÔME

The fate of two of the most promising Spanish politicians as Spain was losing it empire in the Americas

Enrique Dupuy de Lôme (1851–1904) During several years he served in a variety of posts including Japan, Belgium, Uruguay, Argentina, the United States, Germany, and Italy. In 1892 he was named Spanish Minister to the United States.

José Canalejas y Méndez (1854-1912) was a Spanish politician, born in Ferrol, who served as 29th Prime Minister of Spain. Previously, He was Undersecretary to the Presidency (1883), Minister of Public Works and of Justice (1888) and Minister of Finance (1894–95).

Dupuy de Lôme found himself having to support policies he personally opposed and to behave cordially to President McKinley. He expressed his private views in a letter dated December 1897 stating that in his opinion the U.S. President-elect was indecisive and irresolute, and that further negotiations with the Cuban insurgents would be futile. The letter reached the Cuban rebels and by February 9, 1898 Secretary Day already had a copy of the letter in his possession. The *New York Journal* printed an English translation of its contents under the banner headline, "*The Worst Insult to the United States in Its History*." By nightfall, the entire nation knew the contents of the letter and McKinley quickly demanded that the Spanish government apologize. The required response was received from Spain on February 14; two days later the Maine lay at the bottom of Havana harbor.

On November 12, 1912, Spanish prime minister **José Canalejas** followed his normal daily routine of walking from home to the ministry of the interior, in downtown Madrid. Two plainclothes policemen accompanied him as bodyguards, but on orders from Canalejas they remained 20 paces behind him. Pausing on his way to inspect books displayed in the window of the San Martin Library, Canalejas was approached and shot repeatedly by 32-year-old anarchist Manuel Pardinas.

USS *VIGILANCIA* was an American liner of 4,115 tons, built by *Delaware River Iron Shipbuilding & Engineering Works*, in 1890 for the U.S. & Brazil Steamship Co. She had a speed of 14.5 knots and accommodations for 100 1st class passengers. From 1898 to 1909, she was in service for the US Army moving troops and supplies. On March 16th, 1917, *VIGILANCIA*, was sunk by the German submarine U-70 (Otto Wünsche). 15 crew were lost.

The view of the impending war between the US and Spain; two magazines from Spain, **Don Quijote** (its cover showing McKinley ready to attack Spain), **La Campana** (the queen of Spain looks across the Atlantic and says: *What a black destiny!*), and **Le Rire** from Paris (showing McKinley looking at a weak minor figure representing Spain).

OUR CONSUL IN HAVANA   118

Letter of Mr. Lee to Mr. Day.
[No. 767] *United States Consulate- General,*
Havana, February 9, 1898.

Sir: I have the honor to report that I have received $1,743.40 from various sections of the country, in addition to the $5,000 first sent, making a total of $6,743.46, which have been placed to the credit of the unofficial fund. Of this amount about $3,000 have been already expended in purchasing food, paying railroad freights on provisions sent away from the city, and the salary and expenses of an agent to attend to the purchase and distribution, who acts with the committee appointed by the government of the city. It will be necessary to keep sufficient funds on hand to meet the expenses necessarily incurred in the work here. Most of the money I have received has been in small sums, the $1,743.46 being contributed by 37 different persons. Last mail brought me $200 from an unknown donor in Baltimore, Md. I do not see any diminution in the numbers of the suffering poor on this island, except by the daily deaths occurring everywhere from starvation. The present population, which has been concentrated at various places under Weyler's proclamation is still there, not daring to go out to their homes in the interior, if said homes were still in existence, so they continue to herd together with no employment and with but little means of subsistence outside of what we are now trying to afford them. The condition of the reconcentrados is worse in the vicinity of the smaller towns, because they can get something by begging in the larger ones, and hence the death rate is greater in the small towns. The fact that the greater majority of these poor people are principally women and children makes the sad story of suffering and death more heartrending.

I am, sir, etc.,
FITZHUGH LEE,
Consul General.

Letter of Mr. Lee to Mr. Day.
[No. 773] *United States Consulate-General,*
Havana, February 10, 1898. (Received February 15.)

Sir: I have the honor to enclose herewith a statement of the condi-tion of some of the small towns in the neighborhood of this city. These reports are made to me by a person I sent to those places for the purpose of ascertaining the numbers and condi-tion of the destitute and starving people in and about said towns. His name is not signed to the report for obvious reasons.

I am, etc.,
FITZHUGH LEE,
Consul General.

[Enclosure in No. 773]

MELENA DEL SUR. The unhealthy conditions of this town and the total want of resources make it completely impossible for the mayor to remedy the present miserable situation of the people, who die in great numbers from starvation, fever, and smallpox, which is vastly spreading, owing to the lack of vaccination virus or the necessary funds to acquire it with.

There are other towns in the same conditions, as, for example, Guinea, Catalina, and Madruga, whose situation could be, in a small degree, relieved if the country people were allowed to leave the town freely in search of food, which is very scarce. In some towns this is entirely prohibited; in others they are obliged to pay a tax, and, not having anything to eat, how can they pay a tax? In every town you visit the first thing you notice is the unhealthy condition of the men, and their total want of physical strength, which prevents them even from making an effort to procure the means of support.

CATALINA DE GÜINES. The condition of the reconcentrados in this town is very sad and desperate. There are no "zones for cultivation," and they are therefore not allowed even with a military pass to leave the town in search of work or food, which latter is so scarce that one must walk 4 or 5 miles before finding a sweet potato. Among these poor there are many who have not even the meanest hut for a dwelling place and who find nobody willing to help them in the least thing. In these districts the liberty given by General Blanco to the reconcentrados is a farce.

GÜINES TOWN. The land near the town which comprises the *"zone for cultivation"* has been rented by four Spaniards, who have done this by means of their wealth and influence in the present situation. They employ the few reconcentrados who are able to work, paying them 30 or 40 cents a day. Nobody can leave the town in search of work without a pass from the military commander, which pass is good for a month only and costs 20 cents. These workmen have to leave the town at 6 in the morning, and not being able to take the meals with them, are obliged to work until 6 in the evening without any nourishment. The same thing happens to all those who go in search of food. The women who leave the town in search of vegetables, even on their own farms, which are now completely abandoned, are sometimes deprived of them on their way back by the guerrillas.

In fifteen days 200 reconcentrados have died in Güines from starvation and total lack of resources. Many of the sick sleep on the floor and in the piazzas. One of the few real protectors of the reconcentrados, in fact a heroic one, is a young man named José Amohedo, whose father and mother have died attending to the suffering poor, and who himself has given up eight houses that belonged to him as dwelling places for the reconcentrados, all the contents of a grocery store that he possessed, and who is actually as destitute as they are, but always attending to those who suffer.

Although McKinley opposed an armed conflict, many Americans who took a hard line against Spain on the Cuban issue put political pressure on Congress. On the one hand, the Republican McKinley had the support of Republican businessmen, as the U.S. had a $30 million investment in Cuban trade and millions of dollars invested in property and real estate. These businessmen either favored remaining uninvolved in the Spanish-Cuban conflict or supported Cuban autonomy within the Spanish Empire. On the other hand, McKinley had many foreign policy opponents. The Democratic Party used the fact that public opinion supported Cuban independence to wear away at the Republicans, who held a majority in both legislative chambers. McKinley preferred to placate rather than defy the *jingoist*[3] members of his own party, including a group informally led by Roosevelt and several Republican Senators. These groups disapproved of the poor humanitarian situation in Cuba, which William Randolph Hearst's press had enthusiastically reported, and they regarded the Cuban rebels as *"Cuban patriots"* trying to overthrow imperial *"cruelty and oppression."* McKinley avoided calling attention to the war in the first year of his presidency, but his policy preferences did not necessarily align with his party's politics.

Unlike the evident success of President McKinley in balancing the opposing views of Republicans and Democrats in regard to the Cuban War issue, Spanish Prime Minister Sagasta and the regent Maria Cristina ruled over a weakened empire and a very unstable political situation. Spain had lost nearly all of its territory in the Americas during the Spanish American wars of independence of the early nineteenth century, and by January 1898, the once great empire was heavily dependent of having Cuba as its only successful territory. To that purpose Spain had established a constitutional monarchy and was willing to turn Cuba into an autonomous region while still preserving their colonial rule. The only problem were two uncertainties: Would Cubans abandon

---

[3] **Jingoism**: extreme chauvinism or nationalism marked especially by a belligerent foreign policy.

their independence efforts and be satisfied with the new concept of self-government offered by its new Autonomist Constitution? How should Spain react if the US decided to get involved?

Some within the Spanish press suggested they give up on the Cuban colony entirely; one article in *La Época* suggested that the government should not ...

> «... *charge forth to a foreign war without being absolutely certain that all pacific measures compatible with national dignity were exhausted.*»

Some Spanish intellectuals, among them *Miguel Correa y García* Minister of War, believed that surrendering to the US and abandoning Cuba could cause insurrection in Spain itself, more so since victory against the US was almost impossible. Those same intellectuals, when faced with the unappealing choice between a costly, humiliating war and an even more humiliating surrender, reached the conclusion that the only way to escape a war was through an astute sort of cooperation with the US, which no one could explain in detail.

Given those circumstances, Ramón Blanco Erenas, the Spanish Captain General, undertook a lengthy trip around Cuba to gather first hand information about the *criollos* acceptance of the new status of autonomy. Using his own sources of information without having to meet with General Blanco, Fitzhugh Lee reported to Washington the results of that trip:

[Telegram.]
From General Lee to Mr. Day.
Havana, February 10, 1898.

Captain-General returned yesterday; met with no success of any sort. Spaniards everywhere unfriendly; rumors of coming demonstration against him here. I think him excellent man, but in unfortunate position. Three serious combats reported within a week; in each insurgents victorious.

A few days after transmitting this telegram to Mr. Day, Lee received a confidential communiqué from General Máximo Gómez, who was in *Las Villas*, at the center of the island, in his task of decimating the Spanish troops and about to advance for the second time towards Havana. Lee immediately proceeded to transmit it to Mr. Day.

[Confidential.]
Letter of Mr. Lee to Mr. Day.
[No. 775] *United States Consulate General*,
Havana, February 15, 1898.

Sir: I have the honor to transmit herewith a letter, with its translation, signed by the insurgent commander in chief and addressed to the President of the United States. The said letter was delivered by a messenger, who at once departed, before I saw or had any communication with him.

I am, etc.

FITZHUGH LEE,
Consul General.

[Enclosure in No. 775] **[Translation]**
William McKinley,
President of the United States.

Sir : The heroic Cuban people possesses, as a characteristic quality of its moral being and developed to a high degree, one of the most noble sentiments, namely, gratitude; whoever has done well for Cuba wins for himself forever the lively recognition of the sons of Cuba's soil.

Your great people have given to the whole world an example of lofty virtue, and to the shame and stain of Spain, not only has it shown compassion before the great misfortunes brought on Cuba by the ferocious Spanish policy, but has extended a helping hand to the unhappy victims of the warfare carried on by the army of that nation.

The gratitude of this people must be on a par with that great and generous impulse, and if Cuba, by its geographical position and the necessity of its commercial existence, is called to maintain, once that it is free, and for the mutual benefit of both countries, closer relations with your great republic than with any other nation whatever, from this day forward Cuba will consider herself bound by a closer tie in the affection it bears for the noble American magnanimity.

However true and minute may be the reports that you have heard, never will you be able to form a just conception of all the bloodshed, the misery, the ruin and the sorrow caused to afflicted Cuba, to obtain her independence, and how the despotic spirit of Spain, irritated to the last degree before the most just of all rebellions, has reveled in the most implacable destruction of everything, lives and property. The nation which at one time accepted the inquisition and invented its tortures lastly conceived the concentration scheme, the most horrible of all means, first to torment and then to annihilate an entire people, and if it has stopped in the path of destruction it is due in great measure to the cry of indignation which the knowledge of such horrors unanimously drew from the States over which you govern.

The people who are saved from extinction and whose evils your gifts assuage are the people for whose liberty we daily shed our blood on the fields of battle; the country whose independence we now conquer at the point of the sword for them is also for us; blood of our blood and flesh of our flesh, we must rejoice with them in their joys as we weep and sympathize with them in their sorrows and grief.

Be not surprised, then, that as the general in chief of this Cuban army I am so deeply moved at the wave of compassion which agitates your noble country, and that I accede to the requests of the patriots I command to appear before you, the representative of the great nation, as the exponent of our immense gratitude.

I have, therefore, sir, to fulfill a conscientious duty by setting forth a fact, which I beg you will please transmit to the knowledge of the persons to whom is recommended the philanthropic mission of succoring the unhappy destitute Cubans, and in order that ignorance of certain antecedents may not deprive many needy ones of the enjoyment of that noble American charity.

This uprising, as absolute master of the country, has never prohibited any citizen, whatever his nationality, from earning his living, and it has happened that as soon as the barbarous concentration decree was derogated innumerable families have left and still leave the city for the field, impelled by hunger to wrest from the fruitful Cuban vegetation the means of relieving the most pressing needs of life.

Those unhappy beings ignore the fact that if the Spaniards, by steel and privation, have shrouded their hearths in mourning, so also it might be said that the flora of Cuba was in mourning, devastated by the bullet and torch.

Wherefore, being in the same circumstances, those unfortunates have the same moral right to participate in the relief furnished to needed Cubans by your generous people. Many a widow, many a mother, many an orphan do we meet in our way who asks of us that we are not able to give but most sparingly, and therefore upon pointing out to them the charity awakened

> in their behalf in your noble nation, I desire to honor myself by offering my services to cooperate in the noble work with all the power and means within the reach of the forces I command.
>
> I am, sir, with the most distinguished consideration,
>
> MÁXIMO. GÓMEZ.

The letter from General Máximo Gómez to President McKinley could not have come at a more fitting time. The day it was transmitted to Washington the American Warship *Maine* exploded in Havana. It deviated attention from Gómez' letter but it had an enormous effect on the curse of the 1895 Cuban War of Independence. The events were now racing at a speed no one could control. On February 8, *Enrique Dupuy de Lôme* had resigned as Ambassador of Spain in the United States; his infamous letter to his friend José Canalejas insulting McKinley had caused an international scandal that fueled anti-Spanish and pro-war feelings in the United States. [4] The personal and confidential letter was published by the *New York Journal*. In the opinion of many, this letter's revelation was one of the incidents to push Spain and the United States towards war. Finally, on February 12, General Máximo Gómez had issued a call to various Cuban autonomist groups for formation of a united effort against Spain.

But by mid February, of course, the most urgent and only important issue became what had happened to the Warship *Maine*.

Beginning in December 1897, the Warship *Maine* had been based at Key West, Florida in response to the Cuban situation, and for six weeks held in readiness to go to Cuba if Lee called for help. When no call for help had been received by the third week in January 1898, the commander of the *Maine*, Captain *Charles D. Sigsbee*, was told to join the other ships of the Navy's North Atlantic Squadron when it arrived there, and go with them to

---

[4] The letter used the type of language that the press and public opinion of Spain had said of Weyler's style, «... It shows once more that McKinley is weak and catering to the rabble and, besides, a low politician who desires to leave a door open to himself and to stand well with the jingos of his party.»

their winter base at the tiny islands of Dry Tortugas at the tip of the Florida Keys. The Squadron arrived at Key West on January 23, 1898, en route to Dry Tortugas, but there they received orders for Sigsbee from Washington, telling him to proceed with the Maine to Havana on a "friendly" visit.

Under the guise of that friendly excuse for a visit was a serious concern on the part of Washington about the security of many Americans living in Havana and the rest of the island.

Whatever the motive, every attempt was made to make the visit appear friendly. The ship arrived in Havana harbor on January 25, 1898. Then, after sitting in Havana harbor for three weeks, the *Maine* was torn apart by one or two explosions at 9:40 PM on the night of February 15, 1898, two days before the ship had been scheduled to leave Havana and return to New Orleans to show the flag at the upcoming Mardi Gras. Out of a crew of 374, approximately 260 Americans were killed.

In response to the destruction of the **Battleship Maine**, Washington sent American troops and warships to intervene in the Cuban revolt against Spanish colonial rule, and to attack other parts of the Spanish colonial empire, including the Philippines.

A calm and precise Mr. Lee, however, continued his stream of information about each and every issue that he had been commanded to report. Thus, the State Department in Washington was kept informed on the whereabouts and all details of the campaign to assist the residents of Cuba with food, clothing and medical support.

Letter of Mr. Lee to Mr. Day.
[No. 785] *United States Consulate General,*
Havana, March 1, 1898.

Sir : I have the honor to report that the distribution of food, medicines, and clothing to the destitute on this island is satisfactorily proceeding. The work has been well organized and systematized under the immediate supervision and direction of Miss Clara Barton, president of the Red Cross Society of the United States, and her active, able, and experienced assistants.

At first the relief was confined to the city of Havana and its surrounding sections. Now that the proper organizations have been formed in the said sections the supplies have been and are being gradually extended to other portions of the island, while some of the sea ports have received the necessary articles direct from New York. Of course, when the number of the poor and destitute is so large it is almost impossible to relieve large numbers in each locality, but I am able to state with confidence that under the present system of distribution the supplies are not lost or wasted, but reach those for whom they are intended.

I am, etc.,
FITZHUGH LEE,
Consul- General.

[Telegram.]
From Mr. Lee to Mr. Day.
Havana, March 3.

Have established fine asylum for destitute small orphans regard-less nationality. Money sent by you will be applied purchase food for said orphans.

FITZHUGH LEE.

Letter of Mr. Lee to Mr. Day.
[No. 795] *United States Consulate General,*
Havana, March 14, 1898.

Sir : I am requested by Consul Barker, of Sagua, to transmit to you certain information contained in a letter received from him, and as the best means of doing so I enclose the latter without date, but received to-day.

I am, etc.,
FITZHUGH LEE,
Consul-General.

Clarissa "Clara" Harlowe Barton (1821-1912) was a pioneering nurse who founded the **American Red Cross**. She was a hospital nurse during the American Civil War, a teacher, and patent clerk. Nursing education was not very formalized at that time and she never attended nursing school, so she provided self-taught nursing care. Barton is noteworthy for doing humanitarian work at a time when relatively few women worked outside the home

[Enclosure in No. 795]

Mr. Barker to Mr. Lee.

Dear Sir : I will thank you to communicate to the Department as quickly as possible the fact that the military commander and other officers of the military positively refuse to allow the reconcentrados to whom I am issuing food in its raw state to procure fuel with which to cook this food. In addition they prohibited this class of people (I am only giving food to about one-fifth of the destitute—the authorities have quit altogether) from gathering vegetables cultivated within the protection of the forts, telling them the Americans propose to feed you, and to the Americans you must look.

Yours, very truly,

WALTER B. BARKER, Consul.

Letter of Mr. Lee to Mr. Day.

[No. 797] *United States Consulate General,*
Havana, March 17, 1898.

Sir: Havana is calm and the Spanish authorities have been particularly friendly to Americans in the capital and the rest of the island. The Maine incident, however, will never be forgotten. I am having a difficult time trying to see Mr. Blanco.

FITZHUGH LEE,
Consul- General.

[Telegram.]

From Mr. Lee to Mr. Day.
Havana, March 24, 1898.

Work of relief progressing most satisfactory. Tomorrow arrangements made for 22 cars of supplies for Cienfuegos, Cárdenas, Sagua, Caibarién, and Santa Clara, and other places. Railroads will carry special trains through free of charge. Have been greatly assisted by Mr. Klopsch.

LEE.

Letter of Mr. Lee to Mr. Day.
[No. 803] *United States Consulate General,*
Havana, March 28, 1898.

Sir: I have honor to report that instructions have been given by the civil governor of Havana that the *alcaldes* and other authorities shall not give out any facts about the reconcentrados, and if any of the American relief committees should make inquiries concerning them, all such inquiries must be referred to him. I was told Mr. Blanco is about cast off Weyler's reconcentration decrees.

I am, etc.,
FITZHUGH LEE,
Consul- General.

Letter of Mr. Lee to Mr. Day.
[No. 809] *United States Consulate General,*
Havana, April 1, 1898. (Received April 5.)

Sir: With reference to the telegram I had the honor to transmit to you yesterday to the effect that the Governor General had issued a decree terminating concentration of the country people, permitting them to return to their homes, and advising their employment on public works, I beg to enclose a translation of the articles of the decree referred to.

I am, etc.,
FITZHUGH LEE,
Consul- General.

[Enclosure No. 1 with Dispatch No. 809]

TRANSLATION OF THE ARTICLES OF GENERAL BLANCO'S PROCLAMATION OF THE 30TH MARCH, 1898, SUSPENDING THE RECONCENTRATION.

Article 1. From the publication of the present proclamation (*bando*) in the Gazette of Havana the reconcentration of country people throughout the island is hereby terminated, and they are authorized to return with their families to their homes, and to dedicate themselves to all kind of agricultural labors.

Art. 2. The boards of relief and all civil and military authorities shall furnish them the means, within their power, to enable the rural population to return to their former places of residence, or those which They may now select, facilitating them the aid which they may respectively dispose.

> **Art. 3.** At the instance of the council of secretaries, and through the department of public works, the preparation and immediate realization of all public works necessary and useful to furnish work and food to the country people and their families who, through lack of means, truck farms, or want of agricultural implements, may not be able to return immediately to the fields, shall be proceeded with, as well as the establishment of soup kitchens, which may settle and cheapen such services.
>
> **Art. 4.** The expenses which the compliance with this proclamation (*bando*) may originate, as far as they may exceed the means disposed of by the boards of relief, shall be charged to the extraordinary war credit.
>
> **Art. 5**. All previous instructions issued regarding the reconcentration of the country people and all others which may be in opposition to the compliance of this proclamation are hereby derogated.
>
> Havana, March 20, 1898.
>
> RAMON BLANCO.

The commotions produced in Washington by the events of February 15 at the harbor of Havana apparently caused the misplacement of some of the correspondence of Mr. Lee to Mr. Day. The Assistant Secretary of State asked his Consul in Havana to re-send some of the missing communications dated from November 15, 1897 to February 8, 1898.

> ***Letter of Mr. Lee to Mr. Day.***
> [No. 810] *United States Consulate General,*
> Havana, April 4, 1898. (Received April 6.)
>
> Sir: With reference to your request of April 3, I am happy to comply and re-send you the requested correspondence.
> I am, etc.,
> FITZHUGH LEE,
> Consul- General.
>
> **[Enclosure in No. 810]**
> ***Letter of Mr. McGarr to Mr. Day.***
> [No. 137] *Consulate of the United States,*
> Cienfuegos, January 10, 1898.
>
> Sir: All the sugar mills in this consular jurisdiction, 23 in number, have been grinding since the first of the month, and at the busy centrales the various industries incident to the gathering of the crop and the manufacture of sugar are in full and steady operation.

Several of the principal estates are owned by American citizens and corporations, and most of their skilled employees are brought from the United States.

The demand for labor on the sugar estates has drawn from the towns a great portion of the unemployed laborers and given employment to the male "concentrados," many of whom were in a state of enforced idleness and destitution. As a consequence, few of them are now seen here and the labor "congestion" has been relieved.

Small predatory parties of insurgents make frequent attempts to fire the cane fields, and it requires constant and active vigilance to prevent their destruction. The dry weather and the high winds prevailing at this season render it a simple matter for one person (who can easily conceal himself in the tall cane) to start a conflagration that will, unless promptly extinguished, destroy hundreds of acres in a few hours.

Hence the almost impossibility with the utmost watchfulness and using every practicable safeguard to prevent some loss of cane by the fires started, often under cover of darkness, by the stealthy incendiaries familiar with the locality and always on the alert for an opportunity to apply the torch.

The sugar crop is the support of all classes and especially of the laboring class, and should it be in large part destroyed a famine in reality would be inevitable.

I am, etc.,
Owen McGarr,
United States Consul.

Letter of Mr. Brice to Mr. Day.

[No. 95] *Consulate of the United States,*
Matanzas, November 17, 1897.

Sir: I have the honor to submit the following report concerning present condition of affairs in this province and city.

New civil governor, Francisco de Armas, assumed the duties of his office Thursday, 11th instant. As the autonomist governor *of this province, his reception was cold and informal. Spaniards,* as well as Cubans, are not in sympathy with proposed autonomy and reforms.

A memorial to Her Majesty, Queen Regent of Spain, extensively signed by leading Spaniards of province, asking that reform bill be not signed. This will be cabled in a day or two.

Starvation.—No relief as yet afforded the starving thousands in this province. Several days ago an order from Captain Gin was given municipal authorities to issue rations and clothing, but no attention is paid the order.

Death rate in this city over 80 persons daily, and nearly all from want of food, medicines, and clothing. As I write this a dead negro woman lies in the street, within 200 yards of this consulate, starved to death; died sometime this morning, and will lie there, maybe, for days.

The misery and destitution in this city and other towns in the interior are beyond description.

A general order has been issued allowing reconcentrados to return to the country, but the restrictions placed hi order are such as to practically prohibit. If they went, what can they do without money, food, or shelter? Only those who can obtain employment on sugar plantations can live. Insurgents say no one will be allowed to grind in province of Matanzas. The situation is indeed deplorable, and I am free to say no real help can be expected from Spanish Government, and the fate of the remaining reconcentrados is slow, lingering death from starvation.

Insurgents are numerous and quite active the past ten days. In an engagement Saturday, 13th, near Mocha, 8 miles from this city, Spanish troops were defeated with serious loss and forced to retreat. Several sugar plantations report cane burned by insurgents, and the general opinion is little or no sugar will be made this season.

I am, etc.,

A. C. BRICE,
United /States Consul.

Pictures taken by U.S. journalists in the area of Güines during March 1897, showing farm houses burned in Cuba to force guajiros to move to the reconcentration camps ordered by the bloody Spanish General Valeriano Weyler

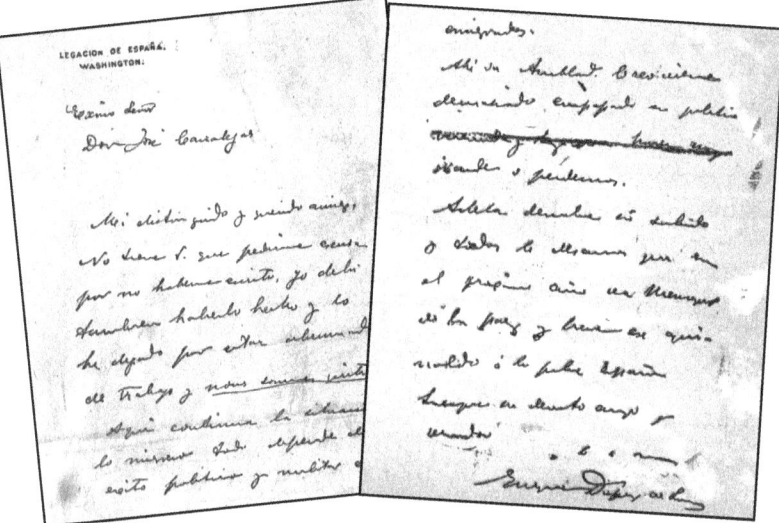

The first and las pages of the letter of **Dupuy de Lôme** to **José Canalejas**.

The **Magazine Puck** and a school book showing the US defending Cuba from the Spaniards and promising Cubans a life of Peace and Prosperity.

Letter of Mr. Brice to Mr. Day.
[No. 97] *Consulate of the United States,*
Matanzas, December 17, 1897.

Sir: I have the honor to report the following Cuban news in this province, taken from personal observation and reliable sources of information:

Concentrados.—Relief offered these and other poor people by Spanish authorities is only in name. I have personally visited (on several occasions) head masters of distributing stations. Two thousand rations were given out, for a few days only, to 8, 100 persons.

There are more than 12,000 starving people in this city to day. One out of 4 (or 6) received the following ration: 2 ounces rice, 1£ ounces tasajo (jerked beef), and sometimes a small piece of bread, per diem. Imagine starving people being relieved by such rations! Even this ration' of food has been discontinued since 11th inst. Death rate has diminished somewhat; now about 63 daily. There are less people to die.

The scenes of misery and distress daily observed are beyond belief Here is one out of hundreds. In a family of seventeen living in an old limekiln, upper part of city limits, all were found dead except three, and they barely alive. A few of the strongest of these people have been sent out to sugar plantations, which expect to grind.

They get 30 cents per day and board themselves. General Blanco's order, allowing reconcentrados, owners of plantations and farms, to return and cultivate crops, etc., is inoperative and of no avail. Several of our American citizens, owners of land, have repeatedly asked the civil governor of this province for permission to return to their homes, and in every case refused or restrictions imposed making it impossible to comply with.

A few plantations are grinding cane. In every case they are heavily guarded by Spanish troops, and have paid insurgents for so doing. Was shown a letter from insurgent chief to owner of a large plantation, in which price demanded for grinding was 2,000 centenes ($10,600 United States gold). It was paid. To make crop of sugar this season money, oxen, and laborers must be had.

I am, etc.,
A. C. BRICE,
United States Consul.

Letter of Mr. Lee to Mr. Day.
[No. 811] *United States Consulate General,*
Havana, April 1, 1898. (Received April 5.)

Sir: With reference to the telegram I had the honor to transmit to you yesterday to the effect that the Governor General had issued a decree terminating concentration of the country people, permitting them to return to their homes, and advising their employment on public works, I beg to enclose a translation of the articles of the decree referred to.

I am, etc.,

FITZHUGH LEE,
Consul- General.

Letter of Mr. Brice to Mr. Day.
[No. 99] *Consulate of the United States,*
Matanzas, January 18, 1898.

Sir: I have the honor to report the following concerning destitute American citizens, Matanzas province:

Up to Sunday, January 9, 1898, weekly rations of food have been

regularly issued, also medicines for sick, and, although there has been more or less hardships and suffering for want of clothing, shelter, etc. (which we were not allowed to supply), none of our people have suffered for food or medicine.

In behalf of these people, I earnestly ask the Department that some prompt measures be taken to further relieve them. They are absolutely helpless—no work, shut up in cities and towns like rats in a trap to starve. We have fifteen or eighteen families (American reconcentrados) who own property in the country, and were they allowed to go to their homes, could make a good living. All these have begged and pleaded with authorities (under Blanco's order) to go, and in every case refused.

Since the 24th of May, 1897, to December 20, 1897, seven months, we have given food and medicines and relief to an average of 305 persons, American citizens, at a cost of $8,175.48 Spanish gold. This amount received from Havana on account of Cuban relief fund to date. We require a little over $800 (bills not rendered) to settle last two weeks' ration bills and three weeks' medicine.

A. C. BRICE,
United States Consul.

[Enclosure in No. 99. J
CUBAN DISTRIBUTION
Circular letter dated January 8, 1898, from Department of State, received yesterday.

This intimates that help is to be extended by the United States to the starving people in Cuba. The news of this relief has been known for the past two weeks and has extended all over the province. This consulate has been overwhelmed with people of all classes asking to be remembered when this relief comes.

I submit a few facts illustrating the Buttering in this province alone. There are in Matanzas Province over 90,000 people who are in actual starving condition and require food, clothing, and medicines.

In addition to above, there are thousands of families (of the better classes, formerly well to do) who to-day are living on one meal a day, and that very scant. They have sold or pawned furniture, jewelry, clothing, etc., to eke out an existence until all is gone, or nearly so. Too proud to beg, they suffer in silence, and many die of starvation. The daughter of a former governor of this province was seen begging on the streets (incognito) of this city. Many of these people call on me privately at my residence asking and praying for God's sake to be remembered when this relief comes from the United States. One has to be here, know and mingle with these people, to fully realize the terrible destitution and misery existing in Cuba. It is to be hoped that this relief from the United States will come quickly, for hundreds are dying daily in this province of starvation. Conditions are dreadful, and no relief afforded by Spanish authorities.

I would advise that food and supplies for this province be sent direct to Matanzas, thus avoiding the railroad freight, drayage, etc. Supplies can be landed direct to warehouses (by lighters), which have been offered free of charge. The figures and facts I have stated indicate the large quantities of food and supplies required to give even temporary relief; also some cash will be required to handle and distribute supplies.

I am, etc.,

A. C. BRICE,
United Slates Consul.
Matanzas, Cuba, January 1S, 1S9S.

Mr. Brice to Mr. Bay.

[No. 100.] Consulate of the United States,
Matanzas, February 8, 1898.

Sir: I have the honor to inform the Department that U. S. cruiser Montgomery arrived in this port February 3, 1898, 10.34 a. m., leaving for Santiago de Cuba on February 5 at 6 p. m. The usual courtesies were extended this consulate; also friendly visits from civil and military governors and other officials of province and city. Return visits made the following day, and their reception by commander and officers on board was a royal one and greatly appreciated. The arrival of cruiser Montgomery, although a surprise, was hailed with delight by all classes,- and sure to be productive of good results.

The striking feature was: Poor people thought vessel was bringing them food from the United States; their disappointment was great.

I am, etc.,

A. C. BRICE,
United States Consul.

Letter of Mr. Hyatt to Mr. Bay.
[No. 405] *Consulate of the United States,*
Santiago de Cuba, November 15, 1897.

Sir: Since my return to Cuba I have availed myself of every opportunity possible to learn what, if any, changes have taken place during my absence.

At first I was disposed to believe that the insurgents were weakening and that the autonomists were coming to the front. Time and further investigation, however, has failed to confirm that view of the case.

The change of policy, as expressed by Captain-General Blanco, is doubtless modifying the feeling of resentment which formerly prevailed and, should the near future prove discouraging to the insurgents, would doubtless smooth the way to pacification. The promised revocation of the order of reconceutration is yet unfulfilled and beggars are very numerous. "*Me estoy muriendo de hambre*" (I am starving) is their most frequent salutation. Generally their appearance confirms their words.

What ought the United States Government do, is a question much discussed, and the answer is usually what the person desires, and sentiment, not reason, makes reply. Among property holders, whether Americans or citizens of other nationalities, there is but one sentiment.

"Hands off," or such active intervention as will quickly terminate the struggle. They greatly deprecate constant agitation, which makes the governing classes enemies to American interests and brings no corresponding advantages. For your information I enclose a military order and a translation of the same, issued by the insurgent general, Calixto García. General García's command extends over more than half of the island, including the provinces of Porto Principe and Santiago, the portions supposed to be in most active rebellion.

Another order is issued by the same authority permitting owners of coffee estates to gather as much as they may need for family use, but none for market.

The present insurgent capital is at San Augustín, between Holguín and Tunas, 135 miles from Santiago.

The local papers, which publish only what has been submitted to censorial examination, admit several engagements of late on those parts of the island heretofore reported as pacified.

I am, etc.,

PULASKI F. HYATT,
United States Consul.

[Enclosure in No. 405]
Military Department of the East,
General Headquarters, Baire, November 6, 1897.
(Third of Independence.)

To the commanding generals of the first, second, and third army corps of eastern Cuba:

Duly informed through the press that the Spanish Government is offering autonomy with the intention by these means to subdue the revolution, or at least to bring about disturbances in our ranks and weaken our cause; this general headquarters reminds you that the spirit and letter of our constitution does not admit with Spain any treaty whatever that is not based upon the absolute independence of Cuba. In accordance with this I will be inexorable, submitting to a summary trial, and will consider as traitors all civil or military officers of whatever rank receives messages, commissions, or has any intercourse with the enemy, as the supreme government of the republic is the only one authorized, and listen to any overtures that may be made, and even the government will only listen to proposals acknowledging the absolute independence of Cuba by the Spanish Government. All persons who come within our lines commissioned by the enemy with proposals to submit to Spain will be tried and punished as spies.

In order to avoid any ignorance being professed on the subject, you will circulate this communication among your subordinates, posting this order during eight days at your headquarters and have it read in the presence of the troops.

Country and liberty.

CALIXTO GARCÍA,
Commander in Chief of the Department of the East.

(Baire is a small village lying about 54 miles from the city of Santiago)

Letter of Mr. Hyatt to Mr. Day.
[No. 407] *Consulate of the United States,*
Santiago de Cuba, November 20, 1897.

Sir : For the benefit of the Department of State I send the enclosed a list of civil officers of the insurgent government of Cuba, elected and installed at Yaya, in the province of Porto Principe October 20.

There is rumor of renewed activity on the part of the rebels of Eastern Cuba, commanded by Gen. Calixto García, and the shipment of all available Spanish soldiers to Manzanillo corroborates the report.

The Spanish residents of the island are becoming very outspoken in favor of closing the war and annexation to the United States. There are numerous inquiries among them of how they can become citizens of our Government. There are also quite a number of Spanish soldiers making the same inquiry. The business Spaniards here declare that they are tired of doing business at a loss, and that peace and prosperity can only come by annexation. Many are greatly disappointed that the United States consul cannot make American citizens of them at once.

With highest, etc.,
PULASKI F. HYATT,
United States Consul.

[Enclosure with No. 407]

List of insurgent officials elected and installed at Yaya Puerto Principe, Cuba,

October 20, 1897:
President, Bartolomé Masó.
Vice-president, Domingo Méndez Capote.
Secretary of War, José B. Alemán.
Secretary of the Treasury, Ernesto Font Sterling.
Secretary of Foreign Affairs, Andrés Moreno de la Torre.
Secretary of the Interior, Manuel R. Silva.
General-in-Chief, Máximo Gómez.
Lieutenant-General, Calixto Garcia.

List of insurgent officials elected and installed at Yaya Puerto Principe, Cuba,

October 20, 1897:
President, Bartolomé Masó.
Vice-president, Domingo Méndez Capote.
Secretary of War, José B. Alemán.
Secretary of the Treasury, Ernesto Font Sterling.
Secretary of Foreign Affairs, Andrés Moreno de la Torre.
Secretary of the Interior, Manuel R. Silva.
General-in-Chief, Máximo Gómez.
Lieutenant-General, Calixto Garcia.

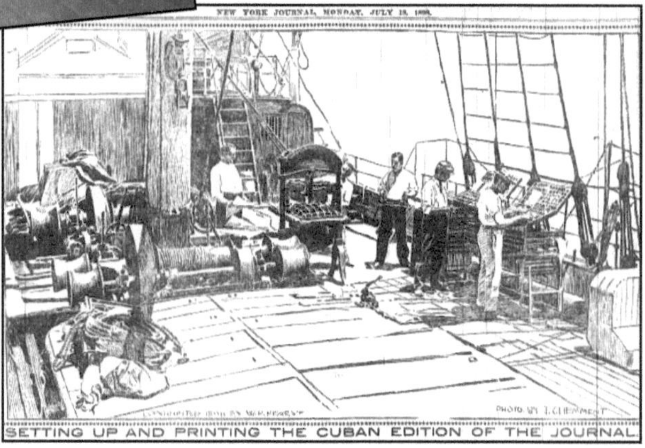

Images from the War of 1895, top to bottom: The ***Warship Maine*** and its crew on the decks; the ***movil printing press*** set up by Hearst on board of a ship, to reach New York earlier than the competition; ***General Bartolomé Masó*** and his Staff in the war zone in Oriente province.

[Enclosure with No. 407.]

Letter of Mr. Hyatt to Mr. Day.
[No. 409.] Consulate of the United States,
Santiago de Cuba, November 26, 1897.

Sir: Yesterday I cabled you as follows: "Day, Washington. All political prisoners freed. Hyatt."

This cable I now confirm. The order of release opened the doors to military prisoners in Castle Morro and a somewhat larger number in the city prison, including persons of different nationalities; but no Americans, all such having been from time to time released by special orders, which is a cause of much favorable comment to our nation. The text of the new autonomy, as published here, is not meeting with favor by the most ardent friends of Spain.

There is, however, a feeling of relief and safety since the change in the Captain-Generalship.

Very respectfully,
PULASKI F. HYATT.

Letter of Mr. Hyatt to Mr. Day.
[No. 410] *Consulate op the United States*,
Santiago de Cuba, December 5, 1897.

Sir : The situation in this part of Cuba is not destitute of activity; nevertheless, it seems to be one of expectancy, both sides posing and waiting to see what will happen in the United States.

There is a more secure feeling since the arrival of Governor-General Blanco, otherwise no perceptible change. The reconcentration order is relaxed, but not removed; but many people have reached a point where it is a matter of entire indifference to them whether it is removed or not, for they have lost all interest in the problem of existence.

A census of the island taken to-day, as compared with one taken three years ago, I feel confident would show that two-thirds of the residents are missing; and the Spanish army would make no better showing.

The rainy season is practically over, and cooler weather is apparent, the thermometer ranging from 70° to 88° F. through the twenty-four hours, in the shade.

His Excellency Enrique Capriles, a former governor of this province, has returned to this post of duty. His former record is a sufficient guaranty of an honorable administration.

Mr. Eigney, an American sugar planter near Manzanillo, was preparing to grind during the coming season. A few nights since the insurgents fired seven cannon shots among his buildings, one ball passing through the roof of his house. Americans were hopeful that they would be allowed to make their crop, and several are making ready to do so; but the action of the insurgents toward Mr. Eigney gives the problem a doubtful aspect. It may have been a personal matter against Mr. Eigney.

The number of destitute Americans fed by this consulate decreased from 89 to 64, but is again on the increase. Since being fed, sickness among them has materially decreased and their appearance has greatly improved.

Very respectfully,
PULASKI F. HYATT,
United States Consul.

Letter of Mr. Hyatt to Mr. Day.

[No. 413] *Consulate of the United States,*
Santiago de Cuba, December 14, 1897.

Sir: Since my last dispatch on the situation in Cuba several military engagements of more or less importance have occurred and the insurgents are claiming to have had the best in the fight; but until an engagement shall take place of sufficient importance to have a controlling influence, I can safely leave the press to report on such matters.

I take it to be a matter of far greater importance that I shall watch the trend of public opinion and its effects on the political situation, for thus far battles have not been the most important factors in the Cuban problem.

Up to the present we have only garbled accounts as to the contents of the President's message, so it is too early to say what its effects will be. I shall, however, watch such results with much concern, as all parties have looked forward to it with deepest solicitation.

The order of reconcentration is now practically wiped out, and, so far as the Spanish Government is concerned, men go about nearly as they please. The insurgents and their sympathizers will unquestionably take advantage of the revocation to get from the towns and cities what they need, and otherwise strengthen their cause. The effect on agricultural pursuits will be disappointing, because the great majority of those who would or should take up the work joined the insurgent forces when compelled to leave their homes, and the portion which came within the lines of reconcentration are women, children, old and sickly people, most of whom seem to have little interest in the problem of life. There is no one to take these people back to the fields and utilize their remaining strength. Their houses are destroyed, their fields are overgrown with weeds, they have no seed to plant, and if they had, they cannot live sixty or eighty days until the crop matures, which, when grown, would more than likely be taken by one or the other of the contending parties.

Many of those who are attached to their families have them within the insurgent lines. Finally, I give it as my opinion, an opinion that I am sure is not biased in favor of Cuba, that Spain will be compelled to prosecute a far more vigorous war than has yet been done if she conquers peace in Cuba. I think I speak advisedly when I say that in this end of the island at least there are many thousand square miles where the foot of the Spanish soldier has never trod. Within this zone the insurgents have their families, carol their horses and cattle and raise their crops. They reach the outside world by methods of their own.

Why Spain with a large body of as obedient and brave soldiers as ever shouldered a gun has not penetrated these grounds and scattered to the four winds the comparatively small body of men who are there, is a question I will not attempt to answer. As I write a man is dying on the street in front of my door, the third in a comparatively short time.

Very respectfully,
PULASKI F. HYATT,
United States Consul.

Letter of Mr. Hyatt to Mr. Day.

[No. 415] *Consulate of the United States,*
Santiago de Cuba, December 21, 1897.

Sir: I respectfully report that sickness and the death rate on this island is appalling. Statistics make a grievous showing, but come far short of the truth.

The principal disease is known by various names. Calentura, baludol fever, la grippe, etc., is thought by physicians to be brought on by insufficient food. I know some that are attacked that have plenty.

These, however, usually make a good recovery, while the others die or make very slow recovery.

The disease is endemic rather than of a zymotic or contageous character. From 30 to 40 per cent of the people are afflicted with it at the present time.

Yellow fever continues in all parts of the island, and smallpox in some places, but are insignificant as compared with the prevailing disease. Out of a total of 16,000 soldiers recently sent to Manzanillo, nearly 5,000 are in hospitals or quartered on the people. I have not learned whether it has attacked the insurgents or not; presumably yes, for Cubans elsewhere are not exempt, as in yellow fever.

An extremely strong effort is being made to increase the strength of the autonomist party. The governor sends for men of supposed influence and asks them to join the party and work to make it successful.

He argues that it is a patriotic duty in which all good citizens should aid.

As yet planters are all at sea as to whether they will grind cane or not. It is no secret that they will have to make terms with the insurgents if they do, and I understand that an agreement by which 50 cents per bag, or about 15 cents per 100, will be paid for Cuban hands off.

Planters say this will leave them no profit, but leave their plantations in better order for future operations.

The three Rivery brothers, American citizens and owners of coffee, cocoa, and orange groves, are about to return to their places. They are absolutely penniless, and say they would have surely starved but for the food issued from this consulate. I shall continue to supply them with food, and issue a month's rations of such food as rice, beans, codfish, crackers, etc., as their homes are over 30 miles away. I have made myself, personally (not my Government), responsible for the transportation of themselves, their families, and goods, as it seemed desirable to get them on their estates as soon as possible.

Dr. Henry S. Caminero, United States sanitary inspector, has just informed me that there are in this city over 12,000 persons sick in bed, not counting those in military hospitals. This is at least 35 per cent of the present population. Quinine, the only remedy of avail, is sold ten times higher than in the States.

Steamers coming to this port mostly give out soup once a day to the waiting throngs.

Fresh meat in our markets sells from 50 cents to $1 a pound.

Very respectfully,
PULASKI F. HYATT,
United States Consul.

Letter of Mr. Hyatt to Mr. Bay.

[No. 418.] Consulate of the United States,
Santiago de Cuba, January 1, 1898.

Sir: I have the honor to say that, from a military standpoint, there is nothing new worthy of report, except the mobilizatien of the Spanish forces to the number of 18,000 in and near Manzanillo, 6,000 of which are in hospital.

Autonomy has been pushed with great vigor, almost or quite to the point of forcing men to join the party, when they could not be hired by a minor office. Planters say this will leave them no profit, but leave their plantations in better order for future operations.

The three Rivery brothers, American citizens and owners of coffee, cocoa, and orange groves, are about to return to their places. They are absolutely penniless, and say they would have surely starved but for the food issued from this consulate. I shall continue to supply them with food, and issue a month's rations of such food as rice, beans, codfish, crackers, etc., as their homes are over 30 miles away. I have made myself, personally (not my Government), responsible for the transportation of themselves, their families, and goods, as it seemed desirable to get them on their estates as soon as possible.

The world press, in both Europe and the
American Continent, took sides for the US,
Cuba or Spain the entire duration of the
War of 1895-1898

The world press, in both Europe and the American Continent, took sides for the US, Cuba or Spain the entire duration of the War of 1895-1898

Dr. Henry S. Caminero, United States sanitary inspector, has just informed me that there are in this city over 12,000 persons sick in bed, not counting those in military hospitals. This is at least 35 per cent of the present population. Quinine, the only remedy of avail, is sold ten times higher than in the States.

Steamers coming to this port mostly give out soup once a day to the waiting throngs.

Fresh meat in our markets sells from 50 cents to $1 a pound.

Very respectfully,

PULASKI F. HYATT,
United States Consul.

Letter of Mr. Hyatt to Mr. Bay.

[No. 418.] Consulate of the United States,
Santiago de Cuba, January 1, 1898.

Sir: I have the honor to say that, from a military standpoint, there is nothing new worthy of report, except the mobilization of the Spanish forces to the number of 18,000 in and near Manzanillo, 6,000 of which are in hospital.

Autonomy has been pushed with great vigor, almost or quite to the point of forcing men to join the party, when they could not be hired by a minor office.

When here, a few days since General Pando sent for a Mr. Lora and said: " You have two active and influential brothers in the rebel army. You must go at once to these brothers and say, Come in and join the autonomist party and they will be provided for by me."

Mr. Lora replied : ." General, I ran away from my home to escape joining the insurgents; my brothers chose to join them. I will obey your command if you desire to sacrifice my life. My brothers would order me shot on the spot if I approached them with your proposition."

General Pando withdrew his command.

Enrique Capriles, who was governor of this province some four years ago, returned to the same position about a month since. He is highly respected by all classes, and has worked with great energy to build up the autonomist party. He resigned to-day and took a solemn oath that he would never again set foot on Cuban soil. He declared himself both discouraged and disgusted.

The problem of sugar making in this province is most discouraging. Climatic fevers still hold about one third of the people in bed. The death rate for the week in this city is 109. I deem myself fortunate in being a physician when called upon to fight life's battles amid such surroundings.

Very respectfully,
PULASKI F. HYATT,
United States Consul.

Letter of Mr. Hyatt to Mr. Hay.
[No. 420] *Consulate of the United States,*
Santiago de Cuba, January 8, 1898.

Sir: I have the honor very respectfully to say that in my opinion the most important question of the Cuban problem to-day is, " Will the people of Cuba accept autonomy as a basis of settlement?"

I have taken great pains to inform myself on this question and to eliminate as far as possible the bias which comes with the sources of my information. That the Spanish Government has made a most energetic and thorough campaign to make autonomy successful there is no room for doubt. Personal appeals of provincial governors and other important officers have been made earnestly and often to the same individuals.

Wholesale removals of Spanish officers from civil positions are made by sweeping orders, with instructions to fill their places with Cuban autonomists. About a week since there came an order dismissing every employee of the custom house in this city, to take effect as soon as proper autonomists could be found to fill their places.

As yet only two have been named, the collector and first deputy. Against these a strong remonstrance was at once sent in, so the entire old corps are still in place.

The newly appointed provincial governor, Lopez Chavez, has been here for several days, but as yet has not taken charge of the office.

In many cases where Cubans are anticipating the acceptance of an office they have sent to the field to ask permission from insurgent officers. It will be seen that Cubans are moving very slow in accepting autonomy.

It is given out that sometime in the month of February there will an election held for the purpose of electing sixty members of the Cuban assembly and eighteen members of the council of administration, while seventeen additional ones are to be appointed by the Governor-General. The lines are supposed to be drawn for or against autonomy.

Cuban leaders declare they will neither make nominations nor go near the polls; so, if they adhere to their purpose, it will be no test of strength, and no recognition of the result will be taken by the men in the field.

Numerous dead bodies at the cemetery are carried over from day to day because the sexton is unable to bury them with his

present corps of assistants as fast as they come.
Very respectfully,
PULASKI F. HYATT,
United States Consul.

Latter of Mr. Hyatt to Mr. Day.
[No. 421] *Consulate of the United States,*
Santiago de Cuba, January 12, 1898.

Sir : I deem it a duty to lay before the honorable Department of State the situation here as affecting American interests, and to enclose herewith an order issued by command of Gen. Máximo Gómez, and a translation of the same, forbidding the grinding of the sugar crop for the years 1897 and 1898.

In this part of Cuba, so far as I can learn, all idea of making a sugar crop is entirely abandoned.

I regret to say that the stoppage of industries, from present appearances, will not halt at the sugar crop, but coffee and other agricultural crops fall under the same ban.

I had hoped that after the reconcentration order was revoked, through the energetic action of the present administration, we would find no trouble in reinstating American industries; but it appears that all of the benefits that should have accrued to our citizens are thwarted by the action of the insurgents, who refuse to allow them to return to their sugar, coffee, and other estates. The Pompo Manganese mines, owned by Americans, would at the present time be a very profitable investment if allowed to operate, are also being held up by the same power.

The three Revery brothers, who I informed you recently I was about to assist in returning to their coffee and fruit estates, got there only to find they could not go to work until permission was obtained from the insurgent commander, which permission seems doubtful, I myself, as I understand my duty, being inhibited from rendering them any assistance at this point.

These, with several sugar estates within my consular district, are held up and becoming more worthless than before.

It is beyond the power of my pen to describe the situation in eastern Cuba. Squality, starvation, sickness, and death meets one in all places. Beggars throng our doors and stop us on the streets. The dead in large numbers remain over from day to day in the cemeteries unburied.

Very respectfully,
PULASKI F. HYATT,
United States Consul.

Spain, through her ministers, often called the attention of the Washington government to the numerous filibustering expeditions which set out from the United States to aid the Cuban insurgents. The Spanish agents seemed to have been more alert than the United States authorities for evidences of such expeditions. The numerous references to such incursions, about which the government in Washington seemed to know little or nothing, and which, when investigated, proved that the Spanish officials were correct in their information and suspicions, seemed to confirm the complicity of the US with the Cuban rebels.

The US law was clear in that regard and Captain General Ramón Blanco on several occasions sent Consul Fitzhugh Lee a copy of these regulations.

Letter of Mr. Lee to Mr. Day. [Confidential]
[No. 821] *United States Consulate- General*
Havana, April 6, 1898.

Sir: I have the honor to transmit herewith a letter, with its translation, signed by Captain General Blanco and addressed to the President of the United States.

I am, etc.

FITZHUGH LEE,
US Consul General

[Enclosure in No. 821] [Translation.]
Letter of Captain General Blanco to Mr. McKinley.
[No. 31] *Government of the island of Cuba.*
Havana, Cuba
To his Excellency the President of the United States:

Sir: On several occasions I have sent letters to your Consul in Havana in regard to incursions in our territory of individuals armed and assisted by US authorities. I have also had the honor of reminding your Consul of the following US law and regulation concerning American assistance to bandits and enemies of Spain that have entered the island of Cuba from US territory:

«*Every person who, within the territory or jurisdiction of the United States, begins, or sets on foot, or provides or prepares the means for, any military expedition or enterprise, to be carried on from thence against the territory or dominions of any foreign prince or state, or of any colony, district, or people, with whom the United States are at peace, shall be deemed guilty of a high*

> *misdemeanor, and shall be fined not exceeding $3,000, and imprisoned not more than three years.»*
> I am, sir, at your service, with the most distinguished consideration.
> CAPTAIN GENERAL RAMÓN BLANCO ERENAS
> Government of the island of Cuba.

Spain claimed that the United States were not cooperating with her, while the US government maintained that it did all that could be reasonably expected of a neutral nation and that its laws were been executed.

Numerous expeditions set out from the United States to aid the insurgents, carrying men, arms, and ammunition. The US neutrality laws did not forbid purely commercial transactions, even if they including arms and ammunition, and it was on this ground that the courts did not condemn or confiscate the many vessels which were detained, even when it was a well known fact that they were destined for the insurgents in Cuba.

Until belligerency was recognized, all such goods were mere articles of commerce and not contraband, and Spain could not exercise the right of visit and search on the high seas, though the United States ships could prevent them from leaving the waters under its jurisdiction. Spain maintained that shipments of arms, etc., to Cuban insurgents were not commercial transactions, and that the US could do better than look the other way.

The reply from Mr. McKinley to Mr. Blanco was made in the form of a letter of Mr. Day to Mr. Lee, a copy of which he was instructed to deliver to the Spanish government in Havana.

> *Letter of Mr. Day to Mr. Lee.* [Confidential]
> [No. 431] *United States Assistant Secretary of State*
> Washington, April 11, 1898.
>
> Sir: Please show a copy of the enclosed letter to Mr. Blanco, Captain General of Cuba, and express our deepest concerns:
> I am, etc.
> WILLIAM RUFUS DAY
> US Assistant Secretary of State,

> *Letter of Mr. Day to Mr. Lee.* [Confidential]
> [No. 431] *United States Assistant Secretary of State*
> Washington, April 11, 1898.
>
> Sir: In regards to the concerns of Mr. Blanco, Captain General of Cuba, I am happy to relate a recent experience that had to do with shipments from the US territory to the island of Cuba.
>
> «*The cargo ship* **Commodore** *became an object of suspicion at New London, Connecticut, in the fall of 1895; when it made a scale in Wilmington, N.C., a shipment of arms and ammunition was sent by express, the express charges being US$942. The arms were taken on board at Wilmington and the ship cleared for Cartagena via Southport, N.C. The Captain of the vessel indicated he did not know what the articles to be shipped were, but that he intended to clear the cargo as mining implements and machinery. About the same time several strange men appeared at Wilmington, but learning of the ongoing proceedings against the ship, they soon disappeared. The ship was detained; the cases marked "hardware" and "agricultural implements" were found to be arms and ammunition, among them being a rapid firing gun of the latest and most improved pattern. It was shown that this gun could be used from the deck of the vessel, and that the ship was equipped with two boats capable of landing four or five tons each. The judge, however, dismissed the libel, refusing to condemn the ship, while no appeal was taken by Belligerency or Insurgency by the United States. The Unites States enjoys a Constitutional separation of powers that impedes the executive branch in cases like this to interfere in the decisions of the courts.*»
>
> Please inform Mr. Blanco of such limitations of power which are an integral part of our Constitutional framework.
> I am, etc.
> WILLIAM RUFUS DAY
> US Assistant Secretary of State,

Both the US and Spain knew that the "*Three Friends,*" the "*Bermuda,*" the "*Dauntless,*" and other ships were among the vessels which made expeditions to Cuba to assist the insurgency. In many cases no proceedings were ever instituted, while in a few cases they were dismissed, in others acquitted, but only in three cases from February, 1895 up to June, 1897, had the parties been found guilty. In no case had the vessel been finally condemned or seized. There were 42 expeditions from June 4, 1895 to May 30, 1897. 21 of these were failures by one cause and another; 6 were partial failures; and 15 were successful.

Aside from correspondence dealing with the expeditions conflict, Consul Lee was aware of the devastation that the policies of the insurgents were causing to agricultural businesses in Cuba and, perhaps with a week or so behind schedule, he reminded Mr. Pulaski F. Hyatt, the US Consul in Santiago de Cuba, to send to Mr. Day the documents he had promised to on his letter of January 12, 1898.

> [Enclosure in No. 421.]
> There is a seal that reads:
> Republic of Cuba, War. No. 43, book 3, folio 150.
>
> The council of the Government in session on the 29th day of last month adopted the following resolution:
> Considering that the working of the sugar estates favor the plans of our enemies, as shown by the marked interest in their last winter campaign, thus injuring the steady headway of the revolution.
> It has been ordered by our Government as a general political measure of war, which today is more than ever imposed upon us, and in accordance with article 22, paragraph 6, of the Constitution to absolutely prohibit the realization of the sugar crop of 1897-98, that this be communicated to the General-in-Chief, with the object that he will dictate the opportune orders for the exact compliance of this resolution, and that it should be published for general knowledge, making known that violators will suffer the punishment prescribed by our laws. What I transcribe to you for your knowledge and exact compliance.
> I am, with high consideration,
> Country and liberty,
> JOSÉ B. ALEMÁN, Secretary of War.
> Palmarito, December 2, 1897.
>
> The enclosure in No. 421 was accompanied by the following message:
>
> ### *Resolution in letter to Gen. Calixto García.*
> I hereby certify that the above resolution authorized by the secretary of war, José B. Alemán, and directed to Gen. Calixto

García, is an exact copy of original on file in the archives of the chief of the military department of Orient.

Lieut. Col. Eduardo Salazar, Auditor.

Baire, December 28,1897.

Letter by Mr. Hyatt to Mr. Day.
[No. 424.] *Consulate of the United States*
Santiago de Cuba, January 22, 1897.

Sir : I have the honor to report that Colonel Masó of the insurgent forces, whose home is in this city, has, at a point west of here, given himself up to the Spanish forces, with one hundred and ten officers and men under his command. I am also enclosing the following communiqué:

CUBAN CORRESPONDENCE.

Citizens of Santiago say that Masó did the same thing in the former rebellion (1868)

The military situation is completely overshadowed in importance by the starving, struggling mass, whose cry is " Bread, or I perish."

This consulate is besieged to an extent that blocks the entrance, and greatly retards business. They have heard that the people of the United States are giving funds for their relief, and have not the patience to wait. I could name three Americans here who contribute monthly over three hundred dollars toward feeding the poor, but it is nothing compared to the people's necessities.

Men, women, and children, homeless and almost naked, roam the streets by day, begging of everyone they meet, or door they pass, and sleeping at night anywhere they can find a place to lie down.

If the present death rate is continued, there would not be a soul left in the city at the end of five years.

For the masses it is speedy help or sure death.

Very respectfully,

Pulaski F. Hyatt,

United States Consul.

Letter of Mr. Hyatt to Mr. Day.
[No. 427.] Consulate op the United States,
Santiago de Cuba, January 31, 1898.

Sir : I desire to inform the honorable Department of State that Captain-General Blanco arrived at this port on Friday night, the 28thinstant, but remained on shipboard until the next morning.

The consular corps called soon after his arrival. Most of General Blanco's remarks were directed to the French and American consuls.

Colonel Marsh, of General Blanco's staff, called upon and dined with me the same evening. He speaks fairly good English, and is a gentle man of rare social qualities. On leaving he said,

«I shall be at all times most happy to use whatever influence I may have with General Blanco in securing a favorable resolution of any matters that you may desire to present to him.»

I told him I was prepared to take advantage of his offer at once, as there had just arrived at the custom-house in this place a quantity of quinine which the collector of customs said he could not deliver duty free without instructions from Havana. The colonel promised to lay the matter at once before the Captain-General, and the quinine, is released, and, as I understand, it is ordered that all future shipments are to be promptly delivered to me, if any shall come.

On Sunday morning the regular passenger train on the Sabanilla and Maroto Railroad, when 5 miles out of Santiago, was blown up by dynamite bombs, exploded by electric wires; two cars were shivered in atoms. Five passengers were killed outright and twenty-two badly wounded, some of whom have since died. It is thought by some that the insurgents believed that Captain-General Blanco was on the train; others said the rebels merely wanted to make clear to the general that they were around and were carefully attending to business.

I am, etc.,
PULASKI F. HYATT,
United States Consul.

Letter of Mr. Hyatt to Mr. Day.
[No. 428.] Consulate of the United States
Santiago de Cuba, February 1, 1898.

Sir: The military conditions here upon the surface are not materially changed, but to one who watches the signs of the times and knows the character of the men who act the drama the situation is not without portent.

The era of good feeling is passing away, while bitter words and cruel acts are again coming to the front. Those engaged in works of mercy are denounced for keeping alive a tribe that ought to be dead. But it cannot be said there is no excuse for harsh judgment. The stoppage of all agricultural pursuits and the blowing up of cars containing innocent people cannot be justified even under the guise of war. Extremists of both sides seem able to dominate the sentiments of their respective parties, while a deep feeling of personal hatred pervades their breasts.

The Extraordinary record of the Dauntless

16 August 1896 - Disembarked in Punta de Nuevas Grandes, Camagüey, under the command of General Emilio Nuñez and Colonel Rafael Cabrera.

13 October 1896 - Disembarked at the delta of the San Juan River, Santa Clara, under the command of General Joaquín Castillo Duany and Miguel Betancourt Guerra. The 32 expeditionaries unloaded a dynamite gun with its shells, 1,100 rifles, 1,000 pounds of dynamite, one million bullets and medicine.

3 January 1897 - Disembarked during its third voyage at the place known as "María la Gorda," in the inlet of Cortés, P. R. It was commanded by General Emilio Núñez and Commandant Rafael Pérez Morales (the cargo was the same brought by the steamer "Three Friends," unable to unload it, in its voyage to the mouth of the San Juan River, Santa Clara). There were numerous expeditionaries and 1,200 rifles, half a million bullets, a cannon with 200 shells, 200 machetes, medical equipment, etc. With the expedition also went a commission of the *New York Journal* with a sword of honor for General Máximo Gomez, a gift of said newspaper.

21 May 1897 - Disembarked in Punta Brava, Manatí, Oriente, under the command of Commandant Serapio Arteaga. The expeditionaries included the Italians Orestes Ferrara and Guillermo Petriccione. Also aboard was Dr. Emilio Luaces, a colonel during the Ten Years' War. Ricardo Delgado then continued to make another landing at the beach of Bacuranao, on the 24th.

30 October 1897 - Disembarked in Punta Brava, Manatí, Oriente, under the command of General Joaquín Castillo Duany.

28 November 1897 - Disembarked with the expeditionaries of Conception Island (Bahamas) and a second voyage with ammunition taken by the schooner *Silver Heel* that awaited in Conception and that disembarked in the mouth of Arroyo Seco, near cape Lucrecia, Banes, Oriente. This expedition included General Nuñez, Luis Rodolfo Miranda and various other expeditionaries.

20 February 1898 - Disembarked in Palizadas, Camaguey, under the command of Colonel Manuel Lechuga y de la Torre.

General Blanco's mild and humane policy meets with but a feeble response from his own followers, while the insurgents laugh at the old man who throws sods and grass instead of stones. Autonomy is already a dead issue, while buying insurgent leaders thus far is not a marked success, the insurgent generals having already imprisoned several officers suspected of venality.

Colonel Marsh, of General Blanco's staff, said recently...

«*Spain fails to comprehend that Cuba has, as it were, two mothers, a political one, which is Spain; a commercial one, which is the United States; and the political mother fails to see that the commercial mother has any rights, while the commercial mother cannot shake off her responsibility, for God has made them next-door neighbors.*»

I do not believe that the Western Continent has ever witnessed death by starvation equal to that which now exists in eastern Cuba.

Very respectfully, etc.,
PULASKI F. HYATT,
United States Consul

Mr. Hyatt to Mr. Day.

[No. 434.] *Consulate of the United States*
Santiago de Cuba, February 16, 1898.

Sir: Wounded Spanish soldiers, about 200 in number, have been brought to the hospital of this city within the last three days. A surgeon who has dressed the wounds of a Spanish captain tells the story this morning as follows :

«*Our command, about 7,000 in number, had been to Holguin and were returning, when at a point near Aguacate, without any notice or knowledge of the presence of the enemy in force, a galling fire opened on us, and, as we could not tell from where it came or see the enemy to return the fire, we were ordered to drop flat on the ground. From this position we returned the fire as best we could for a time on an unseen enemy, who finally withdrew.*»

The captain admitted a loss of 300 in killed and wounded on the Spanish side, and says they have no knowledge of the loss inflicted on the insurgents.

CUBAN CORRESPONDENCE. 59 43

Sixteen hundred new troops from Spain arrived at this port last night, among them quite a number of young doctors just graduated.

Very respectfully,
PULASKI F. HYATT,
United States Consul

United States Consulate,
Santiago de Cuba, February 25, 1898.

From the New York Central Relief Committee.

Gentlemen: I desire to make a brief report of the first four days' work in distributing the 101 cases of evaporated cream, 65 cases condensed milk, 100 bags of rice, 104 cases of codfish, 6 boxes of bacon, 208 bags flour, 43 barrels of beans, pills, drugs, etc.. which I received in due time by steamship Niagara.

As stated in a previous communication, a committee of 30 of the best ladies of this place divided the city into 15 districts, with two ladies to each district. These issue rations tickets according to the number of needy persons in each house. These tickets are honored under the direction of a committee of gentlemen and myself, and a liberal week's rations are issued to each. To prevent imposition we are obliged to refuse all who do not come with tickets from the ladies. The first day, rations were issued to 379; second day, 579; third day, 1,083; fourth day, 1,027; total, 3,068. Each ration being for seven days, which makes a total of 21,482 for one day. As near as I can judge only about one-half of the people who need help have yet received their first rations, and the codfish and beans will give out before we get around the first time. Have given moderate quantities to the eleemosynary institutions of the city, and sent some to the mining and other towns nearby. We are trying to make both food and medicine do the most good possible. It takes six or eight policemen to keep the crowds in order.

I am obliged to spend some money for labor, cartage, transportation, cable incidentals, etc.

CUBAN CORRESPONDENCE.

There are numerous people in a distressed condition. I would not advise sending any more medicine except quinine for the present. Everything sent has been of a superior quality. The Highland brand of condensed cream and flour are specially fine. The medicines have had almost miraculous effects. Should you make further shipments, keep beans, rice, and codfish in the foreground, but everything comes in play. Smallpox has again broken out, and I have requested Surgeon General Wyman to send to you for me a quantity of vaccine virus. Should it come to hand I will thank you to furnish me with a moderate quantity.

I am, gentlemen, with highest consideration, your most obedient servant,

PULASKI F. HYATT,
Santiago de Cuba
United States Consul.

Letter of Mr. Hyatt to Mr. Bay.
[No. 439.] *Consulate op the United States*
Santiago de Cuba, March 24, 1898.

Sir: Three sugar estates owned or managed by the house of Brooks & Co. are making sugar on a small scale, but have little faith in their ability to go ahead. These plantations are located near Guantánamo.

Property holders, without distinction of nationality, and with few exceptions, strongly desire annexation, having but little hope of a stable government under either of the contending forces, and they view with regret the indifference, nay, repugnance, of the American people to such a union, and still hope that a combination of circumstances will yet bring it about; but such a move would not be popular among the masses.

On Sunday last an election was held in this city to elect officers to hold an election on the 27th instant. No one seemed to know anything about it until it was over, and the autonomists won the election. A member of that party told me that ".we met quietly and done our voting.

«*There is no evidence that the people in general intend to take any part in the coming election. Circulars are now out urging the people to turn out and sustain the government, to the end that peace and prosperity may speedily come.*»

Very respectfully,
PULASKI F. HYATT,
Santiago de Cuba
United States Consul.

Letter of Mr. Jova to Mr. Day.
[No. 261.] *Consulate of the United States*
Sagua la Grande, November 11, 1897.

Sir: It may not be improper that I give the Department my impressions of the status of affairs here concerning the new policy promised by Spain to this island.

By the attitude openly demonstrated against autonomy from the two only existing parties that have to decide its results, the Cuban separatists, including the armed men in the field and their supporters in the towns, and the Spanish conservatives, with followers in Cuba and Spain; the former refusing anything but independence, the latter encouraging its members to strongly protest, not solely against autonomy, but even "reforms,"- which they have rebuked as contrary to their constitution, I can not help to foresee that far from improving the actual condition of things it will make it more and more critical.

I have left aside without consideration a new factor on the political arena, " annexation," not being able to calculate its magnitude on account of the legal prohibition of that doctrine resulting in the secret endeavors of the adherents, but it is well seen that it is growing stronger every day, principally among the Spaniards. The autonomist part to day in this district does not exist. In very rare exceptions one partisan may be found loyal to that platform; more so now, in view of Captain-General Weyler's work. It may be said that it is only nominal.

The Reformists have divided themselves so much' that its members are to be found in any of the other parties. They are ready to adopt the flag of the more favorable side, turning out thus a very weak association. Spain has to depend on these two last nominal and feeble corporations for the implantation of its new course of action. Taking all these facts into appreciation, it is hard to see in what way is Spain going to establish this new system. It will always be a parasite without stable foundation, without basis, singly maintained by a very infirm, insignificant auxiliary.

In the meantime the reconcentrados, the majority innocent beings, who have had, and even now have no notion of the cause of this revolution, who had no more aspiration than to till their little farms, continue perishing. It is difficult, it may be said almost impossible, to be able to describe the extension and intensity of such tremendous suffering, of such iniquitous, unjust, and sinful imposition, to annihilate thousands of women and children. If this Godless combination should be accurately represented it would seem an exaggeration induced by stirred fellow-feeling. With sensibility in the heart moving among them, the unceasing crowd of famished beggars, one can scarcely do more than commiserate the undeserved misfortune. To express, to delineate the afflictions, the anguishes witnessed at every step, would require much to write, and no lavish of colors could approach the reality to fiction.

No history in the world, ancient or modern, can be compared an instant to this frightful, dreadful suffering. Perhaps civilization has not seen the like of it. In conclusion, I beg to be permitted to state that, in my humble judgment, the efforts toward the enforcement of reforms or autonomy will prove altogether futile; and, of course, in consequence of this failure the few reconcentrados that have survived will not be allowed to go freely to their devastated farms, prolonging thus this unbearable situation.

I have, etc,
JOHN P. JOVA,
Sagua la Grande
US Vice-Consul.

Letter of Mr. Barker to Mr. Day.

[No. 270.] *Consulate of the United States*

Sagua la Grande, December 13, 1897.

Sir : Confident of the desire of the Department to keep in touch with affairs under the new regime, I beg to submit the following:

In order either to qualify or confirm my No. 204, of the 20th instant, wherein I stated the claim made by the authorities that the people were cultivating the soil, rations issued daily to the needy, and protection given to the mills so as to grind the present crop was not in accordance with my observations, I have within the past few days visited five of the principal railroad towns in this consular district, i.e., Santa Clara, Cruces, Esperanza, Jicotea, and Santo Domingo. The destitution is simply too harrowing to recite and must become intensified each day.

The death rate for last month shows an increase of about 25 per cent. In these towns I got my information from the mayors of each. From them I learned that while an issue of food, running from three to five days, had been made, beginning on the 28th ultimo, consisting of 3 ounces bacon or jerked beef and 6 ounces rice for adults, with half this allowance for children under 14 years, the pittance given was sufficient only for one-fourth to one tenth of the starving. No further relief has been given up to date. On the contrary, the mayors of Santa Clara, Cruces, and Santo Domingo are authority for stating the Captain-General had ordered that after the 8th instant any issue of food to the " concentrados " be discontinued. I enclose herewith a clipping from a local paper of Santa Clara confirming this. I have also read it in more than one other Spanish journal.

The mayor of Santa Clara stated to me that the Captain-General a week since directed him to call on the commissary of the army for 5,000 rations for relief purposes, which he said was sufficient to feed the suffering people but for one day. This officer's answer was he could not do so, as all Government supplies on hand would be required to feed the army. The mayor stated, also, that in presenting this order to the military commander he was ordered by him under no circumstances to give food to anyone having relatives in the insurrection, which he informed me would exclude 75 per cent of the destitute. I know that in Sagua and other points orders for food have been given on the commissary departments of the army, but invariably refused, as being needed for the soldiers. I reiterate, however sincere be the authorities to provide for the large number of "concentrados" who dare not return to the country, the fact that they are utterly powerless to do so cannot be disguised.

All efforts so far to obtain relief by popular subscription have met with signal failure. The Cubans are too poverty-stricken, while the Spaniards, who own the wealth, will contribute nothing.

In my recent trip I found that the Spanish soldiers are not only suffering for necessary food, but I was often appealed to by these pitiable creatures for medicine. One has only to look upon them to be assured of the needs complained of.

In view of the foregoing facts, known to me from personal investigation, I desire to renew the suggestion made to the Department in a previous dispatch, that the dire destitution and distress of the people appeals for immediate assistance to a charitable, Christian people, with which I sincerely hope the Department may not deem ill-advised to acquaint the people of the United States, when such a response will be made as will bring succor to a starving populace.

CUBAN CORRESPONDENCE.

It is proper that I inform the Department that, added to the universal destitution, the guerrillas continue to attack and kill the noncombatants. As stated, the guerrilla chiefs Carreras, Olavarieta, and Lazo are, if possible, more active in their cruel warfare on "*pacíficos*."

I am, etc.,
WALTER B. BARKER,
Sagua la Grande
Consul.

Reconcentrados in Santa Clara assisted by the **American Red Cross.**

The nature and the subject matter of Mr. Lee's reports to Washington changed radically, of course, after the incident of the US Frigate Maine in Havana.

In January 1898, the Maine was sent from Key West, Florida, to Havana, to protect U.S. interests during the 1895 Cuban War of Independence. Three weeks later, at 9:40 PM, on February 15, 1898, an explosion on board Maine occurred in the Havana Harbor. Later investigations revealed that more than 5 long tons (5.1 t) of powder charges for the vessel's six- and ten-inch guns had detonated, obliterating the forward third of the ship. The remaining wreckage rapidly settled to the bottom of the harbor. Most of Maine's crew were sleeping or resting in the enlisted quarters, in the forward part of the ship, when the explosion occurred. In total, 260 men lost their lives as a result of the explosion or shortly thereafter, and six more died later from injuries. Captain Sigsbee and most of the officers survived, because their quarters were in the aft portion of the ship. Altogether there were 89 survivors, 18 of whom were officers. On 21 March, the U.S. Naval Court of Inquiry, in Key West, declared that a naval mine had caused the explosion.

To this day, the cause of Maine's sinking remains a subject of speculation. In 1898, an investigation of the explosion was carried out by a naval board appointed under the McKinley Administration. The consensus of the board was that Maine was destroyed by an external explosion from a mine. However, the validity of this investigation was immediately challenged. George W. Melville, a chief engineer in the Navy, proposed that a more likely cause for the sinking was from a magazine explosion within the vessel. The Navy's leading ordnance expert, Philip R. Alger, took this theory further by suggesting that the magazines were ignited by a spontaneous fire in a coal bunker. The coal used in Maine was bituminous coal, which is known for releasing firedamp, a gas that is prone to spontaneous explosions. There was stronger evidence that the explosion of Maine was caused by an internal coal fire which ignited the magazines. This was a likely cause of the explosion, rather than the initial hypothesis of a mine. The ship lay at the bottom of the harbor until 1911. A cofferdam was then built around the wreck. The hull was patched up until the ship was afloat, then towed to sea and sunk a few miles at sea. The Maine now lies on the sea-bed 3,600 feet (1,100 m) below the surface.

There were two separate investigative bodies looking at the causes of the sinking of the Maine:

The ***Spanish inquiry***, conducted by Del Peral[5] and De Salas, collected evidence from officers of naval artillery, who had examined the remains of Maine. Del Peral and De Salas identified the spontaneous combustion of the coal bunker, located adjacent to the munitions stores in Maine, as the likely cause of the explosion. However, the possibility of other combustibles causing the explosion such as paint or drier products was not discounted. Additional observations included that:

- *Had a mine been the cause of the explosion, a column of water would have been observed.*
- *The wind and the waters were calm on that date and hence a mine could not have been detonated by contact, but only by using electricity, but no cables had been found.*
- *No dead fish were found in the harbor, as would be expected following an explosion in the water.*
- *Munitions stores do not usually explode when a ship is sunk by a mine.*

The conclusions of their report were not reported at that time by the American press.

A second investigative body was a US Naval Inquiry ordered by the United States Government shortly after the incident. It was headed by Captain William T. Sampson and it became known as ***Sampson Board's Court of Inquiry.***

---

[5] Captain **Don Pedro del Peral y Caballero** was assigned by Spain as Judge in Charge of the investigation of the Maine disaster. Lieutenant **Don Javier de Salas** was chosen by Peral to be Secretary of the enquiry.

Ramón Blanco y Erenas, Spanish governor of Cuba, had proposed instead a joint Spanish-American investigation of the sinking. Captain Sigsbee had written that

«...*many Spanish officers, including representatives of General Blanco, now with us to express sympathy.*»

In a cable, the Spanish Minister of Colonies, Segismundo Moret, had advised Blanco...

«... *to gather every fact you can, to prove the Maine catastrophe cannot be attributed to us.*»

The **Sampson Board** concluded that Maine had been blown up by a mine, which, in turn, caused the explosion of her forward magazines. They reached this conclusion, based on the fact that the majority of witnesses stated that they had heard two explosions and that that part of the keel was bent inwards. The official report from the board, which was presented to the Navy Department in Washington, D.C. on 21 March, specifically stated the following:

- *At frame 18, the vertical keel is broken in two and the flat keel is bent at an angle similar to the angle formed by the outside bottom plating. [...] In the opinion of the court, this effect could have been produced only by the explosion of a mine situated under the bottom of the ship at about frame 18, and somewhat on the port side of the ship..* (part of the court's 5th finding)
- *In the opinion of the court, the Maine was destroyed by the explosion of a submarine mine, which caused the partial explosion of two or more of her forward magazines."* (the court's 7th finding) and
- *"The court has been unable to obtain evidence fixing the responsibility for the destruction of the Maine upon any person or persons."* (the court's 8th finding).

The USS Maine entering the port of Havana on January 25, 1898

The ruins of the USS Maine in the port of Havana on February 15, 1898

The location where the Maine sank was enclosed in a cofferdam, on June 16, 1911; the wreck was raised, fixed so that it would float and towed to high seas in from of Havana, and sank again.

The Sampson Board investigating the Maine incident.

A page on the **Satirical Magazine Judge**, published in the US by former **Puck Magazine** writers.

At the request of the State Department, Fitzhugh Lee recommended several individuals to be deposed by the Senate Committee in charge of the investigation of the Maine disaster. They were accepted by Washington and travelled individually to that city starting on the third week of February, a few days after the blowing of the Maine in Havana. The list included:

On February 21,
Mr. Carl P. Koop, a Tobacco Merchant familiar with the situation in Cuba.

On March 31,
US Navy Robert B. Bradford, a torpedo expert,
US Navy Charles D. Sigsbee, Captain of the Maine,

On April 7,
Mr. François Laine, New York Sun Correspondent

On April 8,
Mr. Benjamín J. Guerra, a Tobacco Merchant, familiar with the resources obtained in the US by the insurgents.

On April 12,
Consul General in Havana, Mr. Fitzhugh Lee himself.

The transcripts of their depositions at the US Senate follows:

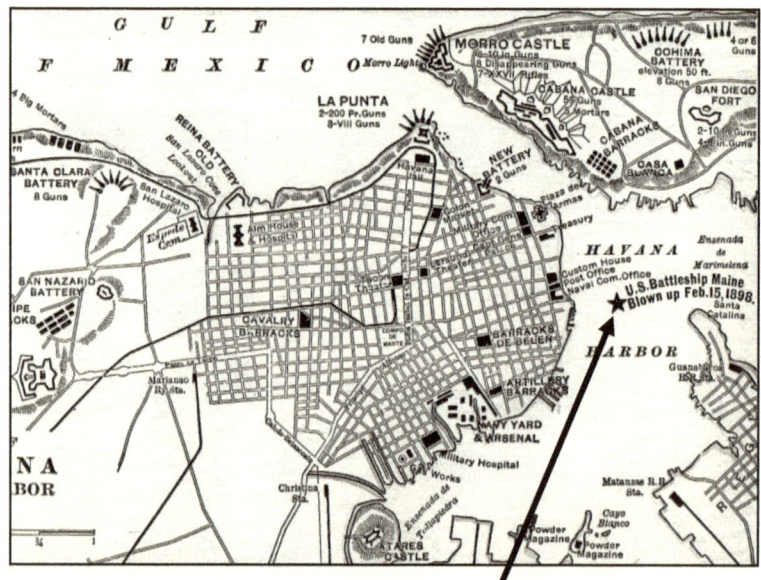

Position of the *USS Maine* in the harbor of Havana at the time of its destruction

STATEMENT OF MR. CARL P. KOOP, FEBRUARY 21, 1898.

Examination by Senator John T. Morgan.
Committee on Foreign Relations of the Senate.

Q. Please state your name, age, and place of residence.
—A. My name is Carl P. Koop, 30 years of age, and resident of Boston, Mass.
Q. What has been your occupation in Boston?
—A. I am in the tobacco business. Buying and selling the raw material.
Q. Have you had trade in Cuba?
—A. Yes; all the time, more or less.
Q. Do you speak Spanish fluently?
—A. I speak Spanish; I cannot say that I speak it fluently.
Q. What are the principal tobacco districts in Cuba?
—A. Vuelta Abajo, and Santa Clara.
Q. When did you make your last visit to Cuba?
—A. I got there on the 6th of January. I left on the 12th of February, a week ago last Saturday.
Q. How did you occupy your time while you were in Cuba?
—A. Largely, of course, looking after my business, and in traveling through
the island from one point to another.
Q. Did you have a permit to travel?
—A. Yes; I had my passport, having been told that it was absolutely unnecessary for an American to have any special pass.
Q. Could you, with the passports, have had access to the lines of the insurgents?
—A. No, I could not; not without some difficulty.
Q. Would the Spanish troops allow you to pass out?
—A. No, the Spanish troops would not allow you to pass out.
Q. Would the insurgents have been willing to receive you?
— A. Yes. I have met the insurgents in various districts. If I went to the lines of the insurgents, outside of the military lines of the Spanish army, I would have had to do it through a great deal of maneuvering and difficulty.
Q. Can you give us a statement of your itinerary through the different provinces?
—A. Well, I left Havana the very day after I arrived from New York, and the first stop I made at that time was at Cárdenas, which is not a tobacco growing place or situated in a tobacco-growing district. I went there to consult with the man from whom I bought some property. I stayed there two days.

Q. What was the condition of the population at Cárdenas?

—A. Something horrible; something beyond all description.

Q. Do you apply that to the reconcentrados as well as to the people who are not affected by that order?

—A. I apply that strictly to the reconcentrados, because the conditions of the other class of the population is altogether different. They have something on which to live; they have their homes, too. The number of reconcentrados forced into Cárdenas amounts to 35,000, out of which about 26,000 have died.

Q. What you saw, then, was a people in a very pitiable and starving condition !

—A. Yes. At one time I saw a woman lying in a doorway in Cárdenas with two dead children lying in her arms, and herself absolutely unable to speak, or even make a motion. She was in the last stages of starvation. Then again, I saw four or five crazy men—lunatics—who were chattering, laughing, crying, cursing—horrible beyond description. And inquiring what brought them to that crazy state from an individual in the Hotel Union there, I was told that it was brought on them by starvation, mainly. With one of them it was the result of finding his whole family starved, and he not able to help them.

Q. Do you know whether any of the benevolent offerings of the United States had reached Cárdenas yet while you were there?

—A. No, they had not.

Q- Can you state any fact which will show that they had not?

—A. I was informed by prominent American officers that they did not have even enough to reach over the city of Havana. Nothing came outside of the city of Havana while I was there.

Q. In what kind of habitations do these people at Cárdenas dwell?

—A. They live in straw huts, as you might call them, built up from the ground about 7 feet high, and covered with straw. They are built like an "A" tent and are called *bohíos*.

Q. While in Cárdenas did you note what was called *"the zone of cultivation"*?

— A. I noticed it very distinctly in going into the city on the railroad and in walking about the country. It is on the other side of a military line and is called zone of cultivation, and no one is allowed to go outside.

Q. Inside of that zone was there any cultivation?—A. It was filled with huts, and not much room for cultivation.

Q. Were there any crops growing?

—A. No. There was no room. There were a few gardens, and little ones at that.

Q. Did you see any vegetables growing?

—A. Yes; something of that kind, but very meager; not even

enough for a population of 2,000, much less a population of 60,000 or 70,000.

Q. From its appearance would you suppose or would you judge that that agricultural zone around Cárdenas would, if cultivated to its fullest extent, enable the reconcentrados who are upon it to live?

—A. Simply impossible.

Q. I suppose Cárdenas is a fortified town.

—A. It is. It is a seaport town and is also fortified with blockhouses in the rear, and has also one or two small forts there.

Q. During the time you were in Cárdenas, did you observe that there was any business being carried on from the outside?

—A. Very little indeed. Everyman whom I interviewed, from the hotel men to the ship brokers, said that business was absolutely at a standstill.

Q. What was the condition of your friend as regards business?

—A. He was a man who was at one time very well off, and even now has some property and manages to get along rather well.

Q. If I get a correct idea of your statements, the land between Havana and Cárdenas was a waste, and the country around Cárdenas a waste!

—A. Yes. I will give you a fuller description. On my journey I passed through the following towns: The first one of any importance was Jaruco, and the condition around there was pitiable, the children and women gathering around the depot and asking for pennies and for bread and crying with hunger. It was too horrible to describe. The next town of any importance was Bainoa, and the condition there was the same. The next town was Aguacate, of seven or eight thousand population, and into this town were forced 10,000 reconcentrados. The condition in this town was something terrible, and I understood from the conductor of the train that in this town out of 10,000 population only about 2,000 lived. The next town was a small one Ceiba—which was in the same condition as the others, the women and children running around the depot begging. The next one was Mocha. This is a very large town, and into it had been forced from eight to ten thousand reconcentrados, and very few of them lived. I remember we had to lay over there for half an hour, and I got out and examined some of the huts. They were all scattered along the railroad track, hundreds of them in a row. I went through a great many rows, and looked into a great many of the huts. They were empty, their occupants having died. About one-fourth of the huts were occupied and the rest unoccupied. The next town was Matanzas.

Q. As you have mentioned Matanzas, please to describe on your visits there what you saw.

—A. Matanzas is one of the worst towns on the whole island. It has a population of 70,000.

Q. Is it a fortified town?

—A. Yes; it has a very large harbor, and in ordinary times does a good business—sugar business especially.

Q. What was the state of business as you observed at the time of your visit?

—A. Absolutely at a standstill. Everything in the way of manufacturing is at a standstill, and the condition of the reconcentrados in Matanzas, what there is left of them, is about as bad as you will find anywhere on the island.

Q. How many had been assembled there and how many were left when you were there?

—A. Somewhere between 35,000 and 40,000; later about 8,000 or 9,000.

Q. You saw them?

—A. I did. As I have said, at every railroad station crowds of women and children gathered around and begged for money and for bread. It is an everyday experience.

Q. What they live upon, I suppose, is alms!

—A. Alms, yes; which they get from strangers passing through the towns. The Government is not making any attempt to feed them, and the local people there are in such a condition that there are few of them who are able to give anything; and those who would have been able to give them something have left the country. In fact, that is the same story of a great many towns. The people who live there and belong there are poor themselves, and are not able to help these people even if they wanted to.

Q. Now, about the *"zone of cultivation"* around Matanzas?

—A. The *"zone of cultivation"* around Matanzas is, of course, considerably larger than around the other towns, but in proportion to the population there is in Matanzas to the proportion of reconcentrados who have been forced in there it is even smaller, I presume, than in some of the other towns. Into that town of 70,000 population were forced 35,000 or 40,000, and that is quite an addition to a town, and for that reason the line of cultivation, while it is larger than in other towns, is simply insufficient for such a population as there is there.

Q. Could you see from appearances that the population of reconcentrados were really deriving any support from these cultivation zones?

—A. It is hard to tell who receives the benefit from these cultivation zones. I am under the impression that most of the products from these cultivation zones were supplied to the city markets. They had not much of a chance to cultivate anything. What they do cultivate is done practically in the street. Between every row of huts there is a road about twenty feet wide, and along in that road, in what you might really call the street, I have seen them try to plant potatoes, etc. I have at various times tried to find out where the vegetables, etc., which were raised inside the military zone went, but was never able to find out. I was always told that they were sent to the markets.

Q. Was that supply of any real consequence toward the support of the population!

—A. It was absolutely insufficient. In all my experiences with the living expenses in the interior of Cuba, I will say that it is something phenomenal, and altogether beyond the reach of ordinary individuals. I have paid at various times 25 cents for a little piece of bread which weighed not more than two ounces. For two eggs and rice I have paid anywhere from 50 to 75 cents; and for a small piece of ice, such as you would want for your glass of water, I have paid 25 cents. Beef and other meats, if they have any, is enormously high in price and absolutely unfit to eat. The only thing they have there on which you could really live is rice and eggs, and occasionally some potatoes; but they are all very expensive.

Q. Are there any other incidents attending your visit at Matanzas that will throw any light on the condition of the people there?

—A. Well, I did not stay so very long at Matanzas, although I was there three different times—merely stopping off to take the next train—and I did not look around so very much ; not so much as I did at other towns.

Q. Proceed.

—A. Guabánana is a town of 8,000 or 10,000 population. This is another miserable town, and the affairs there are in a very bad state. A great many were driven in there, but I have not the exact figures, having given it to a party in Havana, and kept no copy.

Q. Now, is that in the sugar district?

—A. Yes.

Q. Did you find any business going on in Guanábana?

—A. Absolutely none; and the condition there was the same as in the other towns; women and children gathering around, all in a starving condition, begging for bread. The next place was Limonar. That was another place in which the condition was very bad. I passed lots of small places of which I made no note. Next place was Coliseo, which also was in a very bad state. The next place was Jovellanos, a railroad center where you change cars for Santa Clara, Cárdenas, and other places; and I have passed through that place seven or eight times on my travels on the island, and during these visits I have had several times a layover of half an hour, and during that time would go and investigate the huts. I found them to be in horrible shape there. The town has a population of, I think, 10,000, and the amount of reconcentrados, I was told, amounted to as many as the population. I was informed that very few of them lived, the death rate being phenomenal. And there, also, you could see half-naked women and children in a starving condition, their feet and stomachs swollen. After studying the disease

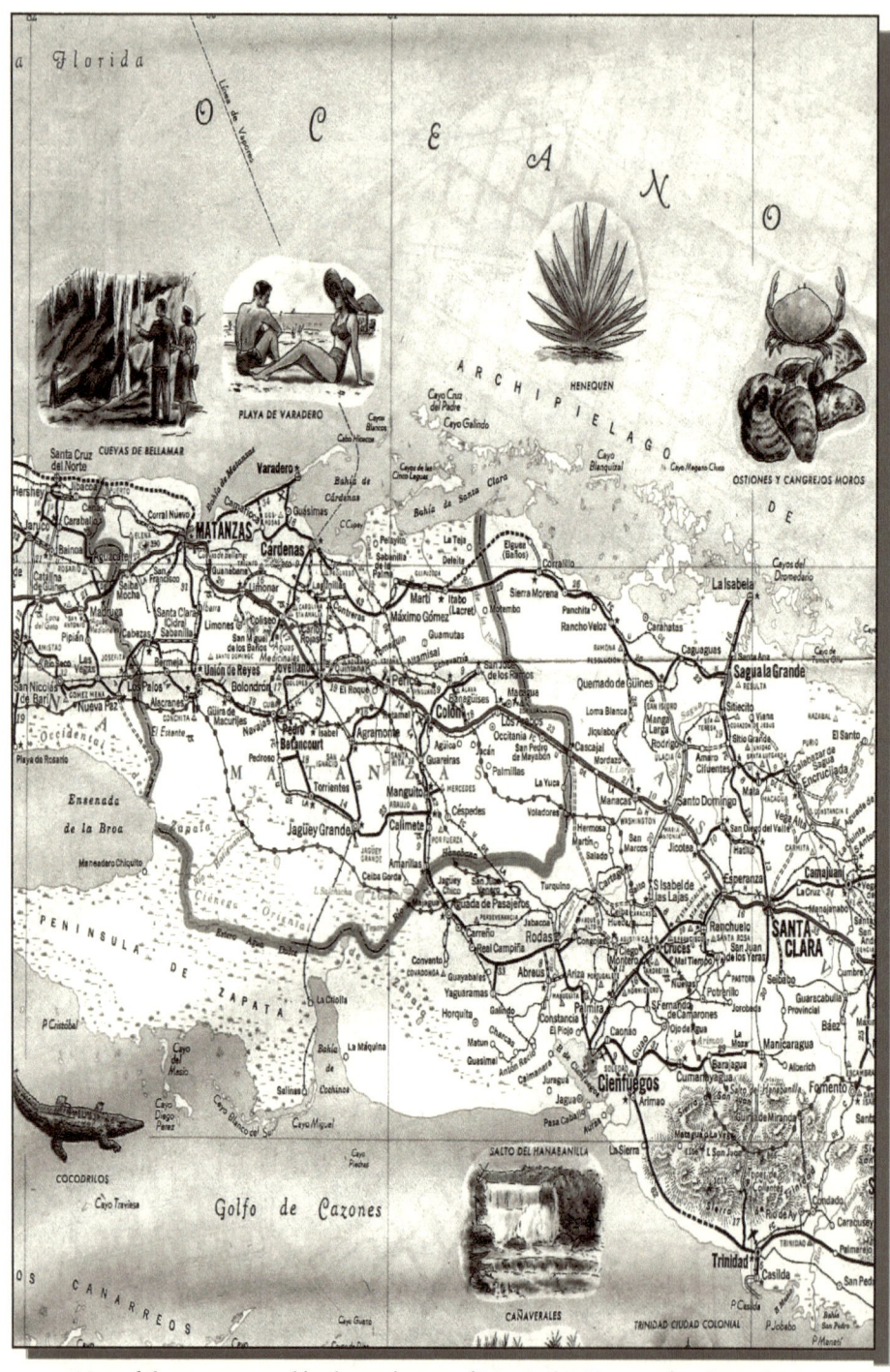

Map of the area covered in the testimony of Mr. Carl P. Koop at the *Committee on Foreign Relations of the US Senate* on February 21, 1898

one could calculate about how long they would live in that condition. I recall another incident. In getting into Jovellanos there was, as usual, a crowd of women and children begging; and four or five little girls came through the train begging. They ranged from three to six years of age. In the car was a Spanish officer, and as the little girls went by one of them brushed against him, and he immediately turned and kicked her in the stomach, knocking her over, and in falling she knocked over the one next to her, and so on until all five of the little girls fell down in the aisle. It was so brutal that I felt like throwing him out of the window, but of course had to restrain myself. Quintana was another town about which about the same story is to be told. It is not so large as some of the other towns. The next town is Perico. I went through it also. The next town Colón. The next one San José. The next is Manguito, and the next Alvarez. At the last-named place the condition was poor—a large amount of concentration to a small population, and nothing left of them. The next town is Mercedita. The next place I visited was Santa Clara, which is the capital of Santa Clara Province, and military headquarters for that province also. It is a town of, ordinarily, a population of fifteen to eighteen thousand, and into that city were driven something like 12,000 concentrados.

Q. How many were there when you visited it?

—A. How many reconcentrados? I have the exact figures. Out of that number 7,829 have died.

Q. From whom did you get this information?

—A. Right from the judge of the civil court. He has to issue certificates for burial for everyone who dies.

Q. Nobody ever knows who else dies?

—A. No; they are gone and that's all. In the State of Santa Clara I saw so much suffering and so many horrible sights that I do not know whether there is any use in relating any of them.

Q. You can state some of the instances which impressed you as being characteristic of the situation.

— A. One of the saddest, if not the saddest, sight I saw was the case of a woman who stood in front of a hotel in Santa Clara, and who dropped dead when I handed her a piece of bread. That was the saddest sight I saw on the whole trip.

Q. Did she undertake to eat it?

—A. She dropped the baby which she had in her arms, grabbed the piece of bread which I handed her, drove her teeth into it and fell over dead. She had a baby in her arms and two little children hanging on to her skirts.

Q. What became of the baby she let drop?

—A. The baby died that night or the next morning. I found out in the morning that it had died; and the other two children died a day or two afterwards.

Q. Died of starvation?

—A. Yes; starvation. of the concentrados in Santa Clara is something beyond description. I traveled around on horseback a great deal and investigated the huts of these people, and all the persons I saw in them were in the last stages of starvation. There was absolutely no food. They were in such a state that even professional nursing would not have saved them. Having stayed in that city for a longer period, and at various times, I, perhaps, investigated it a little closer than I did the other towns, due probably to the fact that I wanted to get out and see something different from what I had been witnessing

Q. Were you out in the zone at Santa Clara?

—A. Yes; and the story is the same as it is of every other interior town.

Q. Let me ask you whether these reconcentrados are permitted to go
outside of this zone to cultivate?

—A. No.

Q. What is the condition of the Spanish soldiery in these various places as to food and clothing?

—A. The ordinary Spanish soldier is in very bad shape. Of course, the officers seem to have plenty, but the ordinary soldier is in a very bad way. You see them begging in the streets in the interior towns quite often. Their clothing is very poor, and they are a sickly looking lot of men.

Q. Young men or old men?

—A. Young men, 15 to 20 years old. Ranchuelo is another town that I visited, and found it in a very bad condition. Cruces is also a town in bad condition. Ranchuelo, Cruces, and Santa Clara are in a state that nobody would imagine. You cannot imagine it. It is simply terrible. Cienfuegos is about the only town in which I can say I saw any business. Of course, it always has been a business center. All the sugar business goes there, and still the merchants complain that there is absolutely no business there. And the condition, as far as the reconcentrados are concerned, is not quite as bad as it is in other localities. Batabanó, which is a seaport town and railroad center, is connected with the boats of the Southern Steamship Company from the eastern part of the island, and to Havana. From Batabanó to Havana I passed through several towns, but made no enumeration, because I was told to stop writing notes on the train.

Q. You were prevented from making notes on the train By whom?

—A. Yes. By Officers of the Spanish army. And that same state of affairs existed several other times during my travels in Santa Clara district. In some of those travels, whenever I had a pencil in my hand and was trying to write down notes, a Spanish officer always came up and wanted to know what I had written down.

Q. What is the distance from Batabanó to Havana?

—A. I do not know exactly, but presume it is about 20 miles; and in that distance there were in the neighborhood of 3,000 soldiers—men on horseback guarding the road.

Q. Were your visits to the large cities mainly for business?

—A. Yes; altogether on business.

Q. Now, is Cuba a fertile country—the parts you saw?

—A. The most fertile country I ever saw.

Q. Suppose those reconcentrados had just been allowed to go out into the country, could they have made a subsistence on the native productions?

—A. Yes; they could have lived alone on the articles which grow in the district of Santa Clara or any other part of the island. There is an abundance of sweet potatoes, bananas, and other fruits which are very nourishing, and which the natives, to a large extent, use in their daily existence.

Q. In passing through the country did you see any herds of cattle?

—A. Absolutely none. All the cattle I saw were strongly guarded by military forces along the railroad, and they were very few at that.

Q. The country had been stripped of its cattle absolutely?

—A. Yes. The price of cattle has increased 200 %, and as I have said before, all the cattle I saw were under a strong guard of Spanish soldiers; and there is no cultivation going on in any part of the island that is not under the guard of the Spanish army, or, rather, Spanish arms.

Q. According to your observations, how do the Spanish get their provisions?

—A. Provisions are sent in from seaport cities somewhat. My observation has been that the Spanish troops suffer almost as much as the native population for the want of food. They are not properly fed. There is no question about that. They themselves acknowledge that they beg for bread. Of course the officers do not come under that category.

Q. From what you saw, and from what you have learned while you have been in Cuba, will you say that there had been any relaxation of the military regulations in respect of those reconcentrados, of this population, since Blanco?

—A. None. Whenever I had an opportunity I made inquiries as regards that point, and was told invariably that the agricultural zone existed just the same.

Q. Did you, at any place you visited in Cuba, ascertain or learn that the Spanish Government was making any provision for the reconcentrados?

—A. Never. I have not, in all the thirty-odd towns in which I have been, I have not heard that the Spanish Government has supplied or helped to supply any starving individual with bread or anything else.

Q. Did you meet with any of our consuls in the interior of Cuba?

—A. Yes.

Q. Did you have opportunity to know whether they had been contributing out of their private resources to the support of these poor people?

—A. All the consuls whom I have met have done a great deal toward the betterment of the starving individuals there out of their private means. I can say right here,

that in all my observations I have felt proud of General Lee and of every consul in whose province I have been ; proud of the way they have treated and helped some of the starving individuals at their own expense.

Q. You think, then, that the purpose of the regulation was really to starve these people to death ?

—A. Yes ; the sole purpose. It is well known that 900,000 of those natives were forced in from their homes, and out of that number 500,000 have died already. Therefore the results have proved the motive.

Q. Did the soldiers seem to have any sort of human regard for them?

—A. Many of the soldiers were mere boys and in such a condition as to be hardly

able to take care of themselves.

Q. I suppose these reconcentrados of whom you have been speaking are natives?

—A. Absolutely all natives.

Q. All natives of Cuba!—A. The majority are white. They are of Spanish, French, and other nationalities, but largely Spanish.

Q. If I comprehend your description of the interior of Cuba, it is a country that is almost entirely wasted and destroyed?

—A. Absolutely. There is nothing at all going on in the interior of Cuba. No houses standing. Ruined sugar estates wherever you look. Wherever there is any sugar growing you will see a force of soldiers guarding it, these soldiers being kept there by the sugar owners, and are therefore able to exist.

Q. It is already then a country laid to waste?

—A. The whole country is a waste.

Q. In the present condition of these people, would it be possible in their weak state that they could survive by the assistance of the fruits of the earth?

—A. A great many of them now, if let loose, would recover at once—women especially, although a great many of them are absolutely too feeble to move much.

Q. Then, you think—it is your opinion—if I understand you, that the failure to relax the orders of Weyler in regard to the reconcentrados of this people to hold them, is still the actual and direct cause of their present starvation?

—A. The only cause.

Q. Are owners of real estate in Cuba, as far as you observed, anxious to dispose of it?

—A. There is a large amount of property which has been absorbed by the American citizens in Cuba; a very large amount of it.

Q. Well, is there an anxiety by those landholders to dispose of their estates?

—A. There is. Some of the Spanish land holders are selling off all they have.

Q. What did you learn about the emigration?

—A. About 400,000 to various American cities from Cuba.

Q. Were they a class of people who had means of emigrating?

—A. They were the people who could get away.

Q. A very large part, then, of that class must have left the island? Those who remained were the poor people and the soldiers?

—A. Yes and Yes.

Q. Did you make any computation of the number of lives that have been sacrificed in Cuba through war, starvation, and disease all put together?

— A. Yes; I have at various times asked that question of officers, and learned that the amount of people who have died from sickness and starvation is somewhere in the vicinity of 600,000. Of course that does not include Spanish soldiers.

Q. Does it include the insurgents?

—A. It does. It includes the deaths in the Island of Cuba, excluding Spanish soldiers.

Q. Among the native Cubans, or those persons who have been a long time residents of the island, did you find any hostility toward the United States?

—A. Absolutely none. Whenever I met any Cubans they were always anxious to do everything they could for me.

Q. Did you have consultation and conversation with men of character and influence?

—A. I did. I have met some of the leading members of the autonomy government, and also some of the present Spanish administration.

Q. Now, without stating with whom these consultations were, what conclusion did you reach as to the popularity of the autonomy movement in the interior towns?

—A. One that any man would come to after having visited the island for even a short while, and that is that autonomy is a matter of indifference there, and it is only believed in by a very few persons, and those are largely concentrated in the city of

Havana. When you come outside the city of Havana you find no autonomy party.

Q. You think, then, that the probability of that form of government being accepted in Cuba is small?

—A. It will never be accepted. It will never be accepted by the Spanish people.

Q. As I understand you, you are not speaking of the insurgents?—

A. No; speaking of the Spanish people themselves.

Q. Were these consultations and conversations with men of such character as to lead you to satisfactory conclusions as to the opinions you have just expressed?

—A. They are, in fact, men of very high standing and leaders of the autonomy movement in the city of Havana.

Q. Did you ascertain in Cuba whether or not the leading men engaged in business pursuits had any confidence in the good faith of the Spanish Government?

—A. There is only one answer to that: Nothing. They have no confidence in the autonomy plan the Spanish Government has so far offered.

Q. Was the subject of an American protectorate in connection with autonomy discussed ?

—A. It was generally discussed by merchants and business men that if they could get an American protectorate with autonomy they might have some confidence.

Q. How do you believe things would be in the event of the success of the insurgent army, accompanied by close and friendly relations with the United States ; what do you believe it would be then ?

—A. I believe that the Island of Cuba would be in a flourishing condition inside of two or three years. There are hundreds of thousands of Cubans who have emigrated. They would return to business on the island, and citizens from other countries would also go there.

~~~

Having examined and corrected the foregoing statements made under oath to John T. Morgan, a member of the Committee on Foreign Relations of the Senate, and having stricken out some passages that are true, but may affect the interest of myself and

> others unnecessarily and dangerously, I make oath that the statement as revised is true to the best of my knowledge, information, and belief.
>
> CARL P. KOOP. [signature]
> February 21, 1898.
> District of Columbia, City of Washington:
>
> Subscribed and sworn to before me this 21st day of February, A. D. 1898.
> [SEAL.] R. B. Nixon, Notary Public.

Senator *John T. Morgan*, member of the
US Senate Committee on Foreign Relations

The next item on the agenda of the *US Senate Committee on Foreign Relations* was to get to the investigation on the sinking of the Maine in the Harbor of Havana. Its first witness was Mr. Robert B. Bradford, a torpedo expert.[6]

> **STATEMENT OF US NAVY COMMANDER Robert B. BRADFORD, March 30, 1898.**
> **Examination by Senator Frye and others.**
> *Committee on Foreign Relations of the US Senate*
> ### By Mr. Frye
> Q. Please state your name and profession.
> —A. Robert B. Bradford; naval officer, at present Chief of the Bureau of Equipment, Navy Department.
> Q. What experience, if any, have you had with torpedoes?

---

[6] In the XIX century, two different armaments were identified by the name **torpedo**. One was the weapon sent under the sea surface to an enemy vessel for the purpose of blowing it out of the water. The second was what is currently known as a *submarine mine*, which is a large charge of dynamite on a floating buoy anchored to the bottom of the sea, under the surface, that would explode upon contact with a passing enemy ship.

—A. I have been on duty at the torpedo station at Newport, R.I., when it was a school of instruction, as instructor and lecturer in torpedo warfare, altogether for a period of about six and a half years, and during that time I conducted a great many experiments with torpedoes and saw a great many explosions and the effect of torpedo explosions on small vessels and various kinds of materials; probably have had more experience than the average naval officer in that direction.

Q. Please state to the committee the several kinds of torpedoes.

—A. At the present day torpedoes are largely employed, under the name of mines, for harbor defense. They were formerly called torpedoes exclusively—during the war of the rebellion they were known as such. Since that time they have received various names in accordance with their usage. Those used for harbor defense are placed under the army and received an army name, and are recognized as such, and are now known as mines or submarine mines. They are the most powerful, because the amount of explosive used for submarine mines is practically unlimited, depending upon the size of the case, which can be made almost any dimensions. It is only limited by methods of handling, such as derricks, etc. The kind of torpedoes used mostly in the Navy are known as electromotive torpedoes, sometimes termed fish torpedoes, and now they are generally or frequently spoken of by the names of the inventors— the Whitehead, the Scwartzkoff, etc. They are all of the movable type, ejected from a tube, and contain, you may say briefly, all the mechanism of a complete steam vessel, provided with engines and motive power, means of steering, and carry in their forward ends an amount of explosive which is limited to about 100 pounds, gun cotton usually, and exploded on contact with any object. They have been very carefully designed and improved for a period of thirty years, so that they are now very perfect pieces of mechanism, mostly used from torpedo boats and torpedo destroyers and torpedo cruisers. They were formerly used in all naval vessels, but with the advent of rapid firing guns, etc., they have been largely discarded for use in tubes above water, except the small vessels which I mention, such as torpedo boats and destroyers. The reason is they are liable to be hit by small projectiles and exploded on board. They are still retained for use in larger ships for tubes under water, where they are protected by the water from shot or by armor. Our cruisers formerly fitted with them are now discarding them for the reasons I have given. Then, of course, there are a great many improvised torpedoes, and a kind that is frequently carried on ships of a small size, and sufficient to destroy or disable larger vessels, carrying from 50 to 100 pounds of explosive, known as electro mechanical torpedoes, carrying a small battery inside with an arrangement that when it strikes the circuit of this battery is completed on an explosive, and they are discharged. They are for the general purpose of fencing in ships that are disabled, or of being planted in narrow passages where enemy's vessels may pass. They are mobile affairs that are carried like any destructive material on board ships of war. Those three are the chief kinds used to-day, but any kind of torpedo can be improvised from almost any water-tight vessel, and are depended upon more or less, but the three kinds which I have mentioned are the perfected kinds.

Q. What is the difference between a torpedo boat and a torpedo-boat destroyer?

—A. Only in size. The destroyer is larger. It has the advantage over a torpedo boat of being more sea worthy and stronger. It is a steamer designed to destroy torpedo boats, being a larger and more powerful vessel. The name indicates the idea of the design. They are capable of being used in rougher water, and they have a larger radius of effective use, carrying more supplies, and more coal, and more men. They carry also more guns and heavier gnus. Torpedo boats of about a hundred tons' displacement carry only small guns and are in every way inferior, but the destroyers are practically only torpedo boats.

Q. And attack a ship in the same way?

—A. Yes, sir.

By Mr. Mills:

Q. Do they attack with torpedoes or guns?

—A. They are chiefly designed to use torpedoes; the guns are mostly auxiliary or incidental.

Q. How far can they send those torpedoes?

—A. They are limited to about 600 yards—the mobile or Whitehead torpedoes, such as I have described.

By Mr. Foraker:

Q. Will they go straight?

—A. They are so perfected that if in perfect order they will go straight. They are subject to deviation from very slight derangement. They are handled very much as though made of glass. They require the greatest care, and will perform a great deal of work if everything is nicely adjusted. Even with the greatest care on board ship we sometimes find in our experiments that they deviate from some unnoticed or unknown cause that we cannot ascertain—probably, in handling, the vertical rudder has been bent somewhat, so slightly we cannot detect it. They go under water some 13 feet, so they cannot be interfered with by shot after once discharged.

They are also liable to be deflected by currents to some extent.

Q. How rapidly do they go?

—A. They go at the rate of from 25 to 30 knots per hour.

By Mr. Morgan :

Q. What is the impelling power?

—A. Two propellers. The motive power is compressed air in tubes. When they are ejected from their tubes, the valve communicating between the air reservoir and the engines is opened,

The Spanish *Bustamante* Torpedo,

The American *Howell* Torpedo,

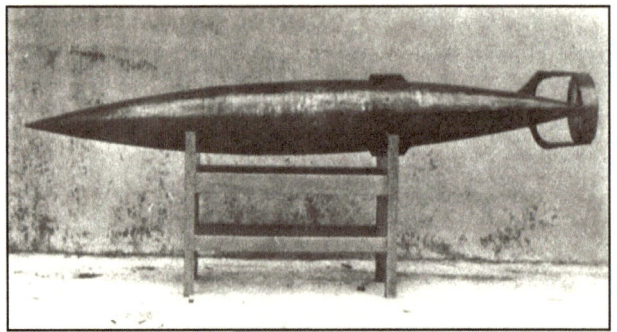

The American *Newport* Torpedo,

Launching a Spanish Mine (aka *Bustamante* quiet Torpedo), 1884

so that they act precisely, you may say, as any steam vessel—automatically.

By Mr. Frye :
Q. Have their own machinery?
—A. Yes, sir; the most perfect that can be built, of the most perfect and best material. They cost from $2,000 to $2,500 apiece, so you may know they are very perfect.

By Mr. Morgan:
Q. Can they be sent from the shore without the assistance of a torpedo tube?
—A. No, sir; they could not be pointed. They could be started with the aid of the trigger. The tube from which they are shot is worked very much like a gun; it is on a pivot, and is carefully adjusted, and allowance is made in firing for the speed of the ship at which they are fired.

Q. I would like to know, briefly, the danger from this Spanish flotilla of torpedo boats and torpedo destroyers?
—A. I am not impressed as much as many naval officers with the dangerous character of torpedo boats and torpedo destroyers. They are frail craft, because everything is sacrificed to speed, and weights are kept down for that reason, and very thin plates used in their construction, very slight frames, and they are easily deranged. I may say that they are boats of possibilities rather than of probabilities. Under certain conditions they are no doubt very formidable. Their chief value in my opinion is in preventing blockades, if in ports that are attempted to be blockaded. They choose their own time of attack, and of course the most favorable time. They are previously groomed up for the occasion, everything in readiness, and they slip out to a vessel outside, and try to get in their work. At sea with a squadron they are so liable to accident and so often deranged that the chances of being effective, in my opinion, are slight. I understand that the present flotilla, crossing from Spain, have been dismantled. That is to say, the torpedo tubes and guns carried on the upper deck have been taken off and are being brought over by the convoying steamer, which is a converted cruiser. That adds to their seaworthiness and stability. With those off they are completely helpless, shorn of any power The destroyers are supposed to be capable of ramming the small boats and destroying them that way. If within the destroying radius of a fleet, of course they can be used in the same way I described in a blockade. For instance, the port of Havana is about 90 miles from Key West or Tortugas. They have high speed. They can slip out at night, get in their work, and return under cover of darkness, and, vice versa, our own could do the same work. We happen to have no destroyers, and our torpedo boats have found it rather rough work crossing the Gulf Stream between those ports.

Q. How long a voyage, on the average, between the Canaries and Puerto Rico?

—A. That depends entirely on speed and the water. It is very difficult to form an estimate. They are coming, no doubt, in a latitude where the weather is very good. The route from Las Palmas, where they left the Canaries, to Puerto Rico is through the trade-wind belt, and there is rarely any bad weather there. I presume they would make somewhere—their speed would be governed largely by the accompanying steamer—say from 10 to 12 knots. I think the distance is about 2,800 miles. Say 10 knots—240 miles a day—that would be about 12 days.

Q. Have you read the testimony taken by the naval board of inquiry?

— A. Only sketches of it in the newspapers. I have not seen the full report as published.

Q. Have you read the accounts of the witnesses who testified as to two explosions?

—A. Yes, I have; and previously in the newspapers.

Q. What do these accounts indicate to your mind was the cause of the explosion?

—A. If you have noticed, the accounts are conflicting as to there being two explosions; some officers state they heard but one. In all torpedo explosions there always, apparently, are two explosions or two shocks. That is universally the case, and it is markedly so with a torpedo or mine on the bottom. The first appears to be transmitted by the land or by the water, and then the next appears to be the emission of this great quantity of highly heated gas into the open air, and in the same manner we have thunder after a stroke of lightning. But that is very well known to people who have exploded torpedoes, that there are always two shocks, and I have been of the opinion generally that those who thought there were two explosions confounded that fact with the idea that there was a second explosion. It seemed to me that

it was quite possible that the explosion of a mine broke the ship in the neighborhood of the magazines—we know the explosion was in the neighborhood of some of the magazines—broke some of the powder cases and dispersed this powder and at the same time ignited it, and this in a measure accounted for the flame about the ship. The result of the divers' work would seem to favor that theory. They found many powder cases broken open and battered up more or less. I do not think myself there was any serious explosion of the magazine from what I have read.

Q. What, in your opinion, did cause the trouble?

—A. A mine—a submarine mine.

Q. Have you any doubt about it, after reading the testimony?

—A. No, sir; I have not.

Q. In your opinion, what kind of a mine must that have been to have the effect shown there?

—A. It must have been a mine of what is termed *"high explosives,"* I think.

By Mr. Gray :

Q. Dynamite?

—A. Dynamite or gun cotton, or any of the modern high explosives. It is possible to do the same with gunpowder.

By Mr. Frye :

Q. What would be the size and weight and general character of that mine?

—A. I am at a disadvantage in answering that question, because I have not seen the wreck and have not read fully the testimony, but there are cases on record where ships—not as strong as the Maine, but metal ships—have been destroyed by the explosion of torpedoes alongside and not in contact, and varying in size from 250 to 300 pounds. In the Chilean war two ships were sunk by an explosion in this manner.

By Mr. Gray :

Q. Were they in contact?

—A. No, sir; not in contact, but a couple of feet at the side and at the surface. They did not have the advantage of the tamping of the water. Of course, the destruction is caused by the release of an immense volume of highly heated gas that escapes to the atmosphere through the path of least resistance. Water being incompressible, and if it is under the ship the path of least resistance is through the ship, and everything must give way to it. It is rather difficult to estimate the amount of explosive, but I would say 300 pounds of modern explosive, in my opinion, would do all the damage that was done to the Maine, and very possibly a less amount.

By Mr. Morgan:

Q. Do you mean dynamite or gun cotton?

—A. Yes, sir; they are included as modern explosives. I notice—I think the opinion was given by Commander Converse, who is a very excellent expert, and who has had almost all his duty on shore in connection with torpedoes—either he or someone else stated they thought the work was done by a slower burning explosive, and I take it to mean—I understand that he meant gunpowder. Gunpowder has a slower action; it is simply combustion as wood burns, while modern explosives, by their fuse, are turned instantly from a solid to an immense volume of highly heated gas, called detonation. The effect of detonation is to rend everything in the immediate neighborhood. Even tamping is sufficient for that, but gunpowder is slower acting.

By Mr. Mills :
Q. How would it be ignited?
—A. By electricity.
Q. Either on shore or on some other vessel?
—A. Yes, sir; it is very simple to do that; it is well understood.
By Mr. Gray:
Q. Do you think it possible for a mine to have been placed there after the ship was anchored with the discipline probably on board?
—A. Oh, yes; I think it was possible.
Q. How?
—A. There are various ways. One, for instance: It could be attached to a line run forward the ship, ahead of it so far it could not be seen, to some point beyond, and then taken back. For instance, here is the bow of the ship [indicating]. Start from a point here. There is the shore line, and suppose we carry a line to that point, run

it across, and come down here. As yon haul in the slack you would have a line taking that -direction. If you knew the distance of the ship from the shore you would know exactly when the torpedo was under the bows of the ship, and you would haul on the line until you reached the proper mark, and the torpedo would be here. [Indicating under the forward part of the ship.] I do not think it would be possible

to prevent it.
By Mr. Davis :
Q. How would you anchor it, then?
— A. Either haul the line taut or allow the torpedo to sink by its own weight.
Q. Can you haul an electric wire so?
—A. Yes, sir; they offer very little resistance; it could be very small, not larger than my pencil.
By Mr. Cullom:
Q. Was that in the mud ?
—A. It is not known. In all probability it was resting on the bottom, and in my opinion it was placed there before the vessel was sent there.
Q. When that was placed there, why, no matter how, or when, how was it to be exploded?
Q. How must it have been exploded?
— A. It was possible to explode it by a trigger line and something somewhat similar to what is known as a friction fuse. The first ship destroyed during the war of the rebel lion was destroyed by a torpedo of that kind. It was at Cairo, and was commanded by Captain, at present Commodore, Selfridge. That was by a trigger

concealed in a rifte pit, and the operator judged by the eye when the vessel was over it, and simply pulled the trigger as you would the lock of a gun. The use of explosives for so many purposes— blasting, mining, everything—is so common that probably anyone who designed to do that work would resort to it. I think it is improbable anything else was used.

Q. Could that have been used without the knowledge of any of the officials at Havana?

—A. Possibly, but not probably.

Q. You have read the descriptions of the vessel given by the divers; did it leave in your mind any doubt as to its destruction having been caused by a mine?

—A. No; I think I have no doubt on that subject; I think it was done by a mine.

By Mr. Morgan :

Q. In the case of a torpedo that works automatically, or by a torpedo localized by itself, would the explosion take place by the impact of the ship ?

—A. Yes, sir ; electricity is not used in these movable, automatic torpedoes. Fulminate is used, and the explosion caused by the impact of a plunger which is driven back into the case of fulminate.

Q. So that when the vessel struck it.

—A. No; this torpedo I am describing progresses until it strikes something and then this plunger is driven back.

Q. Are mines ever used of this kind?

—A. Yes; contact mines; they are both mechanical. I mean the operation of exploding it is not connected with the of operation of electricity. They are electro mechanical where both forces are brought in play, applying to torpedoes which must be tipped over by the object striking it. The electric torpedo or mine is one where the operator must close the circuit by a key.

Q. I notice in the examination by the judge advocate that questions were asked of the witnesses, particularly the officers aboard the ship, as to whether she had the same bearing or heading at the moment of explosion as she had been accustomed to having at the same hour of the day on preceding days, and they said there was a difference?

—A. This question was asked because if the torpedo had been placed at a certain point—the ship was riding to a buoy- -in order that the torpedo should do the utmost damage, it would be necessary for the ship to be over it, and as she swung about it was possible to explode it without doing much damage, but if a time was selected when she swung exactly over it, it would destroy her. Of course, a very little distance makes a great difference in the amount of damage done. The radius of effective damage is not very large, not nearly so large as the radius a ship would describe in swinging around a buoy.

By Mr. Davis :
Q. Was it moored by the stem or stern?
—A. Stem.

Q. Did she swing with the wind and tide and what would be the arc?
—A. Yes.

By Mr. Cullom:
Q. What would be probably the length of a submarine mine with 300 pounds of explosive material in it?
—A. They are very frequently made the shape of a sphere. Those placed on the bottom are commonly flat, while the buoyant are spherical.

Q. How large are the conducting wires by which these explosions are made ?
—A. That is very variable. Cables laid down prepared for use with permanent systems are armored.

By Mr. Lodge :
Q. Would the ordinary torpedo be sufficiently powerful to produce the result produced in the Maine ?
—A. In my opinion it would not. I so stated immediately after the report of the damage done to the Maine.

Q. Was there not opportunity to determine the exact hour on previous nights when it would be over the torpedo?
—A. The winds at Havana are generally north to east; those are the prevailing winds. The currents are small. I have read, though I do not know that it is true, that the ship had never headed before in the direction she did at the time of the explosion.

By Mr. Foraker :
Q. I have heard it said that boats were running in and out that harbor almost within shaking hands distance from the battle ship, and that, on a night for instance, a boat could go in there and slip something under it without the call of the sentry?
—A. Perhaps I have not made myself clear in one respect. I discussed and described regular submarine mines for harbor defense. I think I also mentioned that modem explosives do not require a strong envelope or enclosure to be effective.

Q. You also said that dynamite or modern explosives might be conveyed in a bag?
—A. Yes, sir, and I want to enlarge on that now. It does not follow of necessity that that damage could not be done in any other way than by the use of a submarine mine. That explosion which destroyed two Chilean ships, there the explosive was

By Mr. Cullom:
Q. What would be probably the length of a submarine mine with 300 pounds of explosive material in it?
—A. They are very frequently made the shape of a sphere. Those placed on the bottom are commonly flat, while the buoyant are spherical.

Images, top to bottom: an American Torpedo factory in **Brooklyn**, 1878;
a Spanish Torpedo Factory in **Ferrol**, Spain, 1893;
Robert Whitehead and his son John, examining a novel American Torpedo in 1894.

Q. How large are the conducting wires by which these explosions are made?

—A. That is very variable. Cables laid down prepared for use with permanent systems are armored.

By Mr. Lodge:

Q. Would the ordinary torpedo be sufficiently powerful to produce the result produced in the Maine?

—A. In my opinion it would not. I so stated immediately after the report of the damage done to the Maine.

Q. Was there not opportunity to determine the exact hour on previous nights when it would be over the torpedo?

—A. The winds at Havana are generally north to east; those are the prevailing winds. The currents are small. I have read, though I do not know that it is

true, that the ship had never headed before in the direction she did at the time of the explosion.

By Mr. Foraker:

Q. I have heard it said that boats were running in and out that harbor almost within shaking hands distance from the battle ship, and that, on a night for instance, a boat could go in there and slip something under it without the call of the sentry?

—A. Perhaps I have not made myself clear in one respect. I discussed and described regular submarine mines for harbor defense. I think I also mentioned that modem explosives do not require a strong envelope or enclosure to be effective.

Q. You also said that dynamite or modern explosives might be conveyed in a bag?—A. Yes, sir, and I want to enlarge on that now. It does not follow of necessity that that damage could not be done in any other way than by the use of a submarine mine. That explosion which destroyed two Chilean ships, there the explosive was placed loosely in a boat with a false bottom, and did so much damage that both ships sunk almost immediately, one while the boat was being hoisted and the other while the boat was being cleared of some tempting provisions on the false deck.

Q. Your belief is that it was destroyed by a mine under the vessel and exploded from the shore?

—A. Yes, sir. Yes.

Q. How far was the ship from the shore?

—A. I have seen it stated that it was about 500 yards, but that is susceptible of exact determination. I think the buoy she was using, No. 4, is given on the charts.

By Mr. Foraker:

Q. Do you know of any regulations of Havana for the use or sale of explosives?

—A. I do not. These are not ordinarily found in stores or toy shops for sale. By no means; particularly in a place like Havana to-day, where fighting is going on more or less all the time in the neighborhood.

Q. You think that mine could not be placed there without the consent of the authorities?

—A. I do—I will change that; I do not think it was probable.

Q. The probability is that it was put there by Government authority, and known to be there by the Government officials?

—A. Yes, sir.

Q. If that flotilla of torpedo destroyers and torpedo boats now on its way from the Canaries could be brought to Havana and placed in the harbor, would it not then become formidable and an increased danger in the naval situation to us?

—A. An increased danger.

Q. I suppose, in a harbor like Havana, when mined at all there is more than one such mine, as a rule? And the electric wires are taken to the shore to the same place, as a rule?

—A. As a rule, in harbor defense the cables are laid to a gallery under water connected with a fort or some secret place. This gallery is always kept secret as far as possible, never given out. For instance, our own forts, fitted with cables and galleries, the precise location is always kept secret. I know our forts are planted and have these galleries, but I do not know where they are; that is very confidential.

Q. Confided only to Government officials—army or navy?

—A. Army exclusively.

Q. Why should not those cables leading to the torpedoes have been destroyed after the explosion?

—A. It was a very simple matter to haul them in.

Q. Do you think the ship could have been blown up by dynamite carried in a rubber bag, or anything of that kind?

—A. I think the probability is against it.

Q. It would have to be done in a small boat, and fired at the time used ?

—A. It has just occurred to me that one theory might be advanced that I have not explained. I spoke of a buoyant mine which is attached to a cable and also to an anchor. Suppose this box to represent the mine, and my pencil a cable attached to an anchor, that is made to explode automatically, so that when a ship, say, swings against it and inclines it a certain amount—a favorite mechanical arrangement is to have a ball inside which rolls down an inclined plane and completes the circuit. This arrangement can be made harmless by disconnecting the battery on shore, and the ship may bump and it will not be exploded, because there is no electric current—it has been switched off on shore. When it is desired these mines shall watch, as it is termed, the current is then put on shore, and they will not then be exploded until struck by some object, and in this instance heeled over. It is not impossible that the Maine might have been destroyed by a mine of that description.

Q. What would be our method of protecting our fleet if we wanted to blockade Havana—shoot at it at a distance—the torpedo boats, destroy them?

—A. We suppose the flotilla to be in Havana and our ships outside endeavoring to blockade, and they came out to attack.

Q. Yes, or we wanted to prevent them from attacking their way—what is our plan of attack to prevent them or destroy them?

—A. I do not know that we have any plan, but if we approached near enough the port to bombard it, of course the ships would be subject to bombardment. The most efficacious, and at the same time the most hazardous way, would be to send vessels in to ram them—light draft vessels that probably would not strike any obstruction.

By Mr. Foraker :

Q. Ram these torpedo boats?

—A. Yes, sir, surprise them and ram them. Of course if they get near enough the ship they are subject to a very severe fire from the secondary batteries, small quick-firing guns, and onslaughts from picket boats. We have no cases on record where, in the daytime, torpedo boats have succeeded in getting within striking distance of well-armed ships.

By Mr. Davis:

Q. So that the fact that the nettings were not let down makes no case against the captain of the Maine?

—A. The Maine had no nets; they never had any in our Navy.

Q. How many torpedo boats have we?

—A. We have six at Key West; three more ready to go in a few days down there; all small though.

Q. Are you familiar with this flotilla that is coming over?

—A. Only in a general way. I believe it is composed of the *Maria Theresa*, a sister boat to the *Vizcaya*, the *Colon*, and a torpedo destroyer named the *Destructor*.

Q. Where is the *Pelayo*.

—A. At Ferrol.

Q. Have they not three more armored ships in dock now? I was told they were still in dock, and would be out between the 15th of April and the 1st of May.

—A. I do not know.

Q. I saw a cable that the *Pelayo* had started for Toulon.

—A. She has been at Toulon, and has been repaired there, at La Seyne.

Q. How do we compare with Spain as to first-class battle ships or first-class armored cruisers'?

—A. We have more battle ships; we have not quite as many armored cruisers.

By Mr. Lodge :

Q. Ours are heavier ships?

—A. Yes, sir; the *Brooklyn* and the *New York.*

Q. In battle ships we are much more powerful?

—A. Very much.

Q. Should you not think it very important in case war was coming to dispose of that flotilla before it reached Havana?

—A. It would be an important advantage. Much depends upon the proposed campaign—what we are going to do; whether it is to be strictly a naval war—whether we are to confine ourselves to marine operations, or whether we are to land troops on the island of Cuba, and what the purpose of the Government is. That ought to be decided first, in my opinion, and then we could decide what to do.

Q. Could we land troops with this flotilla at Havana?

—A. I would not advocate it. Warfare cannot be carried on now as it used to be, where a fleet could go in under the guns of a fort and land troops and bombard the fort and town and take possession. The lesson of the Maine proves that such forts must be taken by attack on shore, with such aid as the ships can give, and some place not mined must be selected to land. The object of the Navy now is to destroy what it can by bombardment and destroy ships. The capture of territory must be left to the Army.

By Mr. Foraker:

Q. How are our ships supplied with ammunition?

—A. Very well.

Q. How is the *Oregon,* compared with others ?

—A. She is the same caliber as others in our Navy.

Q. What would happen if she were ordered around from Callao? What length of time would she require to make the voyage?

—A. I have not the distances at my finger ends. You all understand the geographical situation of these islands. In the west the islands of Key West and Dry Tortugas, where we hope to keep coal enough, are only 90 miles from Havana, and ships operating around the west end of Cuba can coal there. The coast of Cuba presents many advantages for small vessels to dodge out from the shore and do a good deal of harm to passing ships. So, it would be dangerous to pass to and fro in order to get coal at Key West, and, also, it is too far to go, it takes too much time to go and come. If you are on the south coast of Cuba the distance is about 900 miles. It is very important to have a coaling station at the east end of Cuba, and right across the Windward Channel is the very excellent harbor of St. Nicholas Mole, which belongs

> to Haiti. We used that as a coaling station in the war of the rebellion, and it did not then require any very urgent defense. I have urged on the Secretary, and I believe it has been communicated to the President, that that port be hired or leased, or obtained in some way, as a coaling station. I would also recommend St. Thomas, a very good port and capable of defense, good anchorage there, smooth water, and I understand that the islands of the Danish West Indies can be purchased for a few millions, probably live or under, I have on good authority, and I should think the purchase of those islands would be cheap at five millions, simply to get the islands, as you would buy a cruiser or anything else.
>
> Q. Do you not think we ought to have those Danish islands anyway?
>
> —A. Yes, sir. If we are going to go ahead ourselves in the West Indies, we must have coaling stations there.
>
> Q. For our own protection ?
>
> —A. Yes, sir.

In response to a letter addressed to him by Senator Frye, asking for his opinion as to the tenability of the statement made in the report of the Spanish board of inquiry on the destruction of the Maine, that one of the grounds for considering the explosion to have occurred on the inside of the vessel, was that no dead fish were found on the following morning, the following letter from Commander Bradford was received by Senator Frye:

> Washington, D. C, March 21, 1898.
>
> My Dear Senator: In reference to your note concerning dead fish about the Maine,
>
> I beg to state, that they always disappear very soon after an explosion. Many of the fish that appear to be dead after a submarine explosion are only stunned, and after a time recover and disappear. I have noticed this a great many times during experiments at Newport. The explosion of the Maine occurred at 9.40 p.m.; I consider that there was ample time for the fish to have disappeared before daylight. I have seen it stated in newspapers that there are very few fish in Havana H arbor on account of its being very foul. I do not personally know this to be a fact, but I do know that the harbor is very foul.
>
> The men at Newport who frequently gathered in the fish after a torpedo explosion so well understood the fact that they must be quick that they were always ready in their boats with their nets, and were the first on the ground in order to scoop up the fish. On one occasion I saw a sturgeon weighing at least 100

> pounds apparently dead after a torpedo explosion, and men went alongside to gather him in, when he suddenly righted, disappeared, and was never seen afterwards.
>
> Yours, very truly,
> ROBERT B. BRADFORD.

The next witness interviewed by the US Senate *Committee on Foreign Relations* on March 31, 1898, was **Captain Charles Dwight Sigsbee** (1845-1923), the commander of the battleship Maine.

In his earlier career Sigsbee had been a pioneering oceanographer and hydrographer, who had developed the *Sigsbee Sounding Machine* which became a standard item of deep-water oceanographic equipment for the next 50 years. He was born in Albany, New York, and educated at *The Albany Academy*. He was appointed acting midshipman on 16 July 1862 and had fought in numerous engagements during the Civil War, taking command of the battleship Maine in April 1897.

In an article in *The Century Magazine* a few weeks after the Maine explosion, he had related his experience:

> «*I was closing a letter in its envelope when the explosion came. The impression made on different people on board the* Maine *varied somewhat. To me, in my position, well aft, and within the superstructure, it was a bursting, rending, and crashing sound or roar of immense volume, largely metallic in character. It was followed by a succession of heavy, ominous, metallic sounds, probably caused by the overturning of the central superstructure and by falling debris. There was a trembling and lurching motion of the vessel, a list to port, and a movement of subsidence. The electric lights, of which there were eight in the cabin where I was sitting, went out. Then there was intense blackness and smoke.*
>
> *None can ever know the awful scenes of consternation, despair, and suffering down in the forward compartments of the stricken ship; of men wounded, or drowning in the swirl of water, or confined in a closed compartment gradually filling with water....*

While in Washington I was directed to appear before the Committees on Foreign Relations in the Senate and the House.... When the investigation took a hypothetical character, I explained a mechanical means whereby the Maine *could have been blown up, and referred to persons who were in a position which would have enabled them to blow her up had they been so inclined....*

We have heard much of the motto, "Remember the Maine*". If we are satisfied that the* Maine *was blown up from the outside we have a right to remember her with indignation; but **without more conclusive evidence than we now have,** we are. not right if we charge criminality to persons. Therefore I conceive that the motto, "Remember the Maine," used as a war-cry would not have been justifiable.»*

What follows is a fairly complete transcript of Captain Sigsbee, who years later retired as Rear Admiral of the US Navy in 1911.

**STATEMENT OF CAPT. CHARLES DWIGHT SIGSBEE, US Navy
March 31, 1898.**

Examination by Senator Frye
Committee on Foreign Relations of the US Senate

By Mr. Frye

Q. What is your full name and profession?

—A. Charles Dwight Sigsbee, Captain, United States Navy, late commanding the United States steamer Maine. I transferred the command at Havana. I held it until I left; the flag was still flying.

Q. What, in your opinion, caused the explosion which destroyed the Maine.

—A. It is, of course, merely matter of opinion. My opinion is that a mine destroyed the Maine, either permanent or temporary.

Q. Please describe what you mean by a mine.

— A.. I mean a large vessel or receptacle filled with explosive matter and submerged at a low depth, so that a vessel can swing over or against it.

Q. How large a mine —of course I am not asking for exact figures— how large and heavy a mine in your opinion would be required to have the effect which was had upon your ship?

—A. The effect on the ship is not known with sufficient accuracy to permit me to state, and, moreover, I think that question is one for an expert, what we would consider in the Navy an expert in matters of that kind. It would, however, undoubtedly take a very large one, but in my opinion no larger than could be planted near the vessel at any time in broad daylight and under direct vision with the means available in Havana for that purpose. This assumes that about 12 men, having mutual confidence and preserving secrecy, would be necessary to plant such a mine.

Q. And that could be done while your ship was preserving the ordinary discipline and watchfulness of a ship in the harbor of an enemy?

—A. Absolutely, in my opinion. I could dilate a little on that if you would like to have it. That [indicating] represents a ship lying at a buoy, that being the buoy. That ship will swing around there. If a mine is planted anywhere in that area, she will swing over that mine in time, it is obvious. Let a vessel come to Havana. She proceeds here and drops a mine there. In time the vessel will swing over it. It could not immediately produce the destruction of the vessel, but in time that vessel will swing over that buoy, and at that time it could be exploded. Let that be a scow with a between decks. There is a tube coming above the water line; there is another. There is the water line. Outside this is a section. There is a bar with two trips on it working with a crank fastened on standards; slings are down there, and a mine can be slung there right under the boat, the slings passing up through two tubes there. From here the wires pass through another tube and are fastened to a reel. That mine can be weighted so the specific gravity is very little more than water. Tugs and lighters are passing and repassing constantly, and all that such a vessel—a lighter, say—has to do is to drop that buoy. It is entirely submerged and makes no wave, has very little specific gravity more than water, hence very little pull on the boat. Now, they have a number of hoys in Havana with derricks on the deck, very slow and very noisy, and they are passing and repassing all the time until late in the evening. A vessel of that kind can go past there every day, and she can go to a. wharf or anchor in the stream, and when you swing over that buoy that vessel can strike the wires and sink you, and she can cut the wires and steam away, or she can drop the wires wherever she pleases.

There was a lot of idle army officers there; I do not charge them with anything, but speak of the possibilities of the case. In this case I have spoken of more than need be. I showed a similar sketch to Captain Sampson, who has also commanded a torpedo station, and is besides an ordnance officer, and I asked, pointing to a vessel, " Could that vessel drop that instantly!" and they said undoubtedly she could, it could be done. I then said, "Can I make report to the Navy Department; will you permit me to say this could be done undoubtedly? The only qualification was that it would take about

The US Press reacted immediately to the news of the Maine blown up in Havana

twelve men to do it. That is the real reason I asked to have the Montgomery taken away. If they were going to do anything to blow us up I wanted to have it done with a smaller vessel. They had no vigilance whatever and no guard over us or our vessels. Their vigilance was great wherever their own vessels were concerned.

By Mr. Gray

Q. No vigilance as regards you?

—A. No; once or twice they played a searchlight on us, but the boats were coming and going all the time, and we would hail them, and they must have heard our hail, but they would refuse to answer the first time and commonly the second time, and then they would finally answer in a rather impudent manner when they did answer. It was a very peculiar thing; they seemed to have no experience of other nations' vessels.

By Mr. Morgan

Q. How would they get hold of the torpedo?

—A. I assume they could make that out of a section of old hogshead, or even a wine pipe. For the short time it was to be down an immense wine pipe, or even two of them, might have been taken, and stealing up to a boat it could have been taken from one boat to another and then dropped in shallow water.

Q. What, in your judgment, was the probability?

—A. I am not certain in my mind whether to attribute it to a temporary mine like that or a permanent one. It is a curious fact that the officers of the deck say we never swung in that particular direction before. The Maine is lying now in about the position she would have taken to play on the Spanish batteries —the Morro and the Cabaña. That is to say, if the Maine had taken a notion to play on the batteries, she would be in that position. Now, I give this merely as a fact; I do not draw any special inference. Here is the mooring point; here is the Spanish admiral's house. The Maine was swinging about in that direction. Now, if a mine had been planted there, where the Maine could play on the batteries, I assume it would have been planted in just that place where the Maine was blown up. If only one had been planted, it would have been just there. If a mine were planted in range from that residence to the buoy, of course, when the Maine swung to that buoy, it would show the mine was under the ship's keel. It was my business to note all these things, but, as for connecting it absolutely with the blowing up of the ship, I cannot do any further than I have stated.

Q. If that ship had swung into position to fire on the castle and a torpedo had been placed, or mine placed, under water so as to blow the ship up in case she did fire, then it would have been placed exactly where you were blown up ?

—A. I would have placed it there.

Q. That suggests the possibility of its having been placed there before yon were located there?

—A. It does.

Q. Has it not occurred to you that very likely it was done so ?

—A. I think if we had. owned the port and had suspected a possible aggressive spirit, I think, we would have done the same thing.

Q. You would have put it right there?

—A. If we only had one mine I should have put it right there.

Q. If that mine had been placed so, how would it have been exploded?

—A. I infer they never would have put a contact mine there that would have been exploded by contact with the bottom of the vessel, because other vessels were coming and going all the time, but an electric mine, having wires leading ashore or elsewhere.

By Mr. Cullom

Q. To have the explosion at a time when they could have control of it?

—A. Yes; the time and opportunity to control it.

By Mr. Frye

Q. If that was the condition, who would be likely to have charge of the electric battery which exploded the mine?

—A. I am unable to say that; I infer the Navy.

Q. An official?—A. I have a certain reason for believing this, which perhaps it would be injudicious to disclose.

By Mr. Morgan

Q. Taking the lights on the ship, which had not been extinguished at the time of the explosion, I understand they would furnish the observer on the shore the position of the ship. Would such an observer be able at night to ascertain that that ship was at that moment in such bearing as she could fire on the batteries?

—A. We have a forward and after light showing, and even without a light he could have seen it by the smokestacks, which are large.

By Mr. Davis

Q. Could have seen at night?

—A. Yes, sir.

By Mr. Frye

Q. No difficulty in determining whether it was over a submarine mine?

—A. No, sir; if there was one there. I have no knowledge whatever that the Spanish authorities blew the ship up; I am merely giving the possibilities of the case.

Q. The Spaniards, in their report of the destruction of the Maine, make a very strong point of the fact that no dead fish were found the next day. What is your judgment about that proposition?

—A. The ship was blown up at 9.40 p. in., and even though there were dead fish, no one knows where they might have gone the next morning. In the next place, I fancy, if any dead fish were available, the reconcentrados would be glad to get them. Again, they say the fish leave the harbor and go to sea at night. I have seen an occasional fish jump in the day time, but the water is very foul and nasty, and I fancy it is a bad water for fish.

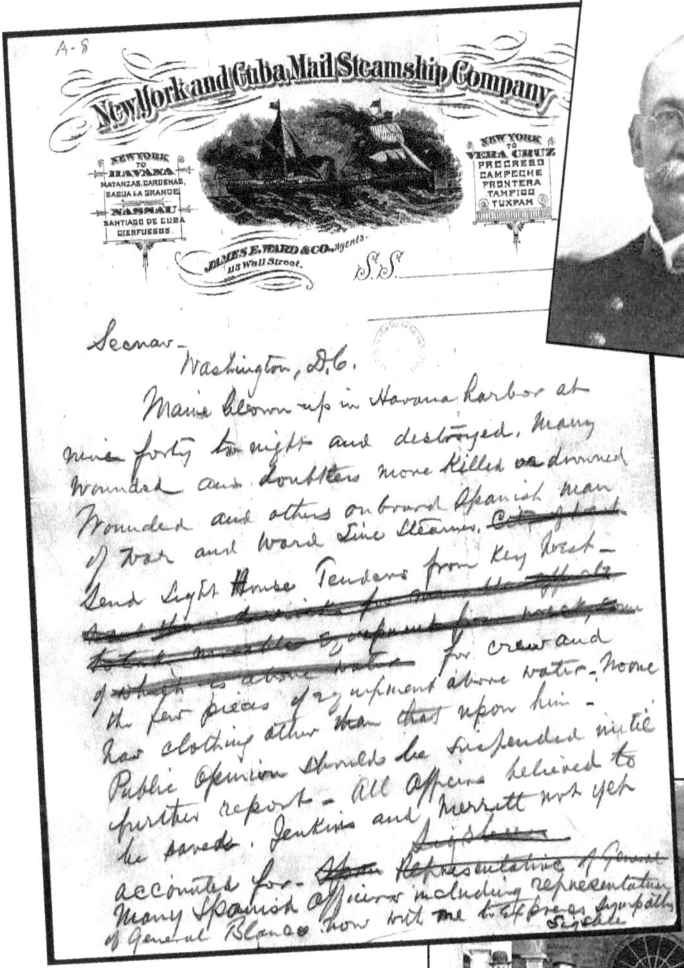

A-8

New York and Cuba Mail Steamship Company

NEW YORK TO HAVANA, MATANZAS, CARDENAS, SAGUA LA GRANDE, NASSAU, SANTIAGO DE CUBA, CIENFUEGOS.

NEW YORK TO VERA CRUZ, PROGRESO, CAMPECHE, FRONTERA, TAMPICO, TUXPAM

JAMES E. WARD & CO., Agents. 113 Wall Street.

S.S.

Secnav—
Washington, D.C.
Maine blown up in Havana harbor at nine forty to-night and destroyed. Many wounded and doubtless more killed or drowned. Wounded and others on board Spanish man of war and Ward Line steamer. Send Light House Tenders from Key West for crew and the few pieces of equipment above water. None has clothing other than that upon him. Public opinion should be suspended until further report. All officers believed to be saved. Jenkins and Merritt not yet accounted for. Many Spanish officers including representative of General Blanco now with me to express sympathy.
Sigsbee

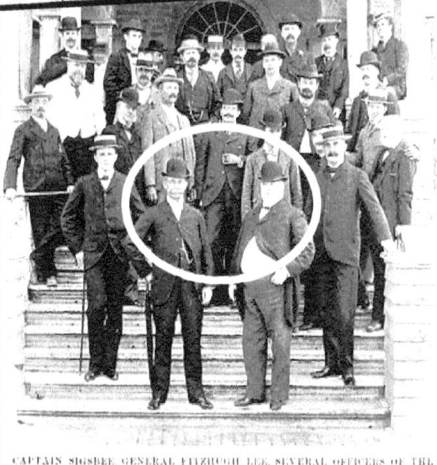

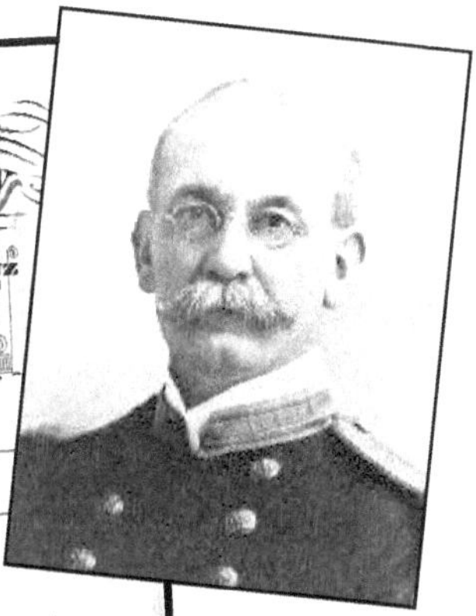

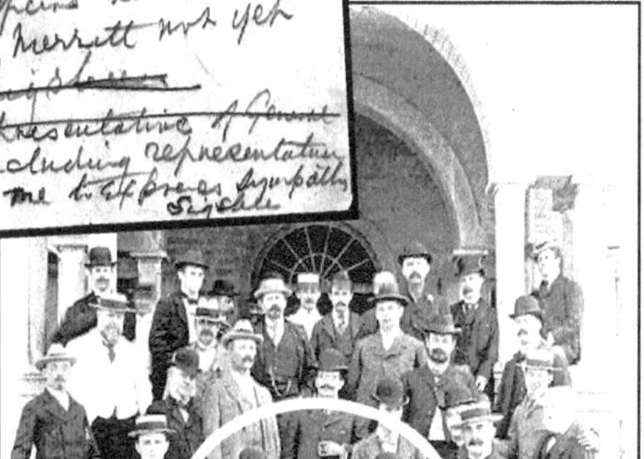

CAPTAIN SIGSBEE, GENERAL FITZHUGH LEE, SEVERAL OFFICERS OF THE "MAINE," AND CIVILIANS AT THE HAVANA YACHT-CLUB

Images, top to bottom:
The ***telegram sent by Captain Charles Sigsbee*** to Washington the day of the blowing of the Maine; the official photo of ***Captain Charles Dwight Sigsbee***, A picture of the Main officers at the Havana Yacht Club in 1898. ***In the circle, Captain Charles Sigsbee and US Consul Fitzhugh Lee.***

By Mr. Morgan

Q. The walls amidships on both sides, to nearly amidships, were broken down?

—A. Especially so; very much disintegrated. It is all gone on the port side.

Q. So that if that was done by an internal explosion the force of the explosion would have gone out through the water?

—A. That is a question, if there was an internal explosion.

Q. If there was, the force of that explosion must have gone through the water?

—A. Yes, sir.

Q. Why would not that have killed the fish?

—A. I think it would. Perhaps not so much, but I think it would have killed them. We regarded that excuse as rather peculiarly Spanish and all that about the wave, etc. They were groping for results and reasons.

By Mr. Frye

Q. I suppose there had been an outward tide from the time they were hunting for the fish until the morning.

By Mr. Gray

Q. Is there much tide?

—A. Very little tidal flow. There is an ebb and flow, of course. If there were permanent wires ashore to the points established by the Government, it is conceivable that somebody may have dragged for those wires at some intermediate point between the station and mine, and having them, may have blown the ship up, or they may have gotten control of the switchboard on shore. They did not like us; that was very plain.

Q. What examination did those Spanish boards make of the accident?

—A. They had not done anything for a week; had not been down at all. Our people laughed at them. Our people kept going down steady, and they a little at a time, and there sat a correspondent of a great American journal in their boat, humbugging them all the time, passing out cigars to them and making fun of them, and they did not know him. They thought he was a great American engineer who did not care much for Americans. When the boatswain came to them with the other boat he transferred to that, and they did not know him. They did very little work on the wreck. It was absurd as compared with our work.

Q. Did you make the examination as thorough as possible?

—A. The examination was made very much under the wishes of the board of inquiry; whatever they wanted they got. We had over the divers all the time commissioned officers. They had part of the time, not all the time, a boatswain. The greatest point on our side was that we had Ensign Powelson. He went to Glasgow to study naval architecture for a year; then he preferred to be a line officer. Of course, the ship was very much disrupted. Whenever any diver would come out Mr. Powelson would take him and have him give, in the first place, exact measurements for the length and breadth and thickness.

He would take his statement, draw a diagram of what he had seen, take it to the detailed diagrams of the ship, and reduce it to a certainty. He would know that a certain beam, forward of a certain place would be, for instance, 3 feet, and abaft it would be 4 feet, and it would be a certain distance from one of the longitudinals, and so on, until he had proved conclusively this was that plate or beam and no other. When the military and naval men come to look at our report and compare it with their report, with the fish story and all that sort of thing, I think a military smile will go around the world.

By Mr. Foraker

Q. Was the ship in the habit of swinging all the way around that circle, around that buoy?

—A. The trade wind—the prevailing wind—is east, and as the sun comes up it blows stiffer and varies less, but during the time we were there it was not so steady in direction, but we commonly tailed to the east with the stern to the Admiral's house.

By Mr. Cullom

Q. That night did your boat swing to the location of the house?

—A. She swung away from the Admiral's house that night.

By Mr. Frye

Q. Was that the first time that vessel swung that way?

—A. Some of the officers said that. I did not notice it. I have not seen the Fern swing once in the direction the Maine swung.

Q. The report of the officers was to that effect!

—A. I think the court reports to that effect.

By Mr. Morgan

Q. What point of the compass is that ship now?

—A. Her bow is twisted to a right angle and shot down in the mud. The general direction is to the northward and westward. The trade winds are to the eastward.

By Mr. Mills

Q. Are they in the habit of docking vessels at the same place as the
Maine?

—A. It was riding to a buoy. When a man-of-war comes in, she makes fast to one of these buoys and swings to a pivot. Captain Stephens, of the City of Washington, that night or the next day said in all his experience he never knew a vessel to be buoyed in just that place, and I think some others said that.

By Mr. Foraker

Q. Do you know what other ships preceded you?

—A. The captain of the City of Washington said he never saw any vessel moored there before. It was almost in the same position as one of the regular plotted buoys, No. 4, and there was nothing to make anyone suspicious.

Q. Were there any torpedo boats in port while you were there?

—A. All the Spanish vessels carry torpedo tubes. The vessel blew up on the port side, and the starboard side was to the Spanish vessel.

Q. I saw a statement in a paper that a Spanish vessel was the last one before you anchored at that buoy?

—A. The *La Gasca* came out and anchored the day before or the second day before we went in. She has torpedo tubes. I was informed several days after the explosion by a Cuban who said his father was an American citizen that the *La Gasca* was General Weyler's dispatch boat, the one used by him in any tour about the waters of the island. The captain of that vessel never called on me. I do not know why. perhaps he thought his was too small a vessel. I permitted myself to suspect him, but I must say I never had anything in the nature of proof.

By Mr. Cullom

Q. Have you examined the testimony sent to Congress?

—A. I heard a great deal of the testimony, but have not read it all, because I have not a copy. I know most of the important testimony. When I found things were going very, very carefully and scientifically in the court, I did not take the trouble to attend all the time. I preferred to be measured by the judgment of other people.

By Mr. Turpie

Q. Before they commenced the examination, did the Spanish Government make any offer of reward for the detection or discovery of persons concerned in the destruction of the Maine"?.

—A. They decided at once, and so stated to me, that it was an accident, and must have been an accident. For a few minutes, say fifteen or twenty minutes, after the explosion, on the City of Washington, they were very anxious to know the cause, and I replied that I must await an investigation; it was perhaps all natural.

Q. They insisted it was an accident?

—A. The Spanish admiral said first it was the dynamo boiler. I said we have no dynamo. He then said it was the boilers, and then I said the aftermost boilers only were used, and the forward boilers had not been lighted for three months. As for the coal bunker alongside the 10-inch magazine, that was in use that day; we were using it. There was a full bunker on the port side next the 15-inch reserve magazine that had been filled for three months, the coal in particularly stable condition, bunkers inspected, and all right. It was the most exposed bunker in the ship with radiating surface, so that it is inconceivable that bunker should have been heated without being noticed.

By Mr. Gray

Q. There was a special examination made?

—A. Yes, sir; and the magazine temperature is taken daily and recorded and sent to the Navy Department for every day in the month.

Q. Do you remember the temperature?

—A. No, sir; for it would not come to me unless it were abnormal. To show you the kind of a man who took the temperature,

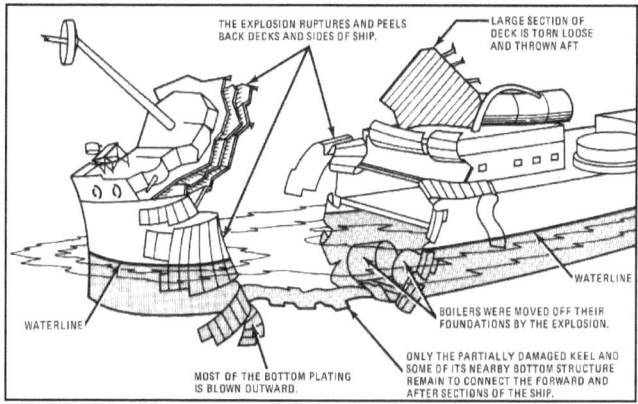

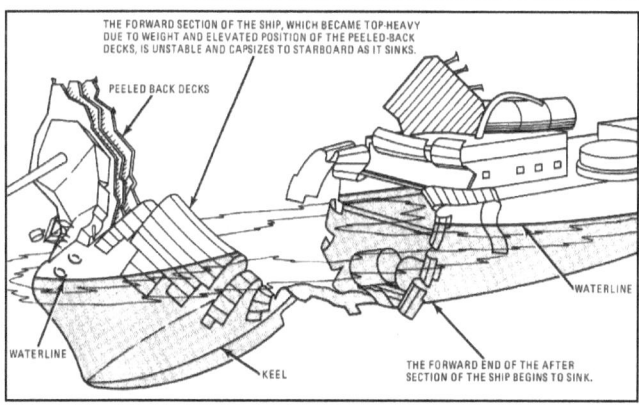

Details of the report sent by US Consul Fitzhugh Lee to Washington in his first report to the Department of State

made the inspection—he was a three-medal man. The gunner was under suspension for insubordination. The gunner's mate, who was a much better man and had three good conduct medals—that meant that for three enlistments he had good-conduct medals. He had been two years under his present enlistment, and every mark under every heading was the maximum, and no punishments recorded against him.

Q. This suspended man had nothing to do with taking the temperature?

—A. No, sir.

By Mr. Gray

Q. Did this man escape with his life?

—A. No, sir; he was killed.

Q. It takes, if I am correct, 300 degrees Fahrenheit to blow up powder.

—A. It takes a very high temperature. We had the brown prismatic powder. I should rather trust the temperature to an expert. The forward magazine was normal; the after magazine, which is near a number of steam tanks and pipes, etc., was often above the normal, the temperature there often being 112, but that gave no concern, for that was well within the safety limit. It might be, on a hot day, 103 or 104, or even 112, and no concern felt.

Q. Do you think it would have been possible to reach that high degree of heat without discovering it?

—A. It is inconceivable. All those compartments are electrically connected with annunciators outside my door. These annunciators are very sensitive, and often ring even when there is nothing there.

Q. In what part of the ship was Lieutenant Jenkins's body found?

—A. The wardroom mess room. Just forward of that is a large compartment. On one side are the torpedo tubes. His body was found opposite that. The ship is very high there, higher than that brass railing. Everything was buoyant and everything rose to the top, and all the loose articles and rubbish was up there, and that shows why it was difficult to get down there to clear away by a single diver.

Q. I ask the question because it is stated he was found in one of the magazines.

—A. No, sir; it was a particularly wide open, beautiful compartment. He was sitting at the mess table.

Q. When the explosion occurred?

—A. Yes, sir. If he had been in the shell room—none of the shell rooms exploded. The after part was not torn or hurt. The plates were torn 10 or 12 feet above the midship section. Forward of that all the damage occurred. Consequently no damage was attributable to anything aft, for there was no explosion there. The Spanish said the war heads exploded. They were all aft. There was but one thing to be taken under suspicion in the Maine.

That was the mere fact that there was a bunker alongside a magazine; but there is not the slightest suspicion of that bunker besides its existence there.

By Mr. Gray

Q. That bunker had been examined that day?

—A. Yes, sir; and I had my hands on it the day before. You had to go in a passage right around three sides of it, and it was the loafing place of the men, where they made their little ships and models and did their playing, so it would have roasted them out if there had been anything of that heat there.

Q. There was an annunciator at your door, anyhow?

—A. Yes, sir.

Q. Is the officer, commissioned or petty, who took the temperature of that bunker that day alive?

—A. Yes, sir; he was examined.

Q. What time of the day was the examination made?

—A. I do not remember the exact time.

Q. What was the custom?—A. Saturday afternoon was the usual time. There was no rigid time to examine; one time was as good as another.

Q. Did you have soft or anthracite coal?

—A. Both kinds. We had soft coal which had been examined at Newport News, and which had been in the ship three months and was very stable. Commonly, we used all the coal from the forward bunkers first, because that brought the ship down in the head. At Key West they made us take in anthracite coal which had been there a long time and they wanted to get rid of it. We were quite as anxious, having got it aboard, to use it as they were, and I wanted to keep all my soft coal, as it was so stable, and that is the reason for retaining the coal in the forward bunkers.

Q. What was your special reason for using the anthracite coal?

—A. It was old, and consequently we could not use it to the best advantage. And the soft coal is better for steam purposes. Besides, t he anthracite had been lying in the air for a long time.

By Mr. Gray

Q. Have you ever made any examinations as to spontaneous combustion?

—A. No, sir; but the English have gone into it with a great deal of particularity. Their tests, 1 believe, show that the gas works along through the layers of coal and through the coal dust, and works along until it strikes a draft of air, which fed it. and ignited it, and in their experiments they found in that way, from a great number of cases, what to expect of it. Captain Wainwright, of the Maine, and formerly head of the office, said he never knew of spontaneous combustion without heat in the first instance.

Q. Do you treat coal with water or anything of that kind when not using it?

— A. No, sir.

Q. State briefly the effect of the explosion upon the keel plates.

—A. The keel plate was driven upward decidedly in one respect. That is given so clearly in the report that I regret to go into it. I left that to the court. It was suggested to me to make the drawing, and I declined because I did not wish to be in it any way.

Q. Can you indicate in those drawings the one showing its existence above the deck?

—A. That is supposed to represent there the keel plate. It is thrown up like that, I think just a few feet below the water line of the vessel. I do not like to go too far in this myself, because I might misjudge something of what the court said. I believe that was one of the strongest reasons for the assumption that that thing could not have been caused by an internal explosion.

By Mr. Davis

Q. How many feet was it blown up from its normal place?

—A. About 30, 1 think, from where it would have rested in the mud in a normal condition.

Q. Showing the force came from below?

—A. I think that was the inference of the court, and would be of anybody.

Q. Is that the bottom of the ship"?

— A. Yes, sir; that is called the keel plate. Instead of having a keel outside it is inside and perfectly flat.

Q. Outside of what you have mentioned, were there any indications of a mine?

—A. Not so far as I know, except indentations of the plate.

Q. A hole in the mud?

— A. Yes, sir; there was that.

Q. No pieces of material in which that mine, if there was one, was incased?

—A. Captain Converse says that would have been destroyed by the explosion.

Q. I saw a statement that some concrete or plaster had been thrown on the awnings or the upper deck of a steamer?

—A. A huge piece was thrown on the City of Washington, a large piece 2 or 3 feet in thickness. That might have come from the blower engines on the berth deck below the upper deck. That was screwed down in a bed of cement in the men's washroom.

Q. Was there any cement in the bottom of the ship?

—A. Yes, sir; all through the bilging there was cement, but my recollection is it was not demonstrated—there was no evidence to show conclusively that cement came from the bottom of the ship.

Q. It might have come from either place?

—A. Yes, sir. I only heard the chief engineer's statement, or rather the constructor, who thought that it came from the bottom of the ship.

Q. There was a double bottom?

—A. Yes, sir.

Q. In the report there is a telegram addressed to Porsythe, Key West, *"Many killed and wounded. Do not send war vessels if others available."* Why, if I may ask, did you say that last?

—A. In the first place, there was a great deal of excitement and I wanted to work along without men of-war and to allay the excitement in the city; and in the next place, if there were any more mines I did not want any more war vessels blown up. Up to that time I had strongly recommended that the Indiana be sent there, just to show them that the Maine was not the only vessel in the Navy or the most powerful. After that time I had no more confidence in the people. Treachery had been shown us, and there was no special care for us; they had not attempted to protect us as we did with the *Vizcaya* in New York.

Q. You spoke of the reconcentrados getting the fish, etc. Did you see any of that class of people in Havana?

—A. Oh, yes, a great many. I was invited to go to see them, but in my position as naval officer I did not care to take part in any political affairs. I desired to have things as peaceful and friendly as possible. I received and entertained out of my own pocket I suppose three or four hundred people on board the ship, but I never accepted any invitations.

Q. Was there any position from which you could have shelled Havana or Morro Castle as advantageously as this"?

—A. We could have shelled the town from any position. That is the position from which we could have brought our batteries to bear on the castle ; one broadside brought to bear on one, and the other broadside on the other.

Q. The committee was yesterday trying to get information as to the rules, or laws, or regulations governing the keeping or disposal of high explosives in the city of Havana. Do you know anything of that?

A. Not strictly, except just before I left there was an arrest made, or rather dynamite was seized opposite General Lee's consular office—so the Spanish papers stated—seized by the authorities; but I fancy that thing must be regulated very carefully where there is an insurrection, and where the custom-house laws are so very strict. General Lee could give you an opinion immediately on that point, but I take it for granted nothing could get in without permission of the authorities.

> Q. Some witnesses testified there was an explosion some time after, supposed to be fixed ammunition.
> —A. I did not notice the separate phenomena of explosion.
> Q. If any magazine had exploded, would not that have caused the explosion of the detached ammunition?
> —A. It ought to have done so. There is much ammunition there now.
> Q. Unexploded?
> —A. Yes, sir; there was some ammunition in the handling room, in the loading room—10-inch shell. We cannot find any of these shells were hurled anywhere; we have no information of that.
> Q. Suppose the explosion had taken place in the magazine, every thing in that magazine would have exploded ?
> —A. I should think so.
> Q. The force would have been confined, and the effect of the gases would have exploded everything?
> —A. Of course very curious things happen
> Q. It would have been very curious if that had not exploded?
> —A. Yes, sir.
> Q. You have no doubt your ship was destroyed by an explosion from the outside?
> —A. I have none whatever—none from the first minute.

On April 7, the testimony of **Honoré François Laine** was secured at a regular meeting of the *Committee on Foreign Relations of the US Senate*. Laine was a serious correspondent of the *New York Sun*, one of the papers that had retained the public trust as opposed to Pulitzers' *New York World* and Hearst's *The New York Journal*, both accused of Yellow Journalism. A February article in *The Sun* «Urged the Public to Be Calm» in the face of «fake reports» by the yellow press:

> «Thus far the question of war with Spain has been made alarmingly sensational only by the few yellow-kid newspapers of the country, which are ready to sacrifice the truth and inflame popular prejudices to open wider markets for the reading of journals which each day must contradict what they published before.»

Reacting to yellow journals coverage of the sinking of the *U.S.S. Maine* (since they jumped to the conclusion that it wasn't an accident), a February 18 letter to the editor of the *New York Times* (not a member of the yellow press) suggested censoring such journals and a February 26, 1898 one-liner in the *Sun* lamented...

> «There is nothing quite so lame as the cheap imitation of yellow journalism.»

Many well known national papers reported about the public distaste for yellow journalism as well: Journalism students across the country asked the public not to buy yellow journals; a group of suburban school teachers in New York, the center of yellow journals, decided that Cuba should be included in the curriculum to «offset the influence of yellow journalism, and thus teach true patriotism,» and the *New York State Art Teachers Association* passed a resolution endorsing the *New York Sun* describing the evils of yellow journalism and the good done by "*clean*" newspaper work.

STATEMENT OF MR. HONORE FRANCOIS LAINE, JOURNALIST
April 7, 1898.
Examination by Senator Gray and others.
Committee on Foreign Relations of the US Senate

Honoré François Laine, being duly sworn, testified as follows:
By Senator Gray
Q. You were in Havana on the night of the disaster to the United States battle ship Maine?
-A. Yes, sir.
Q. Please state how long you had been there and what was your occupation.
-A. I arrived in Havana on the 1st of January of this year at 6 o'clock in the morning, on the steamship *Olivette*, as correspondent of the *New York Sun*, and I was in that capacity in Havana until the 4th of March, when I was expelled by the Spanish authorities, who have never notified me why they have done so.
Q. You had been a resident of Havana before that time, had you not?

-A. Yes, sir; I was born in Cuba and I lived in Cuba until I was 10 years old.
Q. Who was your father?
-A. Damaso Laine.
Q. A planter?
-A. A planter in the Province of Matanzas.
Q. And your mother was an American?
-A. My mother was an American, from Wilmington, Del.
Q. What was her name, please?
-A. Mary Garesche.
Q. The family had lived in Wilmington before?
-A. Yes, sir; the Du Pont Powder Works used to belong to them. They had powder works.
Q. Your father was a French citizen?
-A. Yes, sir.
Q. You were a French citizen ?
-A. Yes, sir. When I was 10 years old they sent me to Georgetown College. Then I studied veterinary medicine in New York.
Q. Veterinary surgery?
-A. Yes, sir; veterinary surgery. When I was 19 years old I graduated, March 4, 1885. I studied that as a sort of sport. I am very fond of horses and thought it best to study that. As to my work in Cuba, I own patents in machinery down there—sugar machinery patents. That was my business, and for that reason I traveled all over the Island of Cuba, and on the whole island. When the war broke out, not having anything to do, I accepted the position of correspondent of the *New York Sun*.
Q. You are familiar with Cuba and with the Spanish language?
-A. Oh, yes, sir.
Q. And French well as English?
-A. Yes, sir; French.
Q. Now, please recur to the night of the explosion. Where were you at the time the explosion occurred?
-A. The American correspondents at Havana at that time had the habit of congregating in the park known as *Isabel la Católica*, in front of the *Hotel Inglaterra*. We used to sit down there and talk and exchange notes. That night I had just returned from the Captain General's palace, the censor's office, and was sitting in the park with some friends when we saw the skies get red, and two or three seconds afterwards we heard a terrific detonation. We took a cab and drove down Obispo street to the wharf of Caballería.
Q. Will you be good enough to indicate on this map [exhibiting] by across with a pencil where you were sitting in the park?
-A. [indicating]. Right here, sir. Here is the *Hotel Inglaterra* [indicating]. From there we took a cab and came down this street [indicating].

Images, top to bottom:
Georgetown University, founded in 1789;
Hotel Inglaterra, across the Isabel II statue in what is today's Central Park.
The **Isabel la Católica Park** in the section of the Prado immediately north of Central Park.

There is the Captain-General's palace [indicating]. The cab stopped there [indicating]. This is a gate [indicating].
Q. The cab stopped where?
-A. At the entrance of the wharf of Caballería.
Q. At the water? On the water front?
-A. On the water front. Then we passed through the iron door there [indicating] and we were on the wharves.
Q. Did you leave your cab there!
-A. .Yes, we paid the man and left the carriage there. Right at the entrance of it there is a large electric pole, what you call
Q. A lamp?
-A. An arc light. That was extinguished.
Q. The light was extinguished?
-A. The light was extinguished.
Q. Then what did you do after leaving your carriage?
-A. Then we got on the wharf, on the water side.
Q. On the water side?
-A. On the water side. There are about 25 or 30 feet, you know. You can walk all around the wharves. These are on the wharves [indicating] and you go inside. There are long wharves.
Q. All along the water front?
-A. Yes, sir; all along the water front. We got to the water front. I saw by the light that it was the Maine that had been blown up.
Q. By what light!
-A. By the light of the Maine. She was burning already; at least, something was burning on the deck that showed me her mast. I could see by that that it was the Maine.
Q. Did you notice any other electric lights extinguished than the one at the entrance?
-A. Every one of them all along here [indicating] was extinguished.
Q. Please state what you did after you left your carriage?
-A. After I left my carriage I saw everybody running in this direction [indicating].
Q. In what direction?
-A. In the direction of the machina.

By Senator Daniel
Q. What is the *machina*?
-A. The *machina* is big shears that they have.
Q. A great pair of tongs for the purpose of lifting masts out of vessels?
How many city blocks were there from where you left your carriage to the *machina*?
-A. About six blocks.
Q. After you entered the iron gate you turned to your right and went along the water front?
-A. Yes, sir.
Q. To the *machina*?
-A. Yes, sir.
Q. And that was toward the Maine?
-A. Yes, sir; it was toward the Maine.

Q. That is where the admiral's house is [indicating]?
-A. It is where the Admiral's house is.
Q. You say when you first entered the gate there was a tall iron pole that had an electric light on it which had been extinguished?
-A. Yes, sir. There are several around here; but this one was distinguished because it was right in the center here [indicating], and I had it in front of me. It was so dark that I noticed it.
Q. Were those around it extinguished?
-A. All were extinguished around there.
Q. Were there a number of electric-light poles along the water front that you traversed on your way to the machina?
-A. I will mark them here [indicating]. There are about twelve all along here.
Q. On the road you traveled!
-A. . Yes, sir.
Q. Were they all extinguished?
-A. . They were all extinguished. The wharf was very dark.
Q. Is this part of the city [indicating] lighted largely by electricity?
-A. Only on the wharves, sir.
Q. What is the lighting here [indicating]?
-A. Gas.
Q. Was that extinguished?
-A. I did not notice that. My attention was not turned that way.
Q. . Did you see any electric lights burning at all along the wharves?
-A. . No, sir.
Q. They were all out?
-A. Yes, sir.
Q. Were you ever down there at any other time in the night time?
-A. Yes, sir.
Q. Did you ever see them out before?
-A. No, sir; I never did. The wharves are always lit up at night, because goods are kept down there and they have to be well watched.
Q. Was this the first time you ever saw them out?
-A. Yes, sir; it was the first time.
Q. In the nighttime?
-A. Yes, sir.
Q. Did you hear any remark at that time or the next day about the extinguishment of the electric lights at the time of the explosion?
-A. I believe the papers mentioned that fact the next day, but mentioned it as the effect of the big explosion. I remember reading also that in a cafe nearby $3,000 worth of damage had been done by the breaking of glass and such things. But I am going to get those Spanish papers and try to send them to you.

Q. Do you know whether the gas lights went out?
-A. I do not, sir.
Q. You have no reason to suppose that they did?
-A. I could not tell you that, sir. When I got down to the wharf my main idea was to look toward the Maine and get a boat to go there. I paid no attention to the city or anything. But I saw this arc light fluttering; I can remember that distinctly.
Q. You saw it fluttering?
-A. You know when an electric light goes out the carbon remains for some time red hot. I just saw that and that made the whole thing look dark. Then that crowd of excited Spaniards hallooing, and all that, impressed me with the darkness of the place.
Q. You drove down Obispo street, which is lighted by gas ?
-A. Yes, sir; it is lighted by gas.
Q. In driving down that street, did you notice whether the lights were out?
-A. I did not. I could not tell you.
Q. If they had been out, would you have been likely to have noticed it?
-A. Yes; I think if they had all gone out I certainly would have noticed it.

ADDITIONAL STATEMENT OF HONORE FRANQOIS LAINE April 7, 1898.

Honoré François Laine, having been previously sworn, further testified at an open session of the Senate as follows:

By The Chairman Senator Davis
Q. Mr. Laine, you are a native of Cuba?
-A. Yes, sir.
Q. What is your age?
-A. Thirty-three.
Q. Your father is a French subject?
-A. A French citizen, sir.
Q. You were educated in this country?
-A. In this country.
Q. Where?
-A. At Georgetown College and Philadelphia.
Q. Is your father a planter?
-A. Yes, sir.
Q. How far from Havana?
-A. Ninety miles.
Q. What became of his plantation?
-A. It has been burned.
Q. By whom ?
-A. By the Spaniards.
Q. When I
-A. . In the month of October, 1896.

Q. Where did you go then ?
-A. I was in prison then.
Q. What became of your father and mother?
-A. They have come to this country. They are living in Tampa now.
Q. Your mother is a native of the United States?
-A. Yes, sir.
Q. Born at Wilmington, Del.?
-A. At Wilmington, Del.
Q. What was her maiden name?
-A. Mary Garesche.
Q. You went from New York to Havana as a correspondent in 1897; did you not?
-A. On the lst of January,1898.
Q. As a correspondent?
-A. Of the *New York Sun.*
Q. Did you make inquiry of the Spanish authorities whether you would be safe in doing so?
-A. I spoke to the Spanish Consul in New York, and I spoke to Secretary Congosto when I arrived there.
Q. What assurance, it" any, did you receive?
-A. Secretary Congosto told me that as long as he would be there nothing would happen to me.
Q. Did you enter upon your duties at Havana?
-A. Yes, sir.
Q. You used to exchange notes with other correspondents for the purpose of furnishing each other news?
-A. Yes, sir.
Q. Did you know a newspaper correspondent by the name of Díaz?
-A. Francisco Díaz ?
Q. An old friend of yours?
-A. Well, an acquaintance. A reporter has a great many.
Q. Was he engaged in Havana at that time?
-A. He was engaged in reporting for the *Unión Constitucional.*
Q. Was that a Weylerite paper?
-A. Yes, sir; a Weylerite paper.
Q. Very radical?
-A. . Very radical.
Q. You have stated to me heretofore some events connected with a letter or a copy of a letter which you received from Mr. Díaz purporting to be a letter which General Weyler had sent to the editor of that newspaper. Now, I wish you to go on in your own way from the beginning, and state the history of that business and what happened to you on account of it.
-A. I met Díaz one night in a room of the *Hotel Inglaterra,* where the reporters used to congregate at night to talk and exchange notes. In talking with him he told me that General Weyler had acceded to become a candidate for the Cortes of Spain for the district of Havana. Asking him how he knew that, he told me he had a copy of a letter of General Weyler. The letter had been written by General Weyler to Santos Guzmán, a lawyer, and

Images, top to bottom:
Muelle de Caballería (Horses) in Havana Harbor;
Muelle de la Machina (crane);
The **explosion of the Maine** as reported by
the *New York Sun*.

head of the Spanish constitutional party in Cuba —the Weyler party. Mr. Santos Guzman had given the letter to Mr. Novo, editor of the paper, the *Unión Constitucional.*

Q. Have you that copy of the letter with you now?

-A. I have not. It is in New York, sir.

Q. Will you furnish it, or a copy of it, to this committee?

-A. Yes, sir. It is in Spanish.

Q. And with it a translation?

-A. Yes, sir.

Q. Both?

-A. Yes, sir.

Q. Go on with your statement.

-A. This reporter, Diaz, saw the letter at the office of the paper there and took a copy of it, which copy he gave me. I do not remember the exact words of the letter.

Q. State the purport of it.

Q. Subject to correction when you send the committee a copy.

-A. In the letter Weyler said

Q. In substance?

-A. Yes; Weyler said that after mature consideration he had decided to run as a candidate for a deputy of the Cortes in Spain. Of course the letter is much longer than that, you know.

Q. Just give the substance of it.

-A. And he gave his reasons why he ran as a candidate and gave some advice to Santos Guzmán on that subject. Then he added that he had read that the Americans were intending to send a warship to Havana; that they had never dared to do so in his time, as he had the harbor well prepared for such emergencies.

Q. Well prepared?

-A. Well prepared for such emergencies, and that he hoped there would be a Spanish hand who would chastise in a fitting way that offense.

Q. Go on with your statement.

-A. The Maine not having arrived then, and knowing nothing at all about the arrival of American ships, that part of the letter had no importance at all.

Q. Was that before you had heard that the Maine was coming?

-A. Yes, sir; it was before that. This was so much so that as to that part of the letter I could hardly understand what he was referring to. The Maine arrived...

Q. What did you do with the letter?

-A. I have got the copy of the letter. I sent the news to Mr. Lee, the US Consul in this country, that Weyler was willing to run as a candidate for the Spanish Cortes.

Q. That was the part of the letter that interested you?

-A. That interested everybody then. Weyler had always said that he was not affiliated to any Spanish party. I kept the letter in my desk; I pigeonholed it in my desk and paid no more attention to it. The Maine arrived on the following day —two days after that.

Q. Two days after you saw the copy of the letter?

-A. Yes; two days after I had the copy of the letter the Maine arrived.

Q. Do you recollect about the date of the letter?

-A. I think it was the 24th, at nighttime.

Q. The 24th of January?

-A. Of January, about 10 o'clock at night. At 10 or 11 o'clock at night he gave me the letter.

Q. But do you recollect the date of the letter?

-A. The letter was written in Madrid on the 8th of January.

Q. Proceed with your statement.

-A. The Maine arrived on the following day, and on the 15th of February it was blown up. I then recalled Weyler's letter. I took it out of my desk and read two or three times over his last paragraphs. I went to see Díaz three times, and tried to get at any price the original letter, and could not do it. A few days after that...

Q. Did he deny the authenticity of the letter when you asked ?

-A. Oh, no. 1 did not see Díaz after that until the time I am going to refer to now. A few days after the explosion of the Maine I met Díaz leaving the palace of the Captain-General as I was entering it. After saluting him he said to me, "*Do you remember the copy of the letter of General Weyler I gave you?*" I told him, "*Yes.*" He said to me, "*What do you think about what Weyler said of the American ship?*" I answered that I thought someone had followed his advice. Díaz, being a Spaniard, looked at me very seriously in the face. I understood right then that I bad made a false step. On the night of the 4th —let me see— Wednesday; if I had a calendar here

Q. There is a calendar here. [A calendar was handed to the witness.]

-A. [after examining the calendar]. On the night of March 4, at 12 o'clock that night, as I was leaving the *Hotel Inglaterra*, I saw two figures on the sidewalk. They were the chief of police of Havana.

and a detective, who I afterwards ascertained had been following my footsteps for several days. As I passed the two figures the chief of police told me, *"Stop, sir; you are under arrest."* A cab was passing by. I was ordered to get in, and the detective took me to the Jefatura, or Police Headquarters. There, after being searched for incriminating papers, I was locked in a small cell incommunicado. An hour after that the chief of police arrived, and said to me, *"Well, we have you secure here at last."* I made no reply to him, and he began to threaten me.

Q. He spoke to you through the bars, did he not?

-A. Oh, yes; I was inside the cell.

Q. What was his language in threatening you?

-A. I think I ought to refer to the cab again and the way.

Q. Oh, yes.

-A. As the detective was paying for the cab that took us to Jefatura I was able to signal to the cabman, who was an acquaintance of mine, to inform my friends that I had been detained. He nodded with his head and I knew that he had understood my sign. He was a Cuban, you know. When the chief of police began to threaten me...

Q. What did he say?

-A. He said to me, *"The secret that I know you know will never be known by others, as they will not know either what has happened to you."* I then replied to him, *"If you think, Colonel"*—he is a Colonel of Police— *"that you can make me disappear as you did Posado and Ariza"* [two young men who had been taken out of the place and killed in the, outskirts of Havana by the Havana police] *"you are very much mistaken, as by this time the French and the American consuls who were my friends know that I am detained."* The chief of police changed his threatening attitude, ordered me out of the cell, ordered two chairs to be brought, and asked me to sit down as he wanted to have a talk with me. He then said, *"I know all about a copy of a letter which you say you have of Weyler. That does not trouble me. What I want to know is what you said to Consul Lee on the 24th of February concerning the explosion of the Maine?"* I answered him that I had not spoken on that subject to Consul Lee. I was ordered to be locked up again in the cell. The next morning I was sent to the Fortress *La Cabana*. On Wednesday March 9, at 11 o'clock in the morning, I was taken out of my cell by a Spanish captain of the Fortress, put on board a Government boat, rowed to the steamer *Olivetti* by Spanish sailors; and that is all. There is not anything more to it.

Q. You were placed on board the *Olivetti?*

-A. That is all. I do not know yet why I had been expelled...

Q. You came to this country?

-A. I came to this country.

Q. You have been here ever since?
-A. Yes, sir; I have been here ever since.
Q. Did you bring that copy of the letter away with you?
-A. Yes, sir.
Q. Where was it?
-A. Being a correspondent of an American newspaper and receiving all sorts of letters from the insurgents and people of that kind, I kept those documents in a secret corner of my room. The Spanish authorities, when they searched my room, were unable to find that.

A friend of mine lived in the same house, the house of an American, Dr. Wilson, and knew where I kept my things. I was able to send him a message from the fortress and tell him to pack all my clothes and send all my papers. My clothes were sent to me, my valise, but the papers were given in a sealed envelope to the agent of the Plant Steamship Company, who delivered them to me on board the steamship Olivetti, and I signed a receipt for them from this young man, named Mr. Miranda.

Q. You signed the receipt for this sealed package of papers on board the Olivetti?
-A. Yes, sir; on board the *Olivetti*.
Q. After the Spaniards had put you there?
-A. Yes, sir.
Q. And that package contained this copy of Weyler's letter to which you have referred?
-A. Yes, sir; and it contained a great many things.
Q. . Where is the copy of the Weyler letter now ?
-A. I have it in New York.
Q. And you will send us the original Spanish copy and a translation?
-A.. Yes, sir.

The following is the copy of the letter referred to above with its translation:

Madrid, Enero 8 de 1898.

Sr. Francisco de los Santos Guzmán, Habana.

Mi distinguido amigo y Correligionario:

Mi opinión sobre la actitud de nuestro partido en Cuba ha cambiado ante los últimos sucesos.

Si yo creí antes que el partido debía dignamente abstenerse de entrar en la contienda electoral, ahora creo que es una necesidad patriótica y un deber que tome parte en esa elecciones. No cabe duda del éxito ni de muestra mayoría en las listas; ni tampoco de que un programa fundado en la defensa del honor nacional había de arrastrar junto con nosotros los elementos tibios; pero sinceramente españoles que se han dejado ilusionar por las combinaciones de Moret y Sagasta y que han tomado por buena moneda y como combinaciones científicas la verdadera y deshonrosa humillación de nuestro pueblo ante el de los Estados Unidos.

Inscriban Uds. en su bandera (la bandera de España) *"revindicación del decoro nacional"* y yo me ofrezco como su candidato. Mi título mayor de gloria, después de haber mandado durante dos años doscientos mil héroes españoles en Cuba, será el de Diputado por la Habana.

Por cierto que he leído últimamente que piensan los Americanos enviar un buque de guerra a esa ciudad. En mi tiempo ni lo soñaron siquiera. Sabían el terrible castigo que les hubiera esperado.

Yo preparé ese puerto para esa contingencia haciendo obras que Martínez Campos había abandonado. Si el tal insulto llegara a realizarse, espero que no faltará una mano Española que se levante para castigar tan ejemplarmente como merece la provocación.

Romero está bien como nunca lo creímos sus amigos y aparte de los disgustos que esta atmósfera de humillaciones me impone lo está también su afmo. amigo y Seguro Servidor,

VALERIANO WEYLER.

Here is a copy of the translation to English of this letter:

His Excellency Don Francisco de los Santos Guzmán, Havana, Madrid, January 8 ,1898.

My Distinguished Personal and Political Friend:

Since the latest events, I have changed my views about the attitude which our political party in Cuba ought to assume. I have thought before that it was more dignified for me to abstain from the electoral contest; I believe now that it is a patriotic duty for us to go to the polls. Our success cannot be doubted; neither can be our majority of voters, nor that, with a program of defense of the national honor, we will

have side by side with us all those lukewarm politicians who, though Spaniards by heart, are deceived by the inside combinations of Moret and Sagasta, and take as scientific solutions of our colonial problems what are really dishonorable humiliations of our country before the United States.

Write on your flag, the flag of Spain, *"Defense of national hon-*

or," and I offer you my name as your candidate. After having commanded during two years 200,000 Spanish heroes in Cuba, the title I shall be more proud of, is that of deputy from Havana at the Cortes of Spain.

By the way, I have read these days that the Americans are pondering about sending one of their war ships to that city. During my command in Cuba they would not even dare to dream about it. They knew the terrible punishment that awaited them.

I had Havana Harbor well prepared for such an emergency. I rapidly finished the work that Martínez Campos carelessly abandoned.

If the insult is made, I hope that there will be a Spanish hand to punish it as terribly as it deserves.

Romero is in better health than his friends could have expected, and notwithstanding how morally sick I feel breathing this humiliating atmosphere, is well, also your affectionate friend and servant.

VALERIANO WEYLER.

Madrid, January 8, 1898.

[This letter was written to Guzmán, who as leader of the *Conservative Party* was famously known as a man *"as Spanish as garlic,"* and was by him turned over to the editor of the ultra Spanish paper, *La Unión Constitucional*, in order that Weyler's candidacy might be announced and favorably commented upon. This was before the Maine had gone to Havana, so there was no immediate significance in that portion of the letter that referred to the preparations to destroy American war ships.]

BUTCHERED CUBANS!

Cuban Concentration Camp, 1895

Concentration Camps

When Valeriano Weyler, also known as "the Butcher", arrived in Cuba, his first act was to create "re-concentration camps" for all Cuban citizens. If any Cubans were found outside these "camps" they were immediately shot and killed. However, living in the concentration camp was not necessarily a better option. These "re-concentration" camps were very crowded and unhealthy. Since Spaniards and soldiers occupied the best accommodations and took the best food. Many Cubans died of disease and starvation.

Weyler's Proclamation of the **Reconcentration Policy**

Blanco's elimination of the **Reconcentration Policy**

Images, top to bottom:
Newspaper reporters in Havana in 1898: **Stephen Crane** seated second from left with a white suit; **Honoré Françoise Laine** standing second from left with a white hat; **Richard Harding Davis**, standing second from right; the **telegram** sent to Washington with the news of the blowing of the Maine; **Valeriano Weyler**: the most hated Spanish officer in Cuba.

In order to clarify all possible details of the US assistance to the insurgents in Cuba, both militarily and economically, particularly because the recurring accusations of Spanish authorities about the multiple expeditions arriving in Cuba from ports in the United States, the *Committee of Foreign Relations of the US Senate*, upon the recommendation of Consul Fitzhugh Lee, requested the presence of Mr. Benjamin Guerra, a well-known tobacco merchant who undertook regular rounds around Cuba as part of his buying strategies. The deposition of Mr. Guerra took place on April 8, 1898, a few days after the Maine incident in Havana.

STATEMENT OF MR. BENJAMIN J. GUERRA, MERCHANT
April 8, 1898.

Examination by Senator Foraker and others.
Committee on Foreign Relations of the US Senate

Mr. Benjamín J. Guerra, being duly sworn, testified as follows :
Questioning by Senator Foraker
Q. Please state your age and residence.
-A. Forty-two years; residence, 104 West Sixty-first street, New York City.
Q. What is your occupation?
-A. Merchant.
Q. What kind of a merchant?
-A. I am a cigar manufacturer.
Q. To what extent have you engaged in the business of manufacturing cigars'?
-A. I have a cigar factory in Tampa, Fla., and one in Key West, Fla.
Q. Do you put your product on the market?
-A. Yes, sir; I have business relations in all the States of the Union.
Q. Of what nationality are you ?
-A. Cuban.
Q. You have resided in Cuba?
-A. Yes, sir; all of my life until the year 1878.
Q. Where have you resided since then ?
-A. In New York City.
Q. Do you now hold any official relation to the Republic of Cuba? And if so, state what it is.

-A. Yes, sir; I am the treasurer of the Cuban delegation.

Q. What do you mean by that term? What is the Cuban delegation and where is it located?

-A. It is the representation of the Cuban Government in Arms in the United States.

Q. Who constitute that delegation?

-A. Mr. Tomás Estrada Palma, Delegate, Dr. Joaquín Castillo, Subdelegate; Antonio Gonzalez Lanuza, Secretary, and myself, Treasurer.

Q. There are four of you, then, in all?

-A. Four in all.

Q. Are there any other official representatives of the Republic of Cuba in the United States?

-A. Gonzalo de Quesada, who is the Charge d'Affaires at Washington.

Q. And anyone else?

-A. Mr. Diaz Albertini, Secretary of Legation.

Q. By whom were you appointed to your present position, and have you any evidence of your appointment?

-A. I was appointed by the President of the Republic of Cuba.

Q. With the approval of his cabinet?

-A. With the approval of his cabinet.

Q. Have you the evidence of that appointment?

-A. Yes, sir.

Q. Will you produce it and allow it to be copied into the record?

-A. Yes [producing a paper]. I have it and now produce it. It is in Spanish. I will have it translated and a copy of it furnished for the record. [The paper was thereupon translated by Mr. Quesada and submitted as follows:

> *[There is a seal which says, "Republic of Cuba. Chancery. Secretary of the Government. Jose Clemente Vivanco, Sec'y of the Government Council and " Chancellor of the Republic of Cuba.*
>
> *"I certify that on page two hundred and twenty-four of volume second of the minutes of the sessions of this council there is copied the following resolution, adopted by the council on the 6th of January:*
>
> *' On motion of the secretary of foreign relations, it is resolved to appoint Citizen Benjamin J. Guerra treasurer of the plenipotentiary delegation abroad. And at the request of the Secretary of Foreign Relations I issued the present certificate. Country and liberty in the free town of Santa Lucia on the 28th of June, 1897. Jose Clemente Vivanco.]*

[There is a seal: Republic of Cuba, Presidency.]

Approved.

(Signed) SALVADOR CISNEROS, *President.*

Q. Do you know whether the Republic of Cuba has issued any bonds at any time since its organization until the present?
-A. Yes, sir.
Q. And if so, to what amount in money?
-A. By the authority and direction of the Government of the Republic of Cuba, Mr. Estrada Palma and myself have caused to be printed bonds to the amount of US$ 3,145,600.
Q. Who authorized the printing of those bonds?
-A. The Government of the Republic of Cuba.
Q. Have you the authority of which you speak, that was given by the Government of the Republic of Cuba to yourself and Mr. Palma to issue those bonds?
-A. Yes, sir.
Q. Will you produce it and allow it to be copied into the record?
-A. Yes, sir; here it is [producing a paper].
Senator Foraker. I will have a copy of it made for the record.
The paper referred to is as follows:

Republic of Cuba, Provisional Government.
Salvador Cisneros y Betancourt, President of the Republic of Cuba, to all whom these presents may come, greeting:

«By virtue of the powers which have been conferred upon me by the constituent assembly, under date of the 18th of September, 1895, I hereby confer upon citizen Tomas Estrada Palma, delegate plenipotentiary of the Government of the Republic, the following powers:

First. That personally, or by means of delegates, he represent the Republic of Cuba before the Government and people of all nations to which he may deem convenient to name a representative, giving him the powers he may deem adequate.

Second. That he may contract one or more loans, to use the money in the service of the Republic, guaranteeing said loans with all the properties and public income, internal or of the customs, present and future, of the said Republic; issuing bonds, registered or to bearer, to the amount he may deem necessary, payable both as to interest and place of payment as he may deem convenient, hereby empowering him to fix the denominations, the rate of interest, conditions of payment of capital and interest, as he may deem most favorable, and to place said bonds on the most advantageous terms, and to pledge them.

Third. To issue paper money in the name of the Republic of Cuba to the amount he may consider necessary, in the form and on conditions he may deem most adequate.

Fourth. To issue postage stamps of the denominations he may judge convenient for the service of the Republic.

Images, top to bottom, left to right:
Bartolomé Masó, Salvador Cisneros, Tomás Estrada Palma;
Benjamín Guerra, Gonzalo de Quesada, José Antonio González Lanuza;
José Castillo Duany, Rafael Díaz Albertini, José Clemente Vivanco.

Fifth. The bonds to be issued as well as the bills shall be signed by the delegate plenipotentiary or the person whom he shall delegate and by the treasurer of the 'Cuban Revolutionary Party,' and shall bear the seals and countermarks which the delegate believes necessary to avoid counterfeits.
Sixth. (Relates to appointment of sub-delegate, who shall act in case of death or disability of delegate.)
Seventh. (Authorizes substitution of power in whole or in part and authorizes appointment of employees.)
Eighth. The delegate may receive, collect, and invest the funds which from any source whatever may come into his hands, doing so in the form which he may judge most favorable to the interests of the Republic, as well as the power to make concessions and celebrate in the name of the Republic all the agreements and contracts, which he may deem beneficial to the interests thereof, which from now on are declared ratified by the Government he represents.

Given in Boston under my signature and that of the Secretary of Foreign Relations and the treasury, the 21st day of November, one thousand eight hundred and ninety-five.
Salvador Cisneros y Betancourt, President.
Severo Pina, Secretary of the Treasury and of Foreign Relations *ad interim*,"

State of New York, City and County of New York:
Leopoldo de Arrastia, being duly sworn, deposes and says:

That he is a notary public in and for the city and county of New York. That he is well acquainted with the English and Spanish languages and has often been employed as sworn translator from the Spanish into the English language, and that he is fully proficient to act as such. That the above is a correct and accurate translation of the power of attorney given by the Government of the Republic of Cuba to Tomás Estrada Palma, under date of the 21st of November, 1895.

LEOPOLDO DE ARRASTIA.
Sworn to before me this 19th of March, 1898.
[seal] LEON J. BENOIT,
Notary Public (377), New York County.

Q. Can you tell us to what extent the bonds which you say have been printed under this authority have been disposed off?
-A. Yes, sir.
Q. Tell us in detail what has become of them—where they are now, if you know?

-A. We have sold for cash, to several people, as per the book I present here to you [producing a record book], US$94,050, and we have disposed of for merchandise, US$828,350, which makes a total of bonds disposed of US$122,400.

Q. Have you any record of the bonds that you have disposed of for cash and merchandise?

-A. Yes, sir.

Q. Where is that record?

-A. Here it is [indicating the record book].

Q. You refer to a book which you have before you?

-A. Yes, sir.

Q. What is the book? What is the name of it?

-A. Sale of Bonds.

Q. Does it contain a complete record of every bond that has been disposed of by you and Mr. Palma?

-A. Yes, sir.

Q. Please explain in detail what that record shows.

-A. This book shows the date of the operation

Q. Of the transaction?

-A. Yes, of the transaction; number of the bonds that are sold, and then here [indicating] how many bonds; then denomination; then marks.

Q. By denomination you mean what amount the bond is?

-A. Yes, sir; what amount.

Q. What do you mean by marks of the bond?

-A. Marks by which we can identify them. Then rate at which the bond has been sold; the name of the buyer, street and number of his residence, city, and State. Here [indicating] are incidental remarks; amount; face value of the bond, and net realized.

Q. That is, the amount of the whole number of bonds sold in one transaction ?

-A. Yes, sir; in each transaction.

Q. Have you any objection to allowing this record to be copied ?

-A. No, sir; but most of it is in Spanish, except the names of Americans and their residence.

Q [examining record book]. I observe that there are a little more than twelve closely written pages in this record book. On that account I will not take the trouble to have a complete copy of the record made, but I should be glad to have a quotation from this book running all the way through the record, showing one of these transactions, simply as a sample of the record that has been kept. I will call your attention to an entry dated May 20, 1896, on page 4. The one I indicate to you I ask you to read that it may be incorporated in the record.

-A. [Reading.] Year. 1896; May 20; marks 18 to 37; twenty bonds of $100 each ; marks 18 to 20, 21 to 25, 26 to 37 ; rate, 50 per cent; name of the buyer, A. Y. Gray, Rutland County,

Middletown Springs, Vt., care of L. and A. Y. Gray, Middletown Springs Bank and Phoenix National Bank of New York; face value, $2,000; net realized, $1,000.

Q. Please state what rates were realized as shown by this record for the bonds which you have sold?

-A. The different rates?

Q. Yes. What is the highest rate you have realized?

-A. Par.

Q. How many of those bonds have you sold at par?

-A. Some six or eight have sold for par. There are some at 6%.

Q. And they have sold at prices ranging all the way down from par to what as the lowest?

-A. The lowest is 20 per cent. Some at 6%; some at 50; some at 75; some at 61; some at 80; some at 90, and others at 50 and 40, and of late, by order of the Government, we are not selling them, at less than 40 per cent.

Q. Can you state without much trouble how many you have sold at 25 per cent?

-A [examining record book]. There are sixteen entries here at 25 per cent.

Q. What is the aggregate amount of the bonds at face value sold at 25 per cent in those sixteen transactions?

-A. Thirteen thousand dollars.

Q. Give the date when those bonds were sold at 25 cents on the dollar, as shown by this record.

-A. From September 12, 1896, to November 1 of the same year.

Q. What is the next entry there?

-A. November 11, 1896.

Q. Run that entry through. What is it?

-A [reading]. November 11, No. 104; one bond of $100; mark 69,618; par; bought by Mr. Joaquin Fortune, of Jacksonville, Fla.; $100 face value; $100 net realized.

Q. Have you sold any bonds at 25 cents on the dollar since November 4, 1896?

-A. Yes, sir; on January 13, 1897, I sold one for that amount.

Q. What prices have you realized usually since November, 1896, as shown by this record?

-A. From 40 per cent up.

Q. So far as this record discloses, you have not made any sale since then for less than 40 cents on the dollar?

-A. No, sir.

Q. This record, as I understand you, shows all the bonds that have been disposed of for either cash or merchandise?

-A. For cash only.

Q. Is there a record of the bonds disposed of for merchandise?

-A [producing a record book[. Yes, sir; here is a book that shows all of the bonds that have gone out of my hands for which no cash has entered into the treasury.

Q. Is this a complete record for every such bond?

-A. Yes, sir; of every such one.

Q. You have now accounted for bonds to the amount of $122,400, of which you have a record. Where are the rest of the bonds that were printed?

-A. One million of those bonds is deposited in the safes of Messrs. August Belmont & Co.

Q. To whom do those bonds belong that are deposited with August Belmont & Co.?

-A. To the Republic of Cuba, and the balance is in my possession.

Q. As treasurer?

-A. As treasurer.

Q. Do any person or persons or any syndicate of any kind own or have any lien or claim upon any of the bonds that are still either in your possession or in the possession of August Belmont & Co.

-A. No, sir.

Q. Are they the sole property of the Republic of Cuba?

-A. They are.

Q. It has been stated in conversation, and possibly in the newspapers, that recently, in the city of New York, someone was offered $50,000 in bonds of the Republic of Cuba as a consideration for coming to New York and rendering some kind of political service. State whether there is any truth in such a statement.

-A. I do not believe there is any truth in that, because nobody from the Cuban delegation has done it, and I do not think anybody has $50,000 of these bonds that can be offered.

Q. Would anyone, except Palma, Castillo, Lanuza, and yourself have authority to make such an offer on behalf of the Republic of Cuba?

-A. Nobody else.

Q. Have any other bonds than those you have described ever been issued by the Republic of Cuba or authorized by the Republic of Cuba?

-A. No other ones.

Q. Have any person or persons other than your delegation any authority to deal in the bonds of the Republic of Cuba?

-A. No, sir.

Q. Then, as I understand you, the total amount of bonds that have been issued by the Republic of Cuba and outstanding is $122,400?

-A. Yes, sir; that is all that have been sold.

Q. And all the remainder of the bonds are still in your possession?

-A. They are all in my possession.

Bonds issued by the **Republic of Cuba in Arms** to secure funds for the Wars of Independence.

Q. Another story has been circulated to the effect that someone here in the city of Washington has been offered $3,0100,000 of these bonds as a consideration for rendering some kind of political service, the kind of service not specified. Is there any truth in that story?
-A. I do not believe there is any truth in it.
Q. Did anyone connected with your delegation make any such offer?
-A. No, sir.
Q. Or have any authority to make any such offer?
-A. No, sir; nobody has any authority to do it.
Q. In the House of Representatives, yesterday, Mr. Grosvenor, of Ohio, made the following statement, replying to Mr. Lentz, who had spoken on the Cuban question:

«*Now, Mr. Speaker, let us see how this situation stands. The gentleman is greatly worried about bonds, and he read the name of John J. McCook in one of his raids this afternoon.*»

«Who is John J. McCook? Whom does he represent? What is he here for? How do he and the gentleman from Ohio stand with reference to this? I will show you that they are parties in a great conspiracy; one wittingly so, the other, I trust, ignorantly so. Who is John J. McCook? is he the legal representative of the Cuban Junta, of New York, behind which stands four bundled millions, more or less, of bonds that can be validated by the recognition of the independence of Cuba by the United States, and they will be destroyed by a policy that drives Spain out of Cuba in the interest of the American people. Do you know John J. McCook, who is referred to here?»
-A. I do not know him personally.
Q. Has he any relation, official or otherwise, to your delegation?
-A. Not to my knowledge.
Q. Has he any relation to the Government of the Republic of Cuba, official or otherwise?
-A. Not to my knowledge.
Q. Does he have any relation whatever to the bonds that have been issued by the Republic of Cuba, concerning which you have testified?
-A. None whatever.
Q. Do you know of any issue of $400,000,000 of bonds, more or less, by the Republic of Cuba?
-A. I know nothing about it, and I do not think there has been any issued except those that I have described.
Q. Do you know anything about the syndicate and the bonds that are referred to by General Grosvenor in the remarks I have quoted?
-A. No, sir.
Q. General Grosvenor further says in these same remarks :

«I will tell you who John J. McCook is. John J. McCook represents an interest running up into the hundreds of millions of dollars, and if he could get the United States to make a recognition of the independence of Cuba and then fight to establish it by the United States, at the cost of a thousand million dollars, the holders of these bogus bonds will realize $400,000,000 and collect the money. That is where the bonds come in.»

Q. I understand you to say there are no such issues of bonds?
-A. I know there are not.
Q. Has the question of bonds or the validation of bonds anything whatever to do with the question of the recognition of the independence of Cuba or with the recognition of the Republic of Cuba as the government of Cuba?
-A. None that I know. There were some gentlemen calling on me in my office a few days ago and asking me what we would take for ten millions of bonds.
Q. Did they say they wanted to buy?
-A. Yes, sir. After consulting with Mr. Palma, I told him that the lowest price we could make them was 40 per cent. Then he made us an offer of 20 cents on the dollar, a cash offer, for the ten million—to give us two million for the ten million —which we refused.
Q. Are there any negotiations pending between your delegation as the representatives of the Republic of Cuba, and any person or persons for the sale of any bonds at this time?
-A. Not to my knowledge.
Q. You are in such a relation to this whole matter that you would know about it if there were any such negotiations?
-A. Yes, sir; the bonds have to pass through my hands; I have to sign the bonds.

The Chairman asks:
Can you say that no such negotiations are being made?
-A. None with my intervention.
Q. We want an answer that is not equivocal. State whether or not any such negotiations are pending.
-A. I think there are not.
Q. If there are, you have no knowledge of them?
-A. T have no knowledge of them at all.
Q. Could they be issued without your knowing about it and signing them?
-A. They could not.
Q. I mean any large transactions.
-A. The bonds could not be issued without my signature.

Q. What did you do with the cash realized from these bonds? I do not want an answer in detail, but just state it generally.
-A. We employed it in the furtherance of the cause of Cuba in the revolution.
Q. Was all the money appropriated in that behalf which was realized from the sale of these bonds?
-A. Yes, sir.
Q. How has the money necessary to carry on the war the insurgents have been making in Cuba been raised?
-A. It has been contributed mostly by the Cubans. $472,617.42 have been received by me as treasurer of the Republic of Cuba from taxes paid by plantations in Cuba to the department of the treasury of the Cuban Republic.
Q. Are the taxes that are collected in Cuba by the Republic of Cuba sent to you?
-A. Yes, sir.
Q. After collection?
-A. Yes, sir.
Q. And you have received from taxes collected in Cuba the amount you have named?
-A. Yes, sir.
Q. Over $400,000?
-A. Yes, sir.
Q. How was that money expended; for the Cuban cause, or otherwise?
-A. It was all expended for the Cuban cause.
Q. Can you tell us what kind of a system of collecting taxes they have in Cuba?
-A. Yes, sir. They have the department of the treasury organized. The Secretary of the Treasury is the head. In every one of the States there is what they call an Administrator of taxes, which corresponds to our collector of customs.
Q. What system of levying taxes has the Republic of Cuba in force there? You have told us of the official who does the collecting. What is the system ?
-A. The system on the sugar plantations is so much per bag of sugar produced. Sometimes it has been 40 cents, and in other years it has been 25 cents per bag. The Government imposed a war tax of 2 per cent on the value given to the plantations in the year 1894.
Q. Upon the value as given in 1894?
-A. As given in 1894.
Q. When you say the Government you mean the Republic of Cuba?
-A. The Republic of Cuba.

Q. Is that tax system uniform in its operation throughout the island"?
-A. Yes, sir.
Q. That is, every man is taxed alike, according to the same principle?
-A. Yes, sir.
Q. And is this system enforced throughout the island?
-A. It is.
Q. Have you tax collectors in all of the different States?
-A. Yes, sir.

The Chairman asks again:
Q. Is that done by virtue of a statute of the Cuban Congress?
-A. Yes, sir.
Q. And not by a military regulation?
-A. Not military at all; the army has nothing to do with it.
Q. Who appoints the tax collectors—the military or the civil government?
-A. The civil government.
Q. Has that civil government, the Republic of Cuba, any other branch of government in operation except this fiscal branch of which you speak?
-A. Yes, sir.
Q. What?
-A. They have the Interior Department.
Q. What does that do?
-A. The head of the Interior Department is the Secretary of the Interior, but there are Governors and Prefects and Subprefects in the different states and districts.
Q. Are those officials whom you mention holding office now ?
-A. They are.
Q. In what way do they get their offices—by election or appointment?
-A. By appointment.
Q. Who appoints them?
-A. The President of the Republic.
Q. You say that they are appointed throughout the island?
-A. Yes, sir.
Q. What is a Prefect? What are his duties?
-A. A Prefect is a kind of a mayor of the district.
Q. Have you any other branch of the Government in operation ?
-A. The Department of War.
Q. Aside from that? I will speak of that presently.
-A. Well, the civil, I mean the Interior Department, assumes the post-office department.

> Q. Has the Republic of Cuba a postal system?
> -A. Yes, sir.
> Q. In operation ?
> -A. Yes, sir.
> Q. What is the nature of that system? How do they transport the mails?
> -A. They have post-houses in all the towns— the small towns— and they transmit the mails by horses—by couriers.

Desembarcos de Expedicionarios

Ruta de la **Invasión de Occidente** planeada y ejecutada por el General Antonio Maceo y secundada y apoyada por el General Máximo Gómez en 1895.
De Baraguá a Mantua

The Staff of President **Bartolomé Masó**:
seated left, **Domingo Méndez Capote**;
standing right, **José Braulio Alemán**;
at the center **President Bartolomé Masó**

On the left: *A military promotion signed by President Masó and General Alemán.*

Q. Have they any postage stamps such as we have in this country?
-A. Yes, sir; they have 2 cent, 5 cent, and 10 cent postage stamps.
Q. Have you any of those with you?
-A. Yes, sir.
Q. That you could show as a sample?
-A [producing a stamped envelope]. Here is a letter addressed to me with two stamps oil it, from Camaguey district, in Cuba.
Q. Will you allow us to put that envelope in the record as an exhibit.?
-A. Yes, sir.
Q. I ask that it be attached as a part of -A's evidence. The envelope referred to is, in facsimile, as follows:
Q. How is it as to an educational system? Have they any?
-A. Yes, sir; they have schools. That is also under the Interior Department.
Q. What is the system of education?
-A. They have primary schools. They have some teaching books that have been printed there in our presses in Cuba.
Q. Do I understand you to say that the Government of the Republic of Cuba has a printing office?
-A. Yes, sir; they have. There are several newspapers printed there.
Q. Does the Government prescribe the books that shall be used in the schools?
-A. Yes, sir. It appoints the teachers, the inspectors.
Q. Does the Government print the school books?
-A. They print the school books—the primary books. We could, perhaps, supply the committee with some.
Q. How are those books distributed, by the Government?
-A. By the Government.
Q. Is the attendance of children at school optional?
-A. Compulsory.
Q. It is compulsory?
-A. Yes, sir.
Q. All children in Cuba, then, under the Government of the Republic of Cuba, are required to attend school ?
-A. Yes, sir.
Q. And are required to be taught in the primary branches, for which the Government furnishes the books ?
-A. Yes, sir.
Q. What kind of a judicial system have they in Cuba, under the Republic of Cuba, if you know?
-A. They have what they call the judiciary corps. That is attached to the army, though ; it is a dependent of the War Department. It is made so by the constitution.
Q. The constitution makes that provision?
-A. Yes, sir; while the war lasts.
Q. Where is the capital of the Republic of Cuba located?
-A. It is in the Province of Camagüey, District of Cubitas. The town is called Agramonte.
Q. Is there a town named Cubitas also?
-A. No, sir; Cubitas is the district where this town is.

Q. What is the population of Agramonte?
-A. Agramonte may have about a thousand inhabitants.
Q. State whether the Republic of Cuba has at Agramonte, where its capital is located, any official Government buildings.
-A. Yes, sir; there is one building for the President, and one for each of the Departments of State, Interior, Treasury, and War.
Q. Are those buildings occupied for official business simply?
-A. Yes, sir.
Q. What is the legislative body of the Republic of Cuba called? What is the name of it?
-A. The Council of Government assumes the legislative faculties of the Government until every two years there is the Constituent Assembly to elect another President and another council body.
Q. The members of the constituent assembly are elected by a popular vote, I understand?
-A. By the people; by popular vote.
Q. And then the constituent assembly thus elected chooses a President?
-A. Yes, sir.
Q. And a Vice-President ?
-A. Yes, sir.
Q. And a Cabinet?
-A. And a Cabinet.
Q. And the President, Vice-President, and Cabinet conduct the Government?
-A. Yes, sir. The Assembly also elects a General in Chief of the army.
Q. Who is the President now of the Republic of Cuba?
-A. Bartolomé Masó.
Q. Do you know him personally?
-A. Yes, sir.
Q. Tell us what kind of a man he is as to character and reputation.
-A. He is a man of great character, known by his honesty and by his literary accomplishments.
Q. Is he an educated, cultivated man ?
-A. He is an educated man.
Q. Where was he educated, if you know?
-A. In Cuba; at the University of Havana.
Q. What is his business?
-A. He was a landowner in Cuba; he is a landowner.

The Chairman asks:

Q. A man of large means?
-A. Yes, sir; of wealth.
Q. Did he own plantations?
-A. He does own them.
Q. Who is the Vice-President?
-A. The vice president is Dr. Méndez Capote.
Q. How old a man is he?
-A. He must be about 45 years old.
Q. What was his business before?
-A. He is a lawyer. He is a doctor in laws.

Q. Was he connected with any university?
-A. The University of Havana.
Q. In what capacity ?
-A. He has been a professor in the University of Havana.
Of the other members of the Government
Q. Yes; speak of them.
-A. There is the Secretary of the Interior, as we call him. He is a doctor, too—a Doctor in Medicine.

The Chairman asks again:

Q. A doctor of medicine ?
-A. Yes, sir.
Q. Did he graduate in this country?
-A. He graduated in Havana.
Q. Well, who is the Secretary of War?
-A. The secretary of war is General Alemán.
Q. Tell us briefly about him.
-A. He was a merchant there. He went into the revolution at the beginning and has been fighting until he was elected Secretary of War. He is an educated man, also; a literary man.
Q. And the Secretary of the Treasury? What was his business before?
-A. He was in business.
Q. A merchant?
-A. Yes; a merchant. The secretary of the treasury is
Fonts y Sterling; he is a lawyer. He is a member of one of the most ancient and illustrious families in Cuba.
Q. A graduate of the university?
-A. A graduate of Havana University.
Q. What is his profession?
-A. Law.
Q. Tell us briefly about the Secretary of Foreign Relations. What was his business before he was appointed to that office?
-A. Moreno de la Torre is a Doctor in Medicine, educated in Spain. He is a young man, known for his energy in all revolutionary affairs in Cuba. He is of a conservative temper, though. That is all I can say about him.
Q. To what extent has the Republic of Cuba governmental control of the Island of Cuba, I mean territorially?
-A. The Government has control, full control, of all the rural districts of the central and eastern parts of the island.
Q. That would be all of Santiago de Cuba?
-A. And Camagüey.
Q. Puerto Príncipe?
-A. Yes; Puerto Príncipe. The Spanish call it Puerto Principe, and we call it Camagüey; and Santiago de Cuba Province outside of a few cities that are held by the Spanish Government.
Q. What proportion of the population of Cuba responds to your Government or shows it allegiance?
-A. In my opinion, 80 per cent of the population of the island are friendly to the revolution.

> Q. What is the population in the provinces of Santiago de Cuba and Camagüey, where you say the Republic of Cuba is in complete control?
> -A. The population is about half a million.
> Q. Are the people in those provinces friendly and satisfied, apparently, with the Government of the Republic of Cuba?
> -A. Yes, sir.
> Q. Would or would not, in your opinion, the Government of the Republic of Cuba be able to administer satisfactorily the civil affairs of the territory of Cuba if they were let alone and allowed to discharge their functions of government without interference by the Spaniards?
> -A. I am positive that they would be able to do it satisfactorily.
> Q. You have told us who constitute the delegation and what other representatives of the Republic of Cuba there are in this country. You have also told us of various other officials who are conducting the Government of the Republic of Cuba. Can you tell us what salaries those officials receive for their services?
> -A. There is no Cuban in the service of the Republic who receives any salary.
> Q. Do you mean to say that the President and Vice-President and Cabinet, who are devoting all their time in the way you have indicated, receive no salaries?
> -A. They receive no salary.
> Q. No official connected with the civil government receives any salary?
> -A. No official connected with the civil government receives any salary.
> Q. How is it as to the army?
> -A. They receive no salary at all.
> Q. Then no officer or soldier in with Gómez receives any salary?
> -A. No, sir; nor Gómez himself, either.
> Q. How many soldiers has Gómez now in his command or under his command?
> -A. In my opinion, in the neighborhood of 35,000.
> Q. Every man works simply for...
> -A. For patriotism.
> Q. That is all. I am much obliged to you.
> -A. You are welcome, sir.

The time finally came to have US Consul Fitzhugh Lee in person testifying before the US Senate. The Consul left Havana in very good terms with the Captain General of Cuba General Ramón Blanco Erenas. Although he had not had many contacts with insurgents, he had enough information provided in good faith by many supporters of the rebellion that had access to Mr. Lee's office.

STATEMENT OF HON. FITZHUGH LEE, US Consul in Havana
April 12, 1898.

Examination by Senator Frye and others
Committee on Foreign Relations of the US Senate

Honorable Fitzhugh Lee, being duly sworn, testified as follows :

By Senator Frye

Q. General, you have just returned from Cuba?

-A. Yes, sir.

Q. You sent to the State Department certain communications touching the ship Maine. Have you any information additional to that conveyed in those communications?

-A. I have not.

Q. Have you any information in relation to torpedoes or anything of that kind in the harbor?

-A. I am informed on very good authority that they have placed within the last month two rows of torpedoes just at the mouth of the harbor by Morro Castle and the switch board is in a room in the Morro.

Q. Had you any information as to the placing of any torpedoes before the Maine was destroyed?

-A. No, sir.

Q. Have you any information in relation to purchases made abroad, or have any communications been made to you by reliable persons of purchases of torpedoes made abroad?

-A. No, sir.

Q. Have you any reason to suppose that the harbor was mined at all before the blowing up of the Maine?

-A. No, sir. No; I had no reason to suspect anything of that sort up to that time.

By Senator Gray.

Q. But since then?

Q. Have you since received any information which leads you to suppose that it was mined before the disaster?

-A. I have seen a letter, and probably you, gentlemen, have also seen it, published in one of the New York papers by a person named Laine, from General Weyler to Santos Guzmán, a citizen of Havana, a very ultra Spaniard, in which General Weyler says that he went on with the placing of the mines in the harbor, which Martínez Campos, his predecessor, should have done. I saw afterwards that General Weyler pronounced the letter a forgery, but I happen to know of a telegram received from Weyler since, and this is the only reason I have to suspect that there were some mines there previous to the entrance of the Maine into the harbor. You have probably seen the letter which Laine published.

Q. We have a copy of it on file.

-A. I see that Santos Guzmán, under the date of March 18, 1898, says to the editor of the Herald: «*I have not received General Weyler's letter dated January 8, to which the New York Herald makes reference in its cablegram of yesterday addressed to me.*» A Madrid dispatch further says: «*General Weyler denies the authenticity of the letter published in New York yesterday in which the former Captain-General of Cuba is alleged to have said that the United States would not have dared to send a warship to Havana while he was in command there, as they knew the terrible punishment that awaited them,*» adding that he had Havana Harbor «*well prepared for such an emergency, having rapidly finished the work that Martínez Campos carelessly abandoned*»

I knew Laine very well. He was expelled from the island about several weeks ago, but I always found him a very upright, honest, straight fellow; and when I saw that he had a copy of a letter from Weyler to Santos Guzmán, of Havana, I thought the chances were that he had a copy of a genuine letter, and that the facts were as stated; so I put some machinery to work and I found this cablegram, which had never been given to the public in any way. Moreover, as to Mrs. Eva Canel. She is quite a noted Spanish woman there, who was a great admirer of General Weyler, during the mob and so on, the riots, hallooing "*Viva Weyler*" and "*Muera Blanco*" (death to Blanco). General Blanco had her expelled from the island and sent to Mexico. Eva Canel and Santos Guzman, which is the very one that Laine refers to in his letter. This is in Spanish, but the translation is as follows: " Grave circumstances cause me to ask you to destroy the last letter of February 18."

Q. Signed by whom?

-A. Signed "Weyler."

Q. Dated when?

-A. There is no date to the telegram I have here, but it says: "In consequence of the grave condition of affairs or circumstances [*deje sin efecto*] the order to destroy the last letter of date 18th February."

Q. Whence does the telegram purport to have been sent?

-A. From Barcelona, I think.

Q. Have you any doubt that is a genuine copy of a telegram from Weyler?

-A. I am satisfied it is a genuine copy of a telegram received in Havana.

Q. From Weyler?

-A. From Weyler.

Q. What is the date of the letter which Laine talks about?

By Senator Foraker

Q. January 18, I believe?

-A. Laine's letter was dated in January, sometime.

By Senator Gray

Q. January 8?

-A. January 8. This asks Santos Guzman, in consequence of grave circumstances which have arisen, to destroy his last letters of the 18th of February. This is simply rather confirmatory. If he had written to Guzmán on the 8th of January, it makes this telegram that much more probable, and that he has also written to him after the 8th of January, and probably there was a very important letter on the 18th of February, which he wanted destroyed.

By Senator Morgan

Q. A few days after the ship was destroyed?

-A. Yes, sir; the ship was destroyed on the 15th. I suppose the news reached Spain probably on the 16th, or something of that sort, and Weyler telegraphed right over.

Q. Have you learned anything about any wire, such as is ordinarily used for torpedo service, ordered from Great Britain, or anywhere else?

-A. I saw a copy of a telegram from Admiral Manterola in Havana, to the Spanish commission, as he put it, in London stating: "Hurry up electrical cables." Whether that referred to wire for submarine mines or torpedoes I do not know. I tried to ascertain if any of the wire or electrical cables had arrived there, but they came on Spanish ships and I could not find out. I have always had an idea about the Maine that, of course, it was not blown up by any private individual or by any private citizen, but it was blown up by some of the officers who had charge of the mines and electrical wires and torpedoes in the arsenal there who thoroughly understood their business, for it was done remarkably well. I do not think General Blanco, the present Captain and Governor General of the Island of Cuba, had anything to do with it. I do not think he had any knowledge of it. I saw him just shortly after the occurrence. I was sitting in my room at the hotel and from the balcony of the hotel I could hear this. I heard the explosion and saw a great column of fire go up in the air. A few moments after ascertaining that it was the Maine, I went right down to the palace and I asked for General Blanco. He came in directly by himself. He had just heard it and was crying; tears were coming out of his eyes. He seemed to regret it as much as anybody I saw in Havana; but I think it came from some of the subaltern officers who had been there under Weyler, and who were probably anti-Blanco anyhow, and who had full knowledge of the business.

Q. General, what have been the orders prevailing in Havana as to the sale of explosives of various kinds?

-A. I have never heard of any explosives being on sale there, or any orders about it one way or the other.

Q. Would they permit explosives to be sold in the ordinary way?

-A. No, sir; I think not. They are very careful about that; so much so.

Q. And have you been so for a long time?

-A. Very; so much so that when Captain Sigsbee wanted to use a little dynamite for the purpose of getting the 10-inch guns from the Maine, they violently objected to it; they did not want him to have any dynamite. I do not think they would allow any private store in Havana to sell dynamite or any explosive materials of any kind.

Q. Have you read the testimony taken by our naval board?

-A. I glanced at it. I have not read it over very carefully.

The testimony of an American Newsman two weeks after the Maine Explosion

On the afternoon of March 1 there was a great demonstration on the water and along the waterfront. Onlookers came and went up for some hours, and the excitement intensified toward sundown. Shortly after sunset the Spanish armored cruiser **Vizcaya** arrived from New York. Her entrance excited great enthusiasm among the Spaniards. Many boats and steamers were present to give her welcome. There were streamers and flags flying on shore, and the wharves were crowded with people. It was reported to me that there were cries of "*Down with the Americans!*"

It was different from an American demonstration a day before. It had been childlike, even pathetic. Americans and British citizens resident of Havana were strolling in the thick of crowds, pressing through the narrow gateway leading from the Machina harbor to the city streets. They knew of the imminent arrival of the **Vizcaya**; they remained serene in the knowledge of that there was a fine US fleet over at Tortugas. The **Maine** was a thing of the past, but the fleet was a thing of the future. By that time the atmosphere at Havana was waxing volcanic with the promise of war, but the Spaniards apparently gave no heed to our fleet, which could then have destroyed Havana in short order.

Cuban Insurgents at the Battle of **La Majagua**; Máximo Gómez troops confronted the Spanish **Victoria Regiment** near Ciego de Avila as it was shown in **"Harper's Weekly"** in June 1897.

By Senator Frye
Q. Were you present in Havana all the time when they were conducting their inquiry?
-A. Yes, sir.
Q. Are you familiar with what was done and what was found?
-A. I am tolerably familiar with it. 1 knew nothing about the report of the board, of course, until it was published, although 1 saw the officers every day. 1 saw them sometimes in town, and L was on board ship almost every day. I do not suppose there was a day they were there that I did not see Sampson and Potter and Maris. You know courts of inquiry in the Navy are like courts-martial in the Army. The officers are sworn, and they do not tell anybody what the findings are.

By Senator Frye
Q. From what you have observed and heard there, have you any doubt as to the explosion of the Maine having been from the outside?
-A. I am satisfied it was from the outside. I cabled to the State Department a few days alter the board assembled that it was almost certain that the explosion took place from the outside. I got that from some of the divers and from Ensign Powelson, and people I happened to meet and talk to about it. I had some little drawings of the ship. A moment ago you started to say something about a telegram from Admiral Manterola to Consul General Lee. It was a telegram to the Spanish commission in London to hurry up the electric cables.
Q. What I want to know is, whether that was before or after the explosion?
-A. I had that telegram. I want to see if I can get the exact date of it. That statement about the Admiral is in my testimony before the board of inquiry. I thought I had a copy of that. I do not remember the date exactly, it was prior to the explosion of the Maine.
Q. About how long prior?
-A. A very short while. You can find that telegram in my testimony before the board ; and I think it is right to say that that testimony about the admiral telegraphing to London, and this dispatch 1 have just given out here from Weyler to Santos Guzmán, were not sent to Congress and were not published, because I sent a telegram requesting the State Department not to do it, as I was afraid the Spanish papers there would republish it and they would probably kill the man that gave it to me, so to protect him I did not want that known at the time. I can get the exact date of it, however.
Q. It is not material.
-A. They have the exact date of it at the State Department.
Senator Gray. You gave it in your testimony before the board?
-A. Yes, sir.

By Senator Clark

Q. But that is not printed. It was withheld at the General's request.

-A. At my request. I ought to state, in justice to the State Department, that I telegraphed the State Department asking them not to have the telegram published, or this one about Weyler, because I was afraid of getting my informant into trouble.

Q. We can get that at the State Department, and I guess we had better do it.

By Senator Morgan

Q. How long, or about how long, after the explosion was it that General Blanco called at your quarters that night?

-A. Before he called at my quarters?

Q. Yes.

-A. You are not referring to my statement that I called at his palace the night of the explosion?

Q. Probably I am.

-A. That was the night of the explosion.

Q. Was that before you went down to the wharf?

-A. The palace is between my hotel and the harbor, and on my way to the harbor I stopped at the palace, about ten or fifteen minutes after the explosion—as soon as I could get down there in a carriage. I called by to see General Blanco.

Q. After you had heard the explosion how long was it before you reached the water's edge?

-A. Ten minutes afterwards I was in the palace, and I spent about five or ten minutes talking to General Blanco. He gave me an order to the admiral to give me one of the admiral's boats to take me right out into the harbor.

By Senator Morgan

Q. When you got down to the water's edge did you see any electric lights burning?

-A. I did not notice that, but I have made inquiries since, and I have ascertained that no electric lights went out. I sent for electric-light men and gas men. Some gas jets went out in one or two places, caused by the shock or something, but I could not ascertain from these men that a single electric light went out.

Q. Captain Sigsbee, in his testimony before the committee, said he was told, shortly after the explosion, by Admiral Manterola that the electric lights in Havana went out simultaneously with the explosion.

By Senator Foraker

-A. In the vicinity of the harbor.

Q. In the vicinity of the harbor. Mr. Laine, who has been before the committee, and who made a very good impression upon us—it corresponds with what you say of him—says he was in the park opposite, or near the *Hotel Inglaterra*, looking toward the water with another correspondent, and that immediately upon the explosion they took a cab and drove to the water front, about

500 yards away, and when he got there he did notice that the electric light on a tall pole at the gate as he went in and smaller ones at the water front to the number of a dozen or more were out.

-A. I did not notice that at all, but I called up the two electric-light men. One of them is a good friend of mine, Carbonel, and then he sent for the person who has charge of the electric lights in Havana, and I had a talk with him. He came to my office. He said he had not heard of any such thing. I said, "I want to know with certainty." He said, "I will go all around and make inquiries, if you please." He was gone but an hour or two in a cab, and came back and said that with the exception of one electric light at a place called Jesus del Monte, right near the harbor, and one other place he mentioned, one place not very far from the harbor, where he thought perhaps the lights might have gone out by the shock, no other electric lights went out.

Senator Morgan. Could you feel the jar of the explosion at the hotel!

-A. No, sir; I was in my room at the hotel.

Q. I wish to ask one more question in regard to the Maine, and then I shall be through, so far as that is concerned. Have you heard since the explosion of the Maine any expression by Spanish officers in relation to it, indicating their pleasure at the fact?

-A. I heard, two or three days afterwards, from various persons who came in, that there was a good deal of rejoicing among some of the officers. Every report I always got said they were drinking champagne, quite a thing to do in honor of the event, and in different portions of the city officers were making merry. I attributed it to the fact that what they considered almost an enemy's battle ship had been blown up, and it was that much in their favor.

By Senator Morgan

Q. Before the explosion, had you heard any threats of or allusions to the destruction of the Maine?

-A. No, sir.

Q. General, did you hear anything of an attempt on the Montgomery?

-A. I heard that there was something of that sort one evening, but I believe upon investigation it was found that it did not amount to anything.

Q. I have asked all I desire to ask about the Maine.

By the Chairman.

Q. Does any member of the committee wish to ask any questions?

By Senator Foraker

Q. You think that no novice could have destroyed the Maine.

-A. Oh, no, sir. The man who did that work was an officer thoroughly acquainted with explosives of all sorts and who knew all

about it. It was very well done.
Q. A man who had expert knowledge, necessarily?
-A. Yes, sir.

By Senator Clark

Q. And who must have had knowledge of the location of the torpedo?
-A. Yes. I never have been certain that the submarine mine was placed there prior to the entrance of the Maine into the harbor. It might have been done afterwards. The Maine was anchored to a buoy by some little chain. A vessel swinging around that way sometimes gets at various places all around the circle. When she would swing off that way, with the bow next to the buoy, and these boats plying about the harbor all the time, anybody could go pretty well in front of her on a dark night and drop one of these submarine mines of 500 pounds. They have fingers, as it were, and as the boat goes around it would touch the finger, which makes contact and explodes the mine. That might have been done after the Maine got in there.
Q. And not be discovered?
-A. Yes, sir; one or two men rowing quietly in a boat could drop it off the stern of the boat on a dark night, though Sigsbee had his patrols out—I do not know what they call them on men of war; sentinels. Still, it might not have been discovered. A boat would not have been noticed, because boats go there always.
Q. Day and night?
-A. Yes, sir ; to a late hour of the night. The harbor is full of these little boats. A mine weighs about 500 pounds, and I suppose it would take two or three men—one man to row and probably three or' four to handle the mine.
Q. Containing 500 pounds of gun cotton ?
-A. And the casing.
Q. And the casing, which weighs something more.

By Senator Gray

Q. What is the population of Havana?
-A. About 250,000.
Q. Of what is that composed, so far as nationality and nativity are concerned?
-A. I suppose about equal parts of Cubans and Spaniards, now. I suppose one-fourth of the population, possibly, are negroes.
Q. Is the Spanish proportion especially hostile to this country ?
-A. No, sir; I do not think they are now. They were. But the Spanish portion are principally the merchants, commission merchants, shopkeepers, and all this agitation is affecting very much their business. A great many of them, whilst they give expression to great loyalty, are really annexationists, because they think it is the only way out of the trouble, and they would much prefer annexation to the United States to a Cuban republic, fearing that discriminations would be made against them in some way, and would rather trust to the United States than to the Cubans.

Q. How as to the Cuban part of the population?
-A. They are generally all for free Cuba.
Q. What is the condition of the reconcentrados out in the country?
-A. Just as bad as in General Weyler's day. It has been relieved a good deal by supplies sent from the United States, but that has ceased now.

By the Chairman

Q. How about the Spaniards?
-A. General Blanco published a proclamation rescinding General Weyler's Bando, as they call it there, but it has had no practical effect, for in the first place these people have no place to which to go; the houses have been burned down; there is nothing but the bare land there, and it takes them two months before they can raise the first crop. In the next place, they are afraid to go out from the lines of the towns, because the roving bands of Spanish guerrillas, as they are called, would kill them. So they stick right in at the edges of towns just like they did.

By Senator Cullom

Q. With nothing to eat?
-A. Nothing in the world, except what they can get from charity; and I am afraid now they are in a dreadful condition, because all they had was the American relief, and that is stopped, you know. The Spanish have nothing to give.
Q. General, what does this cessation of hostilities spoken of in the last few days amount to?
-A. Nothing; practically nothing—the armistice, you mean?
Q. Yes; so called.
-A. It amounts to nothing.
Q. Do you know the conditions of it?
-A. I saw General Blanco's proclamation, which said the Queen Regent, at the request of his holiness, the Pope, had issued an armistice; but that is not worth the paper it is written on, because a truce or armistice between two contending forces requires the consent of both before it can be of any practical effect, and it will not have the consent of the insurgents.
Q. What offer did he make to the insurgents?
-A. This occurred just about the time I left, and I do not know. I suppose he just relies upon that proclamation. He says the various Spanish officers in different parts of the island will see that it goes into effect.
Q. Why do you say, General, that it will not receive any attention from the insurgent forces?
-A. Because every attempt so far to make terms or to make peace or to buy the insurgents or their leaders has met with signal failure; and whatever may be said about old General Gómez, he is, in my humble opinion, fighting that war in the only way it can be done—scattering his troops out—because to concentrate would be to starve, having no commissary train and no way to get supplies. They come in sometimes for the purpose of making

Images top to bottom:
Officers and Spanish troops in Cuba in June, 1897.

some little raid, where he thinks it will do something; but he has given orders, so I have always been informed, not to fight, not to become engaged, not to lose their cartridges; and sometimes when he gets into a fight each man is ordered not to fire more than two cartridges. When General Weyler was there he went out after him sometimes, and they would move up a column and fire, and sometimes the flank of the column, and the Spanish soldiers would deploy and throw out skirmishers, and the Cubans, like Indians, would go into the woods, valleys, and mountain sides, and scatter out, and wait until the Spanish troops were gone. Then the Spanish troops would countermarch and go back to town, 3 men killed and 10 or 12 wounded.

Q. You think the insurgents would not accept any such terms?
-A. No, sir; I do not think it would be safe for any Spanish officer to go out under a flag of truce. They could not buy the insurgents. Every time they went out to buy them they killed them.

Q. How much provisions have they in store for the army? How long can they maintain their forces there without bringing in more provisions?
-A. Senator, they are living there almost from hand to mouth.

Q. Who?
-A. The Spaniards, and the citizens in the town of Havana also. I made some inquiries on that point just before I left. They have a good many barrels of flour and a good deal of rice and some potatoes, but not a great many, and a little lard; but everything that the town of Havana has received in the last four or five or six months has been from the United States by steamers from New York, New Orleans, and Tampa.

Q. Can they get no subsistence from the island?
-A. Nothing more than from this floor [indicating].

Q. That is what I supposed.
-A. The way the insurgents do is this : They have little patches of sweet potatoes—everything grows there very abundantly in a short time—and Irish potatoes and fruits. They drive their pigs and cattle into the valleys and hillsides, and they use those and scatter out. That is the reason why they all scatter out. A great many are planting. The insurgents plant crops in many parts of the island. Speaking about an armistice, they have not been interfered with much since General Blanco came there. With the exception of the campaign of General Pando in the eastern part of the island, there have been very few military operations inaugurated by the Spanish. So it has been practically a sort of a truce for some time—the insurgents because they did not want to fight and because it was against orders to fight, and the Spanish soldiers.

Q. Suppose Havana was blockaded, so that no provisions could come in, the people there would have no way to get any?
-A. None whatever. The town would surrender in a short while.

Q. What percentage of the population of the island is Cuban?
-A. About one million five or six hundred thousand people. About one-third of those are negroes. Take off 500,000 and that

will leave 1,000,000 the Cubans being out of that 1,000,000 all except about 300,000.
Q. About 70 per cent?
-A. Yes; I think all but about 300,000.
Q. Are all the Cubans friendly to the insurgents?
-A. I never saw one who was not.
Q. They are all friendly to them?
-A. Yes.
Q. What kind of men are the Cubans in the city? What character of men are they?
-A. There are some very good ones there and some are very trifling. It is like almost every population. The wealthier classes and the best educated and all those have generally left the island. They left nearly three years ago, when the war broke out. They are in London and Paris and many of them are in New York. I understand that 40,000 of them are in the United States.
Q. I wish to ask you, if you please, about the people we have been feeding in Cuba, on your requisition, from the Treasury of the United States. About how much of the appropriation of US$50,000 have you expended?
-A. Forty-five thousand dollars. There is US$5,000 left.
Q. Who got the benefit of it?
-A. American citizens.
Q. Do you mean native or adopted?
-A. Native American citizens and naturalized citizens.
Senator Morgan. Were they in Havana chiefly or in the country?
-A. All over the whole island.
Q. Was it a matter of actual necessity to feed them, or was it just a matter of kindness?
-A. They were practically in the condition of all the other inhabitants of the island. They have had very little if any business to work at. There were not a great many sugar plantations in operation nor tobacco places and that kind, and they were suffering like everybody else. This money was applied for the relief of Americans, and then afterwards they got up a general relief for everybody, for the reconcentrados, as they call them.
Q. Did the Spanish army get any of the supplies sent from the United States?
-A. No, sir; occasionally they might have gotten a little here and there.
Q. We noticed that in one of your reports (I think it was a report made to you by a consul; I cannot refer to it from memory at this moment of time) a statement was made to the effect that the people all through those settlements were not permitted to go outside of the line of concentration back to their homes.
-A. Yes, sir.
Q. That was the fact?
-A. Yes, sir; they have only recently been permitted to do so by a proclamation of General Blanco.

Q. How recently?
-A. Not quite three weeks ago.

By the Chairman

Q. Has General Blanco begun to relieve the reconcentrados, as has been said ?
-A. Very little, indeed. They distributed some down there when the matter was first agitated, but it was a drop in the bucket.
Q. How long ago was that?
-A. That was possibly eight or ten months ago, when they were first considering the relief of those reconcentrados.
Q. What is the condition of the Spanish soldiers there in the island ?
-A. Very bad.
Q. As to clothing and subsistence, how are they?
-A. They are badly clothed and very badly fed; not well organized; not drilled. Nobody ever saw Spanish soldiers drill.
Q. If Spain has really appropriated $600,000 for the sustenance of the reconcentrados, as it is stated, do you believe that that will be given to those people, and that their own soldiers will be left to starve?
-A. Oh, no. There will be very little of it paid to anybody.

By Senator Foraker

Q. What will become of it?
-A. They will divide it up here and there—a piece taken off here and a piece taken off there. I do not believe they have appropriated anything of the kind. I see those things on paper always.
Q. You would have no confidence in it and would not advise us to have any confidence in it?
-A. Not a particle.
Q. Let me ask you, if you please, as to those persons whom you have been supplying with subsistence there from the Treasury of the United States. Now that you have come from the island, what provision is made for their support?
-A. Well, a great many of those, Senator, have departed from the island, but still there are a few scattered about here and there. There is no provision at all for them any more than there is for the reconcentrados.
Q. So they will be passed in among the starving classes unless they are relieved ?
-A. Yes. If the US $5,000 had been used before we came away, they would have that now; but they will just have to take their chances with the reconcentrados of what is there of food from the American relief fund.
Q. If it is our duty to feed those people there in Cuba, I suppose we shall have to be active about it in order to give them relief?
-A. Yes ; they are suffering and starving there now every day. The Spanish cannot feed them.
Q. Now that you and the other consuls have come away from the island, who would have charge of the distribution of food down there ?

The press in Spain in 1898 lamented the removal of Weyler from Cuba and refused to concede Spain had anything to do with the blowing of the Maine

Old American newspaper called "**The Call**" covering the blowing up of the USS Maine shortly before the Spanish-American War. Notice the propaganda-type sub-headlines, *"Four Hundred and Twenty of Uncle Sam's Brave Boys Are Killed"* and *"One of the Most Awful Disasters That Have Ever Overtaken the American Navy and Spain is Open to Suspicion"*. They are evidently propaganda to gain public approval for the war.

-A. I thought perhaps Miss Clara Barton would, because she came back there; but, very much to my surprise, she turned around and came out the same day we did, bringing every Red Cross. We had a warehouse from this fund that was contributed by the people of the United States, and I saw the warehouseman, a man named Edwell, that I had put there, on the boat. I asked him what he did about the warehouse. He said he just shut it up; that there was not a great deal left in it, and that he gave the key to the person who owned the property.

Q. Did Miss Barton give any reason for leaving?

-A. She thought there was going to be war and she had better get out. She told me coming back that the Red Cross policy was to go behind the guns and not in front of them.

Q. What, in your judgment, is the possibility of Spain conquering the insurgents and restoring peace to the island?

-A. I do not think there is the slightest possibility of their doing it at all in any way.

Q. Provided they do not starve them all to death?

-A. The same condition of things existed when Mr. Cleveland asked me to go down there last June a year ago. I gave him a report three weeks after I got there in which I told him there was no chance in my opinion of the Spaniards ever suppressing that insurrection nor was there any chance of the insurrectionists expelling the Spanish soldiers from the island. That report is in the State Department somewhere to-day, and if I had to write it over I would not dot an "i" or cross a "t," although I have been there nearly two years since then.

Q. Let me call your attention in this connection to a letter written by you to the State Department on the 13th of December last. If you have no objection, I should like to have it go into the record.

-A. I have no objection at all. It is on the same line I have been talking upon.

The letter referred to read as follows:

United States Consulate-General,
Havana, December 13, 1897.

Hon. William E. Day,
Assistant Secretary of State, Washington, DC.

Sir: I have the honor to make the following report:

First. In my opinion there is no possibility of Spain terminating the war here by arms.

Second. Or by autonomy —real or pretended.

Third. Or by purchasing the insurrection leaders, as recently attempted.

Fourth. Or, as far as I can see, in any other way.

Fifth. The contest for and against autonomy is most unequal. For it, there are five or six of the head officers at the palace, and

twenty or thirty other persons here in the city, who, it is said, desire to hold the offices to be created under autonomous forms; at least, such is my information. Against it, first, are the insurgents, with or without arms, and the Cuban non-combatants. Second, the great mass of the Spaniards, bearing or nonbearing arms, the latter desiring, if there must be a change, annexation to the United States. Indeed, there is the greatest apathy concerning autonomy in any form. No one asks what it will be, or when, or how it will come. I do not see how it could be even put into operation by force, because as long as the insurgents decline to accept it, so long, the Spanish authorities say, the war must continue. I am compelled to say, therefore, that in my opinion autonomy does not now, if it ever did, exist as a factor in the solution of the Cuban problem. I am obliged to say, too, that in spite of published manifestoes the government of this island has not been able to relieve from starvation the Cuban population driven from their homes by the Weyler edict, and no longer attempts to do so. I am, sir, your obedient servant,
FITZHUGH LEE,
Consul-General.

Q. I wish to call your attention to the enclosure in your dispatch of November 27, 1897. In your letter you say: One of two gentlemen who visited the reconcentrados after they were concentrated in Las Fosas, or the ditches in this city, handed me to-day the enclosed paper. The names of the two gentlemen are not signed to it for obvious reasons. I do not care about the names; I suppose they are of no value to us; but do you know the gentlemen? I
-A. Oh, yes; they are very reliable. I did not give the names because I thought perhaps if the document was published, or something of the kind, as the Spanish papers repeat everything, these men would be possibly arrested.
Q. Have you any reason to doubt the entire accuracy of that statement?
-A. No, sir; it is correct, in my opinion.
Q. General, what is your opinion of the insurgent government?
-A. I have never thought that the insurgents had anything except the skeleton form of a government—a movable capital. I asked them one day why they did not have some permanent capital, and I think they gave a very good reason. They said it would require a large force to protect it and defend it, and they could not afford to mass up their men there; that the capital and the government offices had to move where they could be safest.
Q. Do you know any of the officials connected with their civil government?

-A. No, sir.
Q. You do not know President Masó or Vice-President Capote or the cabinet?
-A. I never had any communication with the insurgents in any way, shape, or form while on the island, except when, to save Colonel Jeruiz's life, I wrote a letter to Aranguren, the insurgent chief.
Q. What is, approximately, the armed force of the insurgents?
-A. I suppose, if you could get them all up and mass them, they would number probably 31,000 or 32,000. The number has been up probably as high as 36,000 or 37,000.
Q. Are they well or decently armed?
-A. They are well armed.
Q. Have they much ammunition on hand?
-A. The ammunition varies. I think now and then a filibustering expedition gets in some way and resupplies them, but I do not think they have a great deal. I presume that must be so, because, as I told you, Gómez issued an order not to fire more than two-cartridges.
Q. What is the force of cavalry?
-A. They had at one time nearly one-third, but they have not so many now. The horses died; it has been hard to get horse feed, and so on ; and they dismounted a great many of them.

Senator Foraker.
Q. How many Spanish soldiers are in the island now?
-A. Capable of making a fight, possibly 55,000 or 56,000.
Q. And they are rather inadequately disciplined and drilled?
-A. Oh, yes; not drilled, not organized.
Q. Not officered well ?
-A. No.
Q. Are they now conducting any offensive military operations at all?
-A. No, sir; they have been going through some form with General Pando, down on the eastern division of the island, at Santiago de Cuba, but I think that has all stopped now. The last information was that Gómez was getting around to flank Pando, and there were some fears entertained for his safety.
Q. It is practically only an army of occupation?
-A. That is about it, sir.
Q. Are the Spaniards confined to the fortified cities?
-A. Yes.
Q. All are confined to the cities?
-A. They do not try to occupy the country.
Q. Not outside the cities?
-A. No, sir; and generally the seaports. They do not want, to get outside of any seaports. The seaports on the southern coast and the northern part are occupied by the Spanish troops and some of the larger towns in the interior. In the rest are the insurgents.

Some of the most important names mentioned in the hearings of the *US Senate Committee on Foreign Relations* in the years during the **Hispano-Cuban-American war of 1895-1898**.

Top to bottom, clockwise:
Vicente Manterola, Rear-Admiral of the Spanish Navy, Head of the *Apostadero* in Havana; **Clara Barton**, founder of the Red Cross volunteering in Cuba; **US Senator George Gray**, Democrat, Princeton and Harvard alumnus; **Rear Admiral Charles D. Sigsbee,** Captain of the US Maine; **US Senator William Pierce Frye**, Republican, prominent and eloquent debater; **Mrs. Eva Canel**, aka Eva Infanzón, popular writer and journalist from Asturias who was very influential with public opinion when she settled in Cuba.
On the right:
US Senator Joseph B. Foraker, Republican, Cornell alumnus, Civil War veteran, famous for his long speeches in Congress.

Q. The insurgents have the rest all around?
-A. Oh, yes; you can go from Havana 4 or 5 miles any day and get to the insurgents.
Q. To what extent do the insurgents control the eastern part — Puerto Principe and Santiago de Cuba?
-A. Nearly the entire portion of both provinces.
Q. What is the population of those two provinces?
-A. I do not know what it is as compared to the others.
Q. Puerto Principe has a population of about 60,000.
-A. Santiago de Cuba is the largest in the island, I suppose. It has always been considered that there were not many Spanish troops there.
Q. The insurgents practically have control?
-A. So when General Weyler published his proclamation stating that the four western provinces were pacified, Gómez published a counter proclamation and said that the eastern provinces were not pacified.
Q. Gómez seems to be a man of a great deal of ability?
-A. Yes; he commenced to fight the war in that way and never has varied, but has gone right on in a straight line. They cannot get him off of it. He goes out a little way, moves in a circle, and comes back to the place where he started.

US troops and Cuban troops under Máximo Gómez fighting together in 1898.

Q. There are probably 300,000 Spaniards in the island population?
-A. I saw it stated the other day at 280,000, and I have seen it stated at 360,000.
Q. Are all the Spaniards hostile to the Cubans?
-A. As a general thing they are.
Q. The Spaniards are hostile to the insurgent government, and the Cubans are friendly to it, I suppose?
-A. Yes, sir.
Q. The line runs about that way?
-A. Yes, sir.
Q. You said a while ago that you were not sure whether this mine was planted before or after the Maine went there. Was there any place about Havana where private persons could have bought this mine and from which they could have taken it and placed it?
-A. No, sir.
Q. Have you any doubt but that it was put there by the Government?
-A. I do not think it was put there by the Government. I think probably it was the act of four or five subordinate officers.
Q. Spanish officers?
-A. Spanish officers, who had knowledge of the location and probably were experts, and had that branch of the service to look after. I do not think General Blanco gave any order about it.
Q. What number of Spanish troops are on the island now, as you estimate the number?
-A. I suppose probably 97,000 or 98,000. There are some 37,000 there in hospitals, and about 50,000, probably 55,000, capable of bearing arms. A Spanish steamer goes back to Spain once every ten days, and they have taken off in the last year 500 or 800 or 900 and sometimes 1,000 Spanish soldiers three times a month. If they averaged only 700 on a steamer, in a month they would take off 2,100.
Q. What was the largest number they ever had there?
-A. They claimed about 210,000 to 237,000 have been sent over.
Q. Is that shown from the official records?
-A. Yes, sir.
Q. When does the rainy season commence?
-A. It commences about the middle of June or the latter part.
Q. What effect would that have upon the Spaniards and the Cubans?
-A. The Spaniards do not conduct any operations at all during the rainy season. The Cubans are acclimated and get along better.
Q. Have any of the reconcentrados been put to work on public works, as has been intimated in the press?
-A. No, sir; there are no public works, and there is no money to pay for them.
Q. Could an American army of occupation go into Cuba with safety now?

-A. Yes, sir.
Q. I mean on account of climate, and so on.
-A. On account of climate and on account of everything else.
Q. Is the Spanish army paid up to date, or is it in arrears?
-A. When I left they informed me that the troops had not been paid for nine months, and the officers for about four.
Q. What has become of Miguel Viondi, who defended Sanguily?
-A. He has been released. He was taken over and kept in one of those African prisons for a long time, but immediately after General Blanco came back he was released. They said they released a great many of those prisoners because they found difficulty in feeding them.
Q. Do you regard that General Blanco was lacking in courtesy to you on your leaving the Island?
-A. General Blanco and I always got along very well together. We were quite friends. I went into the palace the morning I left as a matter of official etiquette, to bid good-bye. I went with the British consul-general. I saw Dr. Congosto, the secretary to the General. I told Dr. Congosto that I had received instructions to leave the island and go to the United States, and I called to pay my final respects and would like to see General Blanco. He asked me to sit down and said he would go and let him know. He went off and stayed about fifteen minutes and came back and said the General said please excuse him ; he was not well and was lying down. I told Dr. Congosto then to say good-bye to him and turned around and left.
Q. Were there any demonstrations of ill will toward you as you left?
-A. When we were coming out on the steamer Saturday evening there was some hallooing, catcalling, and whistling, and some Spanish expressions, *"Mean cowards, running away,"* and so on. I think that was confined to the lower order of men, however.

By the Chairman.
General, we are very much obliged to you. Thanks.

The bust of **Miguel F. Viondi**, outstanding lawyer and scholar, Cuban patriot, defender of Sanguily, deported to Spain for his sympathies with the insurgents, very close friend of José Martí. Viondi has been forgotten by the marxist regime in Cuba and his bust, placed in a park in Guanabacoa in 1923, is heavily damaged because of lack of maintenance and total neglect.

After the deposition of Mr. Fitzhugh Lee to the US Senate Committee on Foreign Relations, several Senators expressed their interest in having copies of all correspondence and minutes of meetings of Mr. Lee with Spanish and Cuban leaders. A request was submitted to Mr. Lee on April 12, 1898, at the end of Mr. Lee's deposition.

> **REQUEST TO HON. FITZHUGH LEE, US Consul in Havana**
> **April 12, 1898.**
>
> **Asked by Senator Frye and others**
> *Committee on Foreign Relations of the US Senate*
>
> **Honorable Fitzhugh Lee**, continued to be duly sworn.
>
> **By Senator Frye**
>
> Q. General, Would it be possible to have copies of all your contacts, by telegram, written communiqués and other official means, as well as transcripts of all your conversations with Spanish and Cuban leaders, starting on February 1st, 1898 to the present date?
>
> -A. Yes, sir.
>
> Q. Will you please send such communications, transcripts and memoranda to the *US Senate Committee on Foreign Relations,* as well as to the *US Department of State?*
>
> -A. Of course, Sir.
>
> Senator Frye: Thanks Mr. Lee.

What follows is a faithful reproduction of all communiqués sent to US Senate Committee on Foreign Relations and to the US Department of State by Mr. Fitzhugh Lee, US Consul to Havana, as well as relevant communications in the opposite direction.

> **[TRANSLATION]**
> **Señor Gullón to Mr. Woodfordd.**
> *Ministry of State,*
> *The Palace,* February 1, 1898
>
> Your Excellency and Dear Sir:
>
> In your Excellency's kind and well-weighed note dated December 20 last, to which I now have the honor to reply, there

are, many and very diverse statements, causing great and special gratification to H. M.'s Government, remarkable for their clearness and expressiveness. Among them the following deserve special mention:

- Those recognizing the value and efficacy of the new principles applied to the colonial policy;
- those admitting the importance and conclusiveness of the information received at Washington from the peninsula and Cuba, tending to prove the sincerity of Spain's desire and exertions for the improvement of conditions and circumstances in that island;
- and the explicit terms in which your Excellency is pleased to say that the prosperity of the cities and the country there is being prompted by the renewal, under the best auspices, of the suspended agricultural and industrial operations.

The satisfaction, however, derived from these, and other similar statements, giving eloquent expression to the recognition of the irreproachable procedures of Spain, is, to a great extent, destroyed or diminished by the blame cast upon the predecessors of the present Government, and still more so by the fact that the numerous and incredible excesses committed by the Cuban insurgents are confounded in the same category, with the conduct of the Spanish regular army, which for nearly three years has been giving proof of its valor and discipline in the defense of indisputable rights and in the obedient fulfillment of orders and plans emanating from other departments. Whatever may be the political views of the men constituting the present Government of Spain, they cannot, without protest, permit your severe condemnation passed upon those who preceded them in power.

As regards the conduct of our army, the note of August 25, 1897, must have made it evident to the candid judgment of the Washington Cabinet that the Spanish troops have never given occasion for reproaches, tarnishing, either in a greater or less degree, the brilliant splendor of their history, and that if any acts, judged from a distance and separately, have given rise to complaints and lamentations on the part of some sensitive and humanitarian spirits, they have proved, when investigated subsequently with proper coolness, to have been the inevitable consequence of war and a comparatively well-restricted object lesson of the calamities and disasters which have always accompanied war in all ages and in all countries, not excepting the United States, as was shown by references of strict historical accuracy in the document to which I have just alluded.

The Spanish Government assuredly does not admit that reasons of proximity or damages caused by war to neighboring countries might give such countries a right to limit to a longer or shorter period the duration of a struggle disastrous to all, but much more so to the nations in whose midst it breaks out or is maintained, as your Excellency voluntarily admits.

If such a limitation of the legitimate and immutable national sovereignty could not be permitted at any time, it must be expected less than ever when a fortunate concurrence of circumstances has enabled the present cabinet of Madrid, while voluntarily fulfilling its engagements and carrying out, when in power, the colonial policy which it advocated when in opposition, to execute the wishes of the loyal inhabitants of Cuba, and to comply with those suggestions which the United States Government has offered repeatedly and officially as the expression of its desire or as its advice as a friend.

The remarkable consideration with which H. M.'s Government constantly entertains the views and doctrines of the United States Government does not suffice to induce it to accept, now or at any future period, the theory which Y. E. is pleased to propound with regard to international duties in the case of intestine rebellions, in repetition of the views expressed years ago by the illustrious Secretary of State, Mr. Fish. The Spanish Government cannot consent to attach so little weight to international friendship as to render that relation between nations almost entirely destitute of mutual obligations, the duties which it imposes being regarded, in every case, as very inferior to those which are derived from neutrality.

Nor could H. M.'s Government refer to the duties of neutrality, as it maintains with the same vigor as ever its well-founded assertion that there is no reason, nor even a semblance of reason, to justify a recognition of belligerency in the Cuban insurrection.

We cannot, however, notice with indifference, that there continues to be acting in New York an organization composed chiefly of naturalized North Americans who, notwithstanding, do not wish to imbibe the spirit of their recently acquired nationality nor the atmosphere of honor and friendship in which their Government breathes; who violate the laws of their new country and abuse the liberty granted them there by conspiring against the country in which they were born, thereby creating a state of hostility which disturbs the intimate and cordial relations which have so long been maintained between Spain and the United States.

It is impossible to see in the noble work of peace which has been nobly and generously undertaken in Cuba, as your Excellency very truly remarks, a sudden creation which can arise in a single night; it must be regarded as a lasting and noble structure, which, to use your Excellency's eloquent words, would be founded upon the rock of justice, not upon the moving sands of self-interest, and which, for its more rapid development, requires the cooperation of friends and the most scrupulous respect of foreigners.

I avail myself, etc.,
PIO GULLON
Minister of State of Spain

Mr. Woodford to the President.
[No. 35.] LEGATION OF THE UNITED STATES
Madrid, February 26, 1898.

Dear Mr. President:

I had an interview yesterday with Messrs. Gullón and Moret at Mr. Gullón's house. It was then arranged that the Ruiz case should be adjusted, without further official correspondence and in friendly manner, between Mr. Polo de Bernabé, the new Spanish minister, and Judge Day at Washington. The minister leaves tonight via Gibraltar and should reach Washington by March 1st.

This arrangement is what Judge Day suggested might be desirable before I left Washington, and is according to the instruction of the State Department No. [125], dated February 8. I have telegraphed Secretary Sherman. As the suggested commercial treaties and the Ruiz matter will be settled at Washington, I think that I have now secured the practical adjustment of every important matter that has been committed to me up to date.

Autonomy cannot go backward. It must go forward and its results must be worked out in Cuba. There is the storm center. The four essentially important things about yesterday's interview with Messrs. Gullón and Moret are these:

I. They have now decided to work in harmony together and Mr. Gullón will help Mr. Moret actively in the matter of the commercial treaties.

II. I had good opportunity to press on them, as I had already urged upon the Queen, my belief that the Cubans got most of their supplies from points outside the United States. They admitted that our patrol of our coasts is now very efficient and that recent supplies had gone from Belgium, Jamaica, etc.

III. As hitherto reported, they cannot go further in open concessions to us without being overthrown by their own people here in Spain. This is what made it difficult to get prompt and satisfactory settlement of the De Lôme matter, and induced them to accept his resignation before permitting me to have an interview. I got Judge Day's telegram on the morning of the 10th, and within an hour had this telegram translated and was in telephonic communication with Gullón's office. He would not see me until the afternoon. The Council of Ministers (which is usually held late in the afternoon) was called at 11 o'clock this morning, and he did not see me until 4 in the afternoon. It is evident that they heard from De Lôme on the 9th.

IV. They want peace if they can keep peace and save the dynasty. They prefer the chances of war, with the certain loss of Cuba, to the overthrow of the dynasty. They know that we want peace if we can get such justice for Cuba and such protection of American interests as will make peace permanent and prevent this old Cuban question from continual resurrection. I told them positively that I regarded the Spanish note of February 1 as a serious mistake; that I should advise all possible delay in answering it; and that whether our answer should be pleasant or disagreeable must depend entirely on practical results in Cuba.

While I do not think that they can make any more direct concessions to us and retain their power here, I do begin to see possible ways by which they can make further concessions to Cuba through the insular Cuban government and so, possibly, avert war.

Faithfully yours,

STEWARD L. WOODFORD.
Minister Plenipotentiary to Spain.

Excmo. Sr. D. PÍO GULLÓN E IGLESIAS.

On the left: **Pío Gullón Iglesias,** was a lawyer, journalist and Spanish politician, Minister of the Interior during the reign of Alfonso XII and Minister of State during the regency of María Cristina de Habsburgo-Lorraine and during the reign of Alfonso XIII.

On the right: **Stewart Lyndon Woodford**, was an American attorney and politician who served as a member of the United States House of Representatives and Lieutenant Governor of New York. In June 1897, President William McKinley appointed Woodford to the post of *Envoy Extraordinary and Minister Plenipotentiary to Spain.*

From Mr. Woodford to Mr. Sherman.
[No. 161.] *Legation of the United States,*
February 28, 1898.

Sir: I have the honor to report that yesterday I telegraphed you in cipher as follows:

Madrid, February 27, 1898. Decree dissolving the Spanish Cortes was signed February 20. New Cortes will meet April 25. — WOODFORD.

The practical effect of this delay in dissolving the old Cortes and assembling the new one on April 25 will be that the rainy season will have arrived in Cuba before the new Cortes gets fairly at work. With the beginning of the rainy season effective movements by the Spanish regular forces in Cuba will be impossible. The Spanish Government will probably base argument on the then condition of military movements as reason for further delay.

Very respectfully, yours,
STEWART L. WOODFORD.

[Confidential.]
Mr. Sherman to Mr. Woodford.
[No. 147.] *Department of State,*
Washington, March 1, 1898.

Sir: The President's message to Congress at the opening of the present session very fully set forth the information possessed by this Government touching the situation in Cuba, both as to its actual condition and its future prospects, and presented as much in detail as was possible under the circumstances the views and policy of this Government in regard thereto.

I review the present situation briefly for your confidential information, solely to aid you in appreciating any statements which may be made to you and in shaping your own discreet course.

First, as to the condition of the war in Cuba. The testimony which reaches me is concurrent as to the absence of any substantial success of the Spanish arms. Meanwhile the insurgent forces continue to control a large part of the eastern region while making demonstrations and forays in the westward parts without substantial check. The recent expedition of General Blanco to the central district appears to have been barren of military results. On the whole, inaction rather than activity has marked the last three months' conduct of the war.

Second. Two months have now elapsed since the installation at Habana of the autonomist government of Cuba. More than two months have now passed since the substitution of Marshal Blanco for General Weyler and the adoption of a modified rule of conduct in the prosecution of hostilities against the Cuban 'insurgents. I am as yet unable to discern the, favorable advances which were gladly anticipated from the changed order of things.

Thirdly, as for the effect of the offer of autonomy upon the insurgents in the held, it must be confessed that no hopeful result has so tar followed. Beyond a few isolated submissions of insurgent chiefs and their following no disposition appears on the part of the leaders of the rebellion to accept autonomy as a solution. On the other hand, the hostility of the Spanish element in Cuba to this or any form of autonomy is apparent, so that the inaugurated [sic] reform stands between the two adverse fires of hostile opposition in the field and insidious malevolence in the very centers of government.

Fourthly, the condition of the island in its financial and productive aspects has not changed for the better. It is rather, if anything, worse. The endeavors of the representatives of the peninsular authority and the domestic autonomist government to relieve the destitution and distress which prevail have been abortive. The policy of concentrating the rural population in and around the garrisoned towns, while leaving their fields and homes to decay and destruction, has worked its inevitable result. The distressing situation of the reconcentrados has appealed very strongly to the generous heart of the American people, and under the initiative of the President every effort has been made to organize and apply systematic relief through private donations here and distribution by the available channels in Cuba. However generously our countrymen have responded to this appeal, their efforts can relieve but a very small portion of the suffering, and that only within the narrow limits of the larger towns and their immediate surroundings. The work of relief is being earnestly pressed, but it is painfully insufficient to meet the situation.

I append for your further information copy of a careful and valuable report made to the Secretary of the Navy by Commander G. A. Converse, commanding the V. S. S. Montgomery, which recently visited the port of Matanzas, in which is recited the situation in that province. This instruction, as I said before, is written for your confidential information and it is not expected that you will communicate any of its statements to the Spanish authorities, but you will bear these facts in mind in your intercourse with them.

Respectfully, yours,
JOHN SHERMAN.

> (**Enclosure No. 1**, from Navy Department. February 24, 1898, with accompaniment.)
>
> P. S. I also append, for your further information, copy of a report from the commander of the Maine, Capt. C. D. Sigsbee, which has just been received.
>
> (**Enclosure No. 2**, from Navy Department, February 2(3, 1898, with accompaniment.)

Cuba's wealth destroyed, abandoned or damaged during the War of 1895 (I)

The processing of coffee stopped; an idle dry dock in the port of Havana; very difficult transfer of coffee production to the markets.

Images, top to bottom:
A group of **reconcentrados** in the city of Matanzas;
A **barracón** (warehouse type building made of thatch to gather reconcentrados in the outskirts of Matanzas;
On the left: Secretary of State **John Sherman**;
On the right: Captain **G.A.Converse** Chief Officer of the USS Montgomery.

[Enclosure No.1 in [No. 147.]
The Secretary of the Navy to the Secretary of State.
Navy Department,
Washington, February 24, 1898.

Sir: 1 have the honor to transmit, for your information, a copy of a report from the commanding officer of the U. S. S. Montgomery from Matanzas, concerning the condition of the population of that province.

Very respectfully,
JOHN D. LONG,
Secretary.

[Subenclosure.]
Commander Converse to the Secretary of the Navy.
U. S. S. Montgomery, At Sea, Lot. 22° 8& A'., Long. 78° & W.

February 26, 1898.

Sir: Complying with the instructions contained in the Department's telegram of the 3d instant I have caused as thorough an investigation as time and circumstances would permit to be made of the condition of the people of the province of Matanzas, with the view of ascertaining the nature and extent of the destitution at present prevailing, and respectfully report as follows:

1. The total population of the province of Matanzas in December, 1897, was estimated to be 253,616. From statistics gathered from the best authorities (official and semiofficial) the total number of deaths in the province due to starvation and the diseases incident thereto have been 59,000. The number of people in the province now in a starving condition is estimated at 98,000, and this number is rapidly increasing.

2. The present population of the city of Matanzas is variously estimated to lie from 50,000 to 60,000 (including the reconcentrados). In the city of Matanzas there have been between 11,000 and 12,000 deaths. Reports from the cemetery show that at the present time the daily death rate averages 46.

3. Within the city limits there are at present about 14,000 people absolutely without food and clothing. Of these 11,000 live in the streets of the city and are wholly without homes or shelter. The remaining 3,000 live in three small villages, located on three hills, just beyond the built-up portion of the city.

4. The distress is no longer confined to the original reconcentrados (the laboring country people, most of whom have already perished), but has now extended to the better classes, who before the war were in moderately comfortable circumstances. Those now begging in the streets are, for a large part, well-to-do people or their children,

5. The citizens of Matanzas have established three places where

they issue rations. The ration usually consists of cooked rice and fish, which is served in tin pans, each pan containing a spoon. The filled pans are regularly arranged for distribution among the limited number (100) who have previously been admitted to the waiting room.

6. The only other public relief is that given to poor, sick children by the management of the emergency hospital, which is under the direction of the volunteer fire department of the city.

7. The Spanish authorities have rendered some assistance to the starving, and on two occasions gave $1,000 toward the relief fund. This was but a small amount, but it is said to have been all that the Government could give.

8. The United States consul has rations sufficient to last about two weeks, when the fund appropriated by Congress will have become exhausted, and then the sufferers will include many American citizens who have hitherto received relief from the consulate.

9. As far as could be ascertained, Matanzas needs a supply of food for 40,000 people for at least one month. Condensed milk for children and invalids, and quinine, sulphate of magnesia, nitrate of potash, and other medicines are desirable. The people in the streets are in urgent need of clothing, as many of them are entirely destitute and others only partially covered with filthy rags.

10. The urgent necessity of immediate relief and assistance cannot be exaggerated. Whenever the officers of the Montgomery landed they were constantly followed by clamoring crowds of starving men.

11. The foregoing information has been derived from my interviews with the civil officers of the province and city; from the United States consul, Mr. Brice; from the United States vice-consul, Mr. Brinkerhoff; from Mr. Dubois, manager of the Matanzas and Havana Railroad, and from Lieutenant-Commander Beehler, of this vessel, who personally visited the small villages in which the reconcentrados are quartered, the parts of the city most frequented by them, and the various places provided for furnishing the relief.

Very respectfully,
G. A. CONVERSE,
Commander, United States Navy

[Enclosure 2 in No. 147.]
The Secretary of the Navy to the Secretary of State.
Navy Department.
Washington, February 26, 1898.
Sir: I have the honor to transmit herewith, for the information of the Department of State a copy of a letter, dated the

8th instant, received in this Department from the commanding officer of the U. S. S. Maine, at Habana, Cuba, in regard to the suffering among many of the inhabitants of the island of Cuba, resulting from conditions of poverty and destitution.
Very respectfully,
JOHN D. LONG,
Secretary.

[Subenclosure.]
Captain Sigsbee to Secretary of the Navy.
U. S. S. Maine (1st Rate)

Habana, Cuba, February 8, 1898.
Sir: I have the honor to make the following report, in conformity with the Department's telegram of February 4, 1898. The telegram reads: *"Report by mail the condition of the people, being particular about destitution."*

1. Doubtless the Department is aware that my information has been derived from the opinions of others rather than from my own observations. Nevertheless my efforts while in Habana have been confined almost wholly to the cultivation of good relations with the people, both Spanish and Cubans, and to the investigation of conditions on the island from different points of view.

2. As to existing conditions, I have found that the disagreement between Spaniards and Cubans is surprisingly small. Variance of opinion appears to be chiefly in regard to causes.

3. The Spanish view concedes great poverty and destitution, but with blame to the insurgents for beginning the war, persisting in its prosecution, and for preventing initially the grinding of the cane.

4. While in the act of dictating the foregoing, I received a visit from a leading Spanish manufacturer of Habana, who has been in the island forty years, and who is really Spanish in his sympathies. He was accompanied by a very intelligent Swiss, who speaks English very well and has been on the island nine and one-half years and is intensely pro-Spanish. I propounded a series of questions to these gentlemen, and they answered me very frankly.

5. The Swiss stated that 500,000 people, or one-third of the population, had died in Cuba since the beginning of the present insurrection. I then asked specifically if the Spanish manufacturer held the same view. The manufacturer, without qualification, replied that he did, but he also claimed that the deaths were due to a condition of war brought on without sufficient grounds by the insurgents, and that the insurgents were, therefore, primarily responsible.

Cuba's wealth destroyed, abandoned or damaged during the War of 1895 (II)

A ruined sugar industry; the mining industry idle; the railroads blocked; the almost impossible transfer of tobacco products to the markets.

6. I asked these two gentlemen if they did not include in their estimate those Cubans who had emigrated. Both replied that they did not. The Cuban assertions as to the number of reconcentrados who have starved varies from 200,000 to 400,000. The lowest figures given to me by anybody, Spanish or Cuban, is 200,000.

7. I conversed today with an American from Boston, who has been in Cuba for six weeks for the purpose of purchasing tobacco lands in Santa Clara province. He has traversed the route between Habana and Santa Clara five times. He has even gone beyond Santa Clara, which is 2(50 miles from Habana. He has been arrested several times by both Spaniards and Cubans. lie presented me with a table showing in one column the number of reconcentrados collected at various towns and in another column the number of them that have died.

8. Since they were not obtained at first hand, and since, according to his statement, General Lee has compiled statistics from the same places, I do not include his table.

9. In one place he followed on horseback a cart in its rounds to pick up the dead. He saw ten dead put in the cart. He states that the revocation of the Weyler edict has but little beneficent effect in its application, because reconcentrados are not now permitted to go outside the *"limited zones of cultivation"* encircling the towns without permits from the authorities, and the permits are limited to a number of days. He stated that nearly all of the suffering people arc Cubans (white people), principally women and children; that the negroes appear to be able to resist the hardships of the period far better than the whites.

10. The deplorable work begun by the insurgents was continued by General Weyler and advanced by him beyond the bounds of recognized warfare and the common sentiment of humanity.

11. The next consideration is the increase of pay given to the Spanish officers in the field in Cuba. They receive two and a half times the pay given them when serving in Spain. This would make it to the advantage of officers to adopt lingering methods of warfare, human nature being weak.

12. The storekeeping class throughout the island is almost wholly Spanish. So are the workmen in the industrial trades. The Cubans, as a people, live directly from the soil. They have lost their homes through destruction by one side or another in this strife. They have sacrificed every possession that could be converted into money whereby to provide food.

13. Autonomy appears to be truly acceptable only to Spaniards who have raised families in Cuba and whose lives and business are linked with the island. The insurgents demand in dependence, and the Spaniards who are in Cuba to make money, and in the expectation of returning to Spain, are irreconcilably in favor of the old order of things. The Spaniards believe themselves to be the superior people. It is not improbable, therefore, that as a last resort Spain would consent to sell the island to the United States, as affording the best prospect for the Spanish people in the island. It is more than probable that the educated class of Cubans would readily fall in with such a policy.

14. The question of annexation has never been seriously presented to the American people, but should it come up, it could be a strong argument to Spain to point out that she could retire with honor in her present financial condition, by assuring to Spaniards in Cuba the benefit of good government with the United States. This argument would not have prevailed a short time ago, but matters are now approaching a crisis in Cuba. This is one question that no one can answer with any certainty. What will follow the failure of autonomy? Beyond asserting that there will be a change of ministry in Spain, no one will pretend to give an answer.

Very respectfully,
C. D. SIGSBEE
Captain, US Navy, Commander USS. Maine.

Mr. Woodford to the President.
[Nos. 36, 37.] *Legation of the United States*

Madrid, March 2, 1898.

Dear Mr. President: Yesterday morning I received a note from Minister Moret, asking interview at my residence that afternoon. He came at 2 o'clock and remained about one hour and a half. At the beginning of our talk he handed me memorandum in his own hand, and then discussed the same, paragraph by paragraph. He came with the knowledge of Senor Sagasta, president of the council, and I think I am justified in assuming that he came with the knowledge of the Queen.

The first matter discussed was that of the alleged landing from the *USS Brooklyn* at San Domingo of Captain *Brownsfield*, of the American Navy. There is no such officer on our Navy list, and I fancy that he meant Captain *Crowninshield*, but I did not indicate this to Señor Moret. He said that the information had come to him as minister of the colonies; that it had been communicated to President Sagasta; but that if it were true that young Garcia was with the American naval officer and on an American war ship it might be a serious matter, and for the present he was leaving the foreign office to learn about it through the usual official channels.

As to the matter of dismissing or sending away newspaper correspondents from Habana and by the action of General Blanco or of the insular government. Minister Moret [endeavored] to get some expression of opinion as to whether my Government would take such action pleasantly and without remonstrance.

Then came the most serious part of our conversation. He asked me to tell him what I knew and thought of General Lee. I replied that I only knew the General slightly, having simply met him on two or three public occasions at New York; that Lee was a graduate of West Point; that he was cousin to Robert E. Lee, who commanded the Confederate forces during our civil war; that he had attained very great distinction as a cavalry officer during the rebellion; that at the close of the war, being ineligible for reappointment to the national army, he had entered political life and been elected governor of Virginia; that he had been a close personal friend of President Cleveland. I added that I believed General Lee had your confidence and that this seemed to me clear from the fact that you had retained him as Consul General, although Lee is a Democrat and you a Republican.

Mr. Moret then said that he thought General Lee disliked Weyler, and I at once rejoined that no American would be satisfied with General Weyler's methods in Cuba, and that if Weyler had not been recalled I should have advised the prompt breaking off diplomatic relations between Spain and the United States, and that, sincere friend as I am of peace, I should have preferred war to the continuance of Weyler's command and methods.

He then insisted that autonomy is making real and effective progress; that it is winning the business classes, the planters, and all the great middle class to its support, and that it will surely succeed if it can have the sympathy of the American Consul General at Habana and the friendship of the United States. Moret believes that General Lee's home and legation are the centers of sympathy for the insurrection. He also said that the present ministry wanted to dissolve the present Cortes in January so as to convene the new Cortes one month sooner, and in March, but that the delay had been due to the request of the insular government, which required the additional month to get the new regime into working order. The new Cortes meets on April 25. The rainy season begins about May 1. Effective military operations will be practically impossible between May 1 and October 1. Last evening I telegraphed you in cipher and translate such dispatch as follows:

Madrid, March 1, 1S98.
President McKinley, Washington:
My Number 36. **Confidential**.

I have just received the following in an informal and unofficial interview, and I communicate it for your personal information as indicating possible line of conduct the Spanish Government may be forced to take.

I quote verbatim:

«A filibuster expedition commanded by Lacret with Morales as second, intended to land at Puerto Rico, was sighted off San Domingo about the 18th of February when several American men-of-war were visiting the island. From one of these ships, the USS Brooklyn, landed at San Domingo Captain Brownsfield, of the American Navy, with a mission for the Dominican Government. With him landed also son of Calixto García, who stayed there and communicated with several filibusters. The USS Brooklyn started away, but Captain Brownsfield remained and embarked afterwards in the USS Montgomery, and with him, in all probability, the son of Garcia too.»

Some of my other observations are as follows:

- Foreign correspondents at Habana, who are a very disreputable set, are doing all they can to raise a war scare between America and Spain, spreading no end of lies and succeeding in exciting a bad feeling.
- In order to attain peace the best would be to send away some of those correspondents.
- The last, but not the least, cause of danger is the behavior of Consul Lee.
- Spain cannot consider him a reliable man, and is entitled to say that his reports are misleading and untrustworthy.
- Consul Lee freely admits that he is corresponding with the insurgents and openly avows that he is deadly against autonomy.
- The insular government distrusts him as well, and is much inclined to solicit his recall.

Memorandum stops here. Spanish minister of foreign affairs ignorant of interview, which was asked by minister for the colonies with knowledge of the President of the Council. Full report by next mail.

Faithfully yours,
STEWART L. WOODFORD.

Segismundo Moret. In 1897 as Minister for Overseas Colonies (*Ultramar*) he decreed the autonomy for **Cuba** in a vain attempt to avoid their secession. He opposed the **war with the United States in 1898**

Mr. Day to Mr. Woodford.
[Telegram.]
US Department of State

Washington, March 2, 1898. (Received March 3.)

President directs me to say, in answer to your telegram of the. 2d instant, Captain Crowninshield visited San Domingo on business entirely disassociated with Cuban affairs. Did not see Garcia or any filibustering expedition. Report has no foundation in fact. The President will not consider any proposal to withdraw General Lee. Even a suggestion of his recall at this time would be most unfortunate from every point of view. Our information and belief is that throughout this crisis General Lee has borne himself with great ability, prudence, and fairness.

DAY.

Mr. Woodford to the President.
[Nos. 38, 39.] *Legation of the United States*
Madrid, March 4, 1898.

Dear Mr. President: Yesterday afternoon I received Judge Day's cipher telegram answering my telegram No. 36 in my correspondence with you. This afternoon I have seen Minister Moret at his house, and have shown him Judge Day's dispatch. Moret is sincerely grateful for the prompt and satisfactory explanation of the Crowninshield incident at San Domingo, and admits that the Spanish naval officer who made the report must be mistaken. This closes the San Domingo incident.

Moret accepts your judgment with regard to Consul-General Lee, and I am sure that no suggestion will be made by the Spanish Government looking toward the recall of General Lee.

I have just telegraphed Judge Day in cipher as follows:

Madrid, March 4, 1898.
Assistant Secretary Day, Washington:

Personal No. 38, Presidential series.

Have shown your dispatch of 3d instant to minister for the colonies. He is entirely satisfied with explanation of the San Domingo incident and grateful for prompt reply. There will be no suggestion of recall of Consul General of the United States at Habana. The minister fully appreciates the situation.

Minister Moret admits that the De Lôme letter was stolen from the Habana post-office by a Spanish clerk employed in that office and who was a spy in the service of the insurgents.

There is nothing further of importance to-day, and, I am.
Faithfully yours,
STEWART L. WOODFORD.

Arent Schuyler Crowninshield (March 14, 1843 – May 27, 1908) was a Rear Admiral of the United States Navy. He saw combat during the Civil War, and after the war held high commands both afloat and ashore. Promoted to captain on 21 July 1894, he was the first Captain and took command of the new battleship *Maine* at her commissioning in 1895. During the 1898 Spanish–American War, had a large part in the United States Naval operations planning.

Images, top to bottom, left to right:
Captain Crowninshield receiving the US Secretary of State aboard the Maine; ***Carlos García Velez***, son of Calixto García Íñiguez in his third wedding. Brigadier of the Cuban Liberator Army, Studied at the Dental School in the Faculty of Medicine of San Carlos, Madrid. Served as Diplomatic representative of Cuba in several countries after the end of the war; Captain **Crowninshield**, in a photo taken when he was promoted to captain in 1894.

As the telegraph equipment in Washington was hectic with a stream of communications from Fitzhugh Lee, the Spanish government was franticly debating how to extricate Spain from a situation in Cuba that was worsening from day to day.

After hours of meetings and consultations by Prime Minister Práxedes Mateo Sagasta with Regent Queen María Cristina, Minister of State Pio Guillón Iglesias, and Juan Manuel Sánchez, Duke of Almodovar del Río, the top decision makers of the Kingdom decided to have a secret meeting at the *Royal Palace of La Granja de San Ildefonso*, known simply as *La Granja,* in the small town of San Ildefonso, located in the hills near Segovia and 80 kilometers (50 mi) north of Madrid, within the Province of Segovia in central Spain.[7]

In preparation for this meeting, the Minister of State asked Ramón Blanco, the Captain General of Cuba, and William Pinkerton, son and heir of Allan Pinkerton, founder of the famous international detective agency, to provide the basic documentation necessary to formulate a cohesive policy of Spain in regard to the US interference and the Cuban situation.[8]

At the meeting in *La Granja*, Sagasta made a meticulous review of Cuba's standing as a colony, as well as the events and policies that had turned the most loyal colony of the Spanish Empire into a serious political and economic problem.

---

[7] ***La Granja*** was the court's main summer palace, and many royal weddings and burials, state treaties, and political events took place within its walls, mostly covered by frescoes by Giambattista Tiepolo and Francisco Bayeu. The area was a favorite hunting grounds for many Castilian kings, due to its location on the forested northern slopes of the Sierra de Guadarrama.

[8] The Spanish Colonial Government had already hired **Pinkerton** to keep track of Cuban rebels within the US. Unknown to Madrid, at the same time the US government used the agency to make sure that international neutrality laws were not violated by American filibustering expeditions leaving the US for Cuba. During one high profile trial of a crew contracted to move supplies and guns to Cuba, it was revealed that undercover Pinkerton agents had been on board. Because the agency's connection to the Spanish government in Cuba Pinkerton agents were also accused of providing the Spanish government with information about American defense plans, an accusation that William Pinkerton loudly denounced as "grossly malicious and tending to create an unjustifiable prejudice." Once the US declared war with Spain, the federal government contracted Pinkerton to provide intelligence for the US against Spain

In a confidential communiqué to Washington, one of the American intelligence agents having access to the discussions at *La Granja* sent a summary of Sagasta's discourse:

> [Confidential]
> From La Granja to M. Day
>
> March 5, 1898.
>
> Sir: the following words were offered today by Mr. Sagasta to the participants in the La Granja summit:
>
> 1. Cuba is a geopolitical aberration. Lying only 90 miles from the Florida keys, at the entrance to the Gulf of Mexico, it is separated from Spain by a vast expanse of the Atlantic Ocean. Yet Cuba remains a colony of Spain. It is governed from Madrid much as it had been governed since it was first occupied and settled by us in 1511.
>
> 2. After the rest of the Spanish American empire disintegrated, nevertheless, Cuba's colonial government gradually turned more despotic. The members of the planter class and the intellectuals who had initially opposed independence then began to show their dissatisfaction. Some, favoring reform over revolution, opted for demanding self-government within the framework of the empire. Others sought annexation to the United States as a means of gaining political and economic freedom while preserving slavery. Neither movement made any headway. Annexation became impractical after the U.S. Civil War.
>
> 3. Cubans were assured representation in the Cortes and some elective institutions at home. Those promises failed to materialize. Cuban society has evolved gradually toward a more egalitarian pattern of racial relations and political aspirations. At the same time, owing to a great influx of Spanish immigrants, about 709,000 between 1868 and 1894, Cuba's population has undergone a process of intensive Hispanization, particularly noticeable in the principal cities.
>
> 4. Cuba's economy has become even more closely linked with that of the United States than it had been earlier in the century. The tobacco industry has been partially transplanted to the North American south. Due to a sharp drop of sugar prices, the old Cuban "*sugar nobility*," has been unable to mechanize and cut costs; it is now disintegrated and has lost its dominant role in the island's economy and society. This facilitated U.S. penetration of the Cuban economy. Sugar estates and mining interests passed from Spanish and Cuban to U.S. hands, and it was U.S. capital, machinery and technicians that helped to save the sugar mills that remained competitive with European beet sugar. Furthermore, as the dependence of Cuban sugar on the U.S. market increased, the Cuban sugar producers were more and more at the

mercy of the U.S. refiners to whom they sold their raw sugar. Over the last few years nearly 90% of Cuba's exports have gone to the United States, which in turn provided Cuba with 38% of its imports. Over these years Spain took only 6% of Cuba's exports, providing it with just 35% of its imports. Clearly, Spain had ceased to be Cuba's economic metropolis.

5. The current war is still raging in 1898, notwithstanding the 220,285 men sent by us to choke it off. At first the rebels were able to wage a successful campaign and push on from the east to the west, where the sugar heart of the island was located. But then we made the mistake of appointed as Commander-in-Chief General Valeriano Weyler, who regained the initiative with the support of substantial reinforcements. Seeking to starve out the rebels operating in the countryside, he herded the rural population into garrisoned towns, where bad and inadequate food and lack of sanitation brought death to thousands of peasants - some 50,000 in Havana province by some accounts. These extreme measures have failed to crush the insurrection, because the rebels retreated to rural areas in the eastern provinces and from there carried on guerrilla operations. The war has now settled down to one of attrition and destruction. We are unable to defeat the rebels and the rebels lack the resources to drive our troops from the island. No one knew for certain how long it would continue.

6. It is true Cuba has developed a well defined Spanish type of society, but a real national tradition has been in the making in the country for many decades. The loyal merchants, speculators, and government officials have also lost their preeminence, and many Cubans have come to hate and despise everything Spanish, thinking only of the corruption and oppressiveness of the Spanish rule. There are also upper class Cubans, and Spaniards who have settle there, who do not share the independence ideas. These elements see the rebellion against Spain as a racial and social struggle for control of the island; they know that upon the withdrawal of the Spaniards Cuba would sink into anarchy, racial warfare, and perhaps an Hispaniola-like division into two parts, seeking annexation to the United States as a means of preserving their wealth.

7. There are no institutions in Cuba endowed with influence and authority, much less the Catholic Church. Since the bishops of the Cuban Church as well as many priests, have identified themselves with the Spanish side during the war, at war's end the Church will be politically discredited as an institution. By now, it has entirely lost its prestige. In 1898 consequently, there is only one political force still operative on the Cuban scene, and that is the partisans of independence, of whom the most compact and substantial component is the liberating army. If Washington enters the Cuban struggle for independence and eventually destroy the rebel military organization and the institutions the Cubans created, Cuba will become a tabula rasa politically once more.

Events precipitated themselves after the *La Granja* conference. The conventional and courteous exchange of claims, protests and justification became acrid and menacing. Spain got tired of asking US for help preventing insurgent expeditions and weapons from reaching Cuba. The US, with a long history of wishing that Cuba were part of their territory, began to seek the right moment to enter the war. They had three aces in their hands: the incident of the Maine , the De Lôme letter and the persistent human abuses in Cuba, particularly since nothing, or almost nothing, was been done to reverse the reconcentration cruelties.

By May 1st, 1898, the "Message to García" had arrived in a rebel mountain stronghold of Cuba -no one knew where, and General Calixto García had agreed to cooperate with an American intervention.

By May 2, Máximo Gómez had come on board and was ready to meet with Rear Admiral William Sampson of the US Navy.

On May 5, the US Senate passed a bill authorizing McKinley to supply munitions to Cuban rebels, and the Spanish Cortes had voted for additional war credits.

Five days later the US torpedo boat Winslow was facing the port of Cárdenas, waiting for orders to sever undersea cable communications with Havana.

At that point in time both Washington and Madrid had access to each other's same confidential and secret telegraphic messages, whether they were coming from Fitzhugh Lee in Havana, from Ramón Blanco in the *Capitanía General de Cuba*, from US Ambassador to Madrid Stewart Lyndon Woodford, from Spain's Minister for Overseas Segismundo Moret or from US current or former Secretaries of State John Sherman and William R. Day.

The following summary was taken from the archives of US Consul in Havana, Fitzhugh Lee, who was probably the individual with the most complete and uninterrupted torrent of information during the days before the initial steps in the War. There was no doubt that the insurgents and the Spanish government had a similar stockpile of documents.

[Telegram]
From Mr. Woodford to Mr. Sherman
Legation of the United States

Madrid, March, 3, 1898.

Spanish minister for foreign affairs sent for me this afternoon, and, after full and most friendly interview, asked me to send the following dispatch, which I give in his exact words. I expressed no opinion, and did not commit my Government in any manner. Spanish request begins here:

> «*The sending of two war ships for the sole purpose of carrying succor to the necessitous inhabitants of Cuba not only seems superfluous, but affords grounds for fearing that their presence in two different ports of the island, situated at a great distance from one another, and rarely visited by men-of-war, might be interpreted, no doubt against the desire of the Government of the United States, as favorable to their plans by those who strive to thwart the will of the majority of the Cuban people, and so prolong a rebellion which is rapidly being quelled by the political and military measures applied soundly. It would therefore be most desirable that the relief prepared in the United States should be sent to Cuba on board merchant vessels.*»

Spanish request ends here.
WOODFORD

[Telegram]
From Mr. Day to Mr. Woodford
Department of State
Washington, March 4, 1898.

Spanish charge presented here yesterday matter covered in yours 3d. Explained to him that vessels are the Montgomery and Nashville, small cruiser and gunboat. Montgomery has called at Cuban ports recently. At request relief committee these ships will take load of supplies Key West to Matanzas and Sagua next week. This is the most prompt and efficient means of getting supplies to people greatly in need.
DAY.

From Mr. Woodford to Mr. Sherman.
[No. 163.] Legation of the United States,

Madrid, March 1898.

Sir: Yesterday afternoon, March 3, the Spanish Minister of State sent me a note asking me to call at his office. I went, and our conversation was interpreted by Mr. Merry del Val for the Spanish minister, and Mr. Moreno of my office for myself. The Spanish minister first expressed his gratification in believing that the President, like the Queen, and myself, like himself, are all working in the interests of peace. He then expressed his belief that all matters of large account were in the way of satisfactory adjustment, and added that he feared most danger from irritation growing out of small things. He then came to the matter in hand; said that he had learned that supplies were to be sent to the reconcentrados in American ships of war; that such ships would appear in ports seldom visited by men-of-war, and that their presence would certainly be misunderstood and would practically aid the rebellion. He then requested me to ask my Government, as a matter of friendship, not to send such supplies in ships of war.

I answered him that I would send, as a request from the Spanish Government, whatever dispatch he would prepare in English and request me to send as coming from himself. I expressed no opinion as to the merit of his request, and did not commit my Government in any manner. I then withdrew from his room and waited until he and Mr. del Val had prepared a request in Mr. del Val's writing, which the minister handed to me.

Accordingly I telegraphed you last evening as follows:
I have the honor, etc.,
STEWART L. WOODFORD.

Mr. Woodford to Mr. Day.
[No. 166.] *Legation of the United States,*

Madrid, March 6, 1898.

Sir: 1 have the honor to acknowledge the receipt this morning of Department dispatch by telegraph in cipher, which I translate as follows:

Washington, March 4, 1898.

Woodford, Minister, Madrid: Spanish Charge d'Affaires presented here yesterday matter covered in yours fourth. Explained to him that vessels are the Montgomery and Nashville, small cruiser and gunboat. Montgomery has called at Cuban ports recently. At the request (of) relief committee these ships will take load of supplies Key West to Matanzas and Sagua next week.

This is the most prompt and efficient means of getting supplies to people greatly in need.
DAY.

My dispatch to which you refer as dated March 4 was delivered at the telegraph office here in Madrid on Thursday evening, March 3, at about half past 9 o'clock, Madrid time. If Señor du Bosc saw you on March 3, he must have had instructions from Minister Gullón at the same time that Gullón was seeing me and getting me to send his re
quest. I can see no just ground of complaint by the Spanish Government because the United States put war vessels at the disposal of charity to feed starving women and children. The United States is not responsible for the policy of reconcentration, with its horrible results of famine, disease, and wholesale murder. Spain has no just cause of complaint, but should be grateful that our people and Government are doing so much to protect Spanish citizens against the results of Spanish methods of administration and warfare. I appreciate all the difficulties of the present Liberal Government, but I am not sure that it is wisest to be over punctilious with them in these matters of detail in the performance of a great work of humanity and charity. I shall be very careful and very considerate in my conversations and correspondence with the Spanish foreign office, but I am inclined to tell the Spanish minister very courteously, but so that he will not misunderstand me, that our Government and people cannot see old men. women, and children dying with starvation by our very shores and not help them in the most prompt and effective manner.

I have the honor, etc.,
STEWART L. WOODFORD.

Mr. Sherman to Mr. Woodford.
[No. 155.] *Department of State*

Washington, March 7, 1898.

Sir: Referring to the Department's instruction No. 147, of the 1st instant, advising you of the present state of affairs in Cuba, I have to enclose for your further information al old copy of a report from the commanding officer of the U. S. S. Montgomery concerning the condition of the population of Santiago de Cuba.

Respectfully, yours,
JOHN SHERMAN.

[Enclosure.]
From Mr. Long to Mr. Sherman.
Navy Department
Washington, February 28, 1898.

Sir: I have the honor to transmit, for your information, a copy of a report from the commanding officer of the U. S. S. Montgomery concerning the condition of the population of Santiago de Cuba.

Very respectfully,
JOHN D. LONG,
Secretary.

[Subenclosure]
U. S. S. Montgomery, Port Antonio, Jamaica,

February 12, 1898.

Sir: Complying with instructions contained in Department's telegram, I respectfully submit the following report of the condition of the people of the Province of Santiago de Cuba, and of the destitution prevailing.

The Province of Santiago de Cuba contained at the last census 267,511 inhabitants; but since the outbreak of the present revolutionary war there have been no reliable estimates of its population.

Before the war the city of Santiago de Cuba had 56,766 inhabitants. This number has been reduced to about 35,000 by departure of most of the able-bodied men to take part in the war. There have been about 5,000 "reconcentrados" quartered upon the city.

The number of deaths in the city for the past four months were as follows: October, 253; November, 320; December, 424; and in January, 486. During the first week of February the mortality was only one-half of the weekly average in January. This marked decrease is partially attributed to the free distribution of quinine through the United States consulate.

The destitution here is not nearly as great as was found in Matanzas. The actual number of "*reconcentrados*" could not be definitely ascertained; but the best authorities state that there are less than 2,000 at present, and they are not in any great distress.

The two mining companies are in need of labor, and give employment and good wages to all who are able to go to the mines and work; consequently, the destitution of the lowest laboring classes is little greater than normal.

There is, however, considerable destitution among the better classes, especially the lower middle classes, who are too proud to ask relief, or to let their poverty be known.

The health of the city is remarkably good at present, and at this date there is not a single case of yellow fever.

There is but one means of public relief in operation. This is known as the "*Cocino Económico*" and is under the management of a German subject, Mr. Michaelson, of the firm of Schumann & Co.

The "*Cocino Económico*" is supported by the voluntary contributions of the citizens of Santiago. The Spanish Government has not aided the charity as yet, but the autonomy governor, Señor Capriles, has recently promised Mr. Michelson that his government would contribute $1,000 toward the maintenance of the "*Cocino Económico.*"

The management of this charity has been highly successful. Cooked rations of soup, meat, rice, and a loaf of bread, which are estimated to be worth 30 cents, are issued for 5 cents and afford relief to those who most need it. These rations are issued in a large building admirably arranged to feed 1,500 people. All who come pay for these rations with five brass checks which can be bought for 5 cents. In many cases the "*Ladies' Relief Society*" distribute these checks when they visit destitute families.

Those who feed in the "*Cocino*" go to a counter and take their choice of either rice and meat, or soup and vegetables, with one loaf of bread. The portions are served on china plates, which are taken to the tables where the purchasers sit and eat. Many are served at an outer counter, where a ration is put in a pail and carried home.

Wood, coal, and stores of provisions are contributed to sustain this charity, and there does not appear to be an urgent need in this city of further assistance from the United States.

Eighty-nine American citizens are now supplied by the United States consul, who daily expects to receive ample additional supplies.

The foregoing information has been derived from interviews with the civil officials; from the United States consul, Mr. Hyatt, and from Lieutenant-Commander Bechler, of this vessel, who personally visited the "*Cocino Económico*" and investigated matters relating to destitution and means of relief.

Very respectfully,
G. A. CONVERSE,
Commander United States Navy, Commanding.
The Secretary of the Navy.

From Mr. Day to Mr. Woodford.
[Personal and Confidential]
March 3, 1898.

Dear Mr. Woodford: I have your favor of the 21st último, as also your note of the 19th último. I have, furthermore read your personal letters to the President, which have kept him so thoroughly advised of the situation. As to De Lôme, I agree with you that that incident is, fortunately, closed. The publication of the letter created a good deal of feeling among Americans, and but for the fact that it was a private letter, surreptitiously if not criminally obtained, it might have raised considerable difficulty in dealing with it diplomatically. As soon as we learned of its authenticity the first cable was sent to you suggesting the recall of the minister. De Lôme had been advised the day before, and cabled his resignation before the letter was brought to the Department. Your prompt and efficient method of dealing with the matter after its serious import was known, and your firm, dignified action in the interview with the minister, no doubt led to the satisfactory termination of the incident. Everybody that I see seems well pleased with it, and no one wished trouble about a matter of this kind.

If a rupture between the countries must come, it should not be upon any such personal and comparatively unimportant matter. We sent you day before yesterday full instruction covering the Cuban situation, as you will see it is bad enough.

The De Lôme incident, the destruction of the Maine, have added much to the popular feeling upon this subject, although the better sentiment seems to be to await the report of the facts, and to follow the action of the President after the naval board has made its report.

Whatever that report may be, it by no means relieves the situation of its difficulties. The policy of starvation, the failure of Spain to take effective measures to suppress the insurrection, the loss of our commerce, the great expense of patrolling our coast —these things, intensified by the insulting and insincere character of the De Lôme letter, all combine to create a condition that is very grave, and which will require the highest wisdom and greatest prudence on both sides to avoid a crisis. Yesterday came your cipher telegram to the President as to Captain Crowninshield, etc. Captain Crowninshield's mission had nothing whatever to do with Cuba. He was accompanied by his son, and not by young Garcia, disembarked from the Brooklyn, came back to Key West, and thence home by rail, after learning of the destruction of the *Maine*, as he wished to be at his post in the Department. The suggestion of the withdrawal of General Lee meets with no favor with the President. Like yourself, the General has been in the midst of surroundings often unfriendly, and has borne himself with dignity, patriotism, and courage, deserving the support, not the disapproval, of the Administration. As to the objectionable newspapers, their sensational and unfounded reports are the cause of as much embarrassment at home as they can be abroad. The only remedy seems to be the sober sense and judgment of the people. There are many things, my dear General, which cannot be written, but we all appreciate how difficult your position is and with what sagacity and fidelity you have discharged its manifold duties. I wish I could have a full talk with you.

It may be that things will take such shape that the President will conclude to send a special messenger to you with full information, which no amount of writing could make available to you. The President highly appreciates your good work, and often speaks of it in the warmest terms.

I beg to add my personal assurances of confidence and esteem, and remain,
Very sincerely, yours,
WILLIAM K. DAY.

The **La Granja Palace** in Segovia. A view from 1898.

Mr. Woodford to the President.
[No. 41] *Legation of the United States*

Madrid, March 9, 1898.

Dear Mr. President: three issues I would like to comment with you

1. A well known Spanish merchant, gave us a family dinner, at which were present his wife and daughter, my wife, daughter, a number of other Americans, and myself. Towards the end of the meeting he turned quickly and put to me this direct question: «*Has the United States ever set any time limit for the suppression of the rebellion?*»

And I answered in these words:

«*Not to my knowledge. It certainly never has done it through me.*»

He then replied:

«*If you, as the representative of Mr. McKinley in Madrid have any influence with your Government I beg you, not as the American diplomat, but as a man, to urge your Government to finish this rebellion, no matter what your Government is re-*

quired to do, before the rainy season begins. This awful condition of affairs in Cuba cannot continue forever. End it at once - end suddenly- end it within the next few days, for no thoughtful Spaniard can tell how long the conscience and humanity of the Spanish people can be held in check.»

2. This morning the papers announce the unanimous passage by the House of Mr. Cannon's bill putting $50,000,000 at your disposal. It has not excited the Spaniards—it has stunned them. To appropriate fifty millions out of money in the Treasury, without borrowing a cent, demonstrates wealth and power. Even Spain can see this. To put this money without restriction and by unanimous vote absolutely at your disposal demonstrates entire confidence in you by all parties. «The ministry and the press were simply stunned.»

3. The Spanish merchant came in this afternoon; said he had repeated our conversation of yesterday evening (March 8) to Minister Moret, but had not yet seen Sagasta. He insisted: «I fear war. My Government fears war. You will not tell the rebels to lay down their arms and this means war.»

I simply replied: «we also fear for the future of Spain if it goes to war with us.»

He shrugged his shoulders, but made no reply.

This evening an American friend called at my house and told me that Spaniards are beginning to talk freely about the hopelessness of the war; about the certainty of the ultimate loss of Cuba, and are discussing quite openly the advisability of selling Cuba if the United States are still willing to buy. I repeat this for what it is worth.

Faithfully, yours,
Stewart L. Woodford.

Mr. Woodford to the President.
[No. 41] *Legation of the United States*

Madrid, March 9, 1898.

Dear Mr. President: Two issues I would like to comment with you.

1. A well known Spanish merchant, gave us a family dinner, at which were present his wife and daughter, my wife, daughter, a number of other Americans, and myself. Towards the end of the meeting he turned quickly and put to me this direct question:

«Has the United States ever set any time limit for the suppression of the rebellion?»

And I answered in these words:

«Not to my knowledge. It certainly never has done it through me.» He then replied:

«If you, as the representative of Mr. McKinley in Madrid have any influence with your Government I beg you, not as the American diplomat, but as a man, to urge your Government to finish this rebellion, no matter what your Government is required to do. This awful condition of affairs in Cuba cannot continue forever. End it at once -end suddenly- end it today, for no thoughtful Spaniard can tell how long the conscience and humanity of the Spanish people can be held in check.»

2. This morning the papers announce the unanimous passage by the House of Mr. Cannon's bill putting US $50,000,000 at your disposal. It has not excited the Spaniards -it has stunned them. To appropriate fifty millions out of money in the Treasury, without borrowing a cent, demonstrates wealth and power. Even Spain can see this. To put this money without restriction and by unanimous vote absolutely at your disposal demonstrates entire confidence in you by all parties. The ministry and the press were simply stunned.

The Spanish merchant came back this afternoon; said he had repeated our conversation of yesterday evening (March 8) to Minister Moret, but had not yet seen Sagasta. He insisted: *«I fear war. My Government fears war. You will not tell the rebels to lay down their arms and this means war.»*

I simply replied: *«we also fear for the future of Spain if it goes to war with us.»*

He shrugged his shoulders, but made no reply.

This evening an American friend called at my house and told me that Spaniards are beginning to talk freely about the hopelessness of the war; about the certainty of the ultimate loss of Cuba, and are discussing quite openly the advisability of selling Cuba if the United States are still willing to buy. I repeat this for what it is worth.

Faithfully, yours,
STEWART L. WOODFORD.

Mr. Woodford to the President.
[No. 43] *Legation of the United States*

Madrid, March 17, 1898.

Dear Mr. President:

On Saturday, March 12, our friend the Spanish merchant came again; said that he had seen Minister Moret again on the 11th; that, according to Moret, it was clear that autonomy would surely succeed if the United States would openly advise the insurgents to lay down their arms; that if we would not do this the rebellion will continue; that Spain would never sell the island; that her honor is involved, and that autonomy having been granted, Spain would never surrender her sovereignty, except by force. All this has evidently inspired Moret. I heard him with kindness, replied with courtesy, and kept my own counsel.

On the other hand, Señor Sagasta, an experienced statesman, a loyal Spaniard, and a faithful friend of the Queen, waits hoping against hope. I think that he would do anything for peace

Images, top to bottom:
Allan Pinkerton, founder of the Pinkertons in 1850; a picture of **Pinkerton agents** that appeared on March 22, 1898, on Page 2 of the *New York Times* with the headline: *DENIAL BY MR. PINKERTON. Agency's Detectives Not Acting as Spies for Spanish Government*; **William A. Pinkerton**, the man in charge during the War of 1895; Spain's Segismundo Moret on a campaign. He was a inexhaustible politician. During the regency of Maria Cristina de Habsburgo, Minister of State, Minister of Development, again Minister of the Interior and Minister of Overseas Affairs; and finally, during the reign of Alfonso XIII, Minister of the Interior.

Images Top to Bottom:
Joseph Gurney Cannon was a United States politician from Illinois and leader of the Republican Party in 1898;
Práxedes Mariano Mateo Sagasta y Escolar was a Spanish civil engineer and politician who served as Prime Minister on eight occasions between 1870 and 1902—always in charge of the Liberal Party—as part of the **Turno Pacífico**, alternating with the Conservative leader Antonio Cánovas. His photo is shown in his office and with all the members of his Cabinet in 1898. Sagasta's political opponents looked at his decisions as a betrayal of Spain. They blamed him for the country's defeat in the war and the loss of Cuba in the *Treaty of Paris* of 1898.

that Spain would approve and accept. Senor Gullón evidently doubts whether peace can be maintained with the United States. I think that the Queen is disappointed and anxious. Well she may be, for she has struggled with admirable courage and wonderful faith for her son and her dynasty.

Faithfully, yours,
STEWART L. WOODFORD.

Mr. Woodford to the President.
[No. 47] Legation *of the United States*

Madrid, March 17, 1898.

The 15th of March has come and gone and peace is not yet secured. I think that the largest holders of the Spanish debt will soon advise the sale of Cuba to the United States. But Minister Moret has now made a speech in which he has taken very positive ground that autonomy will succeed. His speech is clever and strong. But even he may change. It is possible that you can buy Cuba and that such contingency may soon arise as may make it advisable for me to be authorized to at least discuss the matter with the Queen, or with Moret, if she or he should broach the subject. I believe that Spain, tired out and exhausted, threatened with practical famine, and confronted with the immediate necessity of tremendous outlay, would thank the Queen for her wisdom and courage should she dare to part with Cuba without war, and would sustain her even if she were compelled to change her ministry to secure this result.

Some way must be found by which Spain can part with Cuba without loss of self-respect and with certainty of American control so that we may give protection to loyal Spaniards and natives alike which each must have if peace is to be assured. You can not abandon those who have been true to you. We cannot as a free people permit those to suffer whose worst crime is that they fought to be free. Only one way has yet. occurred to me, and this has not been thought over sufficiently for me to do more than to suggest it tentatively. May I suggest it?

I have advised, respectfully but earnestly, against annexation and against any protectorate, and have worked only for peace. This was the keynote of my interview with the British and other foreign Ambassadors last September and October. I have hoped that autonomy might be successful and might bring peace. It now seems almost certain that autonomy cannot succeed. This means that the present hell of famine and anarchy may continue in Cuba during all the coming summer.

Should autonomy be supported by the great body of the educated and property-holding whites of Cuba, it will probably be strong enough next autumn to prevent effective good government by the insurgents. The native Cubans and the Spanish residents are divided into hostile factions. Corruption in official rule has been for centuries the curse of Cuba. I pray that no conditions may arise under which we shall be responsible for the practical peace and good government of the island unless we have full power of ownership which shall enable us to compel good government. I have at last come to believe that the only certainty of peace is under our flag and that with courage and faith we can minimize the dangers of American occupation and assure the blessings of American constitutional liberty. I am thus, reluctantly, slowly, but entirely a convert to the American ownership and occupation of the island. If we recognize independence, we may turn the island over to a part of its inhabitants against the judgment of many of its most educated and wealthy residents.

I therefore ask your permission to present these ideas should the opportunity ever be offered. Whatever I might do in such contingency would be done tentatively and subject in all things to your constant knowledge and direction. Should your judgment not approve my present request, such knowledge will still be helpful, whatever may be the contingencies of the future.

Faithfully yours,
STEWART L. WOODFORD.

[Enclosure: Words by Minister Moret, March 9, 1898]
(Published in *El Día* of March 11)

Mr. Woodford to the President.
[No. 49] Madrid. March 18, 1898

Dear Mr. President:

At noon I learned that the Council of Ministers had held a long and heated meeting; that the Ministers of War and Navy had advised immediate action by Spain, urging that each day of delay increased our preparation for war and lessened any possible chance of Spanish success: that Moret had argued for peace; that Sagasta had finally and positively declared for peace on any terms at all consistent with Spanish honor; that the peace party had triumphed and that the Ministers of War and Navy had withdrawn their threats of possible resignation.

You know, and I need not further assure you, that in all things I am,
Faithfully, yours,
STEWART L. WOODFORD.

From Stewart L. Woodford to Mr. Day
[No. 193.] *Legation of the United States*

Madrid, March 27, 1898

Assistant Secretary Day, Washington: Telegraphic instructions, signed "Day," dated March 25, received Saturday evening, March 26. Do the words *"full self-government"* mean actual recognition of independence, or is nominal Spanish sovereignty over Cuba still permissible?

Instruct me fully as to what the words "*with reasonable indemnity*" mean and imply.

Under Spanish constitution, ministry cannot recognize independence of Cuba or part with nominal sovereignty over Cuba. Cortes alone can do this and Cortes will not meet until April 25. If I can secure immediate and effective armistice or truce between Spanish troops and insurgents, to take effect on or before April 15, will this be satisfactory?

It is possible that I may induce Spanish ministry to submit the question of an early and honorable peace to the Cuban Congress, which will meet at Havana on May 4, and that Spanish Government will give such Cuban Congress all necessary authority to negotiate and conclude peace, provided such authority shall not dimmish or interfere with the constitutional power vested by the Cuban constitution in the central government. If I can secure these two things with absolute and immediate revocation of concentration order may I negotiate? I believe that an immediate armistice means present and permanent peace. Also I believe that negotiations once open between insurgents and the Cuban government some arrangement will be reached during the summer which the Spanish home Government will approve, and that Cuba will become practically independent or pass from Spanish control. President of Council of Ministers wishes personal interview as to armistice, but I will not see him until after I get your reply to this telegram.

I have, etc.,
STEWART L. WOODFORD.

From Stewart L. Woodford to Mr. Day
[No. 43] *Legation of the United States*

Sir: The President instructs me to say that we do not want Cuba. He also instructs me to say, with equal clearness, that we do wish immediate peace in Cuba. He suggests an immediate armistice, lasting until October 1, negotiations in the meantime being had looking to peace between Spain and the insurgents, through the friendly offices of the President of the United States.

He wishes the immediate revocation of reconcentration order, so as to permit the people to return to their farms, and the needy to lie relieved with provisions and supplies from the United States, the United States cooperating with the Spanish authorities, so as to afford full relief.

I have paused and waited for President Sagasta's reply.

He said that he agreed with you in thinking any discussion of

Officers in the White House receiving telegraph communications during the War of 1895-1898;
two cartoons showing **Uncle Sam** defeating a terrified Spain and young **Alfonso XIII** playing in Cuba while receiving a huge bullet of *retribution* from an American War Ship.

the respective views held by the two nations to be inopportune and useless at such a conference.

He spoke first of the condition of the reconcentrados, calling my attention to the fact that this condition was inherited from the old ministry; then stated that the present government is arranging to furnish employment for such as are able to work, and to supply the necessities of the feeble men and of the women and children. He made no serious objection to the United States assisting in this work of charity, and gave me to understand that this part of your request would be promptly and satisfactorily met.

He then mentioned the loss of the Maine, and expressed his appreciation of the manner in which you had presented the subject to Congress, and added that he believed your method of dealing with this question would enable the two Governments to examine and adjust the matter in some way honorable and fair to both nations.

He then took up the question of the armistice, saying that he is in thorough accord with you in desiring early and honorable peace. He suggested that there are difficulties in the Spanish situation here in the Peninsula which I, as a stranger, could hardly understand, which made it almost impossible for the Spanish Government to offer such an armistice, but that if it were asked by the insurgents it would be at once granted; that the insular congress would meet on May 4, when the insular government could make such a proposition; that only six weeks would intervene before that time, and he hoped that the United States, which had waited so long, would now wait for these few weeks; that the offer of autonomy had been accompanied by firm declaration that Spain would employ military operations in aid of civil reforms; that these operations are now being successfully conducted, and that he hoped that the rebellion would be largely reduced before the Cuban Congress met.

I replied substantially that the sober sense of the American people insisted upon immediate cessation of hostilities; that the recent speech of Senator Proctor, who is one of the most conservative and reliable of our public men, had so convinced American public sentiment that longer prosecution of the war must now be prevented.

I then asked them for an answer to the two suggestions which I had made, and upon their saying that they would give the matter careful consideration, but that they must have full time for deliberation, I told them, with all possible kindness of manner and courtesy of language, that I hoped to have a further interview with them on Thursday afternoon of this week, March 31, when I trusted 1 should receive satisfactory reply to my suggestions.

They reluctantly agreed to meet me on Thursday afternoon at the president's office.

I have, etc.,
STEWART L. WOODFORD.

From Mr. Woodford to Mr. Day.
[Telegram] *Legation of the United States*

Madrid, March 30, 1898.

Dispatch from Mr. Moret which reached me March 28 instant at half past 10 in the evening, and which I translate as follows:
WOODFORD, Minister, Madrid:
Your cable 27 received. Full self-government with indemnity would mean Cuban independence which we will oppose. As to other matters, see Sunday telegram. Very important to have definite agreement for determining peace after armistice if negotiations pending same fail to reach satisfactory conclusions.
MORET.

From Mr. Woodford to the President

Madrid, March 29, 1898.

President McKinley, Washington:
My No. 60. Have had conference this afternoon (Tuesday) with president of the council, the minister for foreign affairs, and minister for colonies. Conference adjourned until Thursday afternoon, March 31. I have sincere belief that arrangements will then be reached honorable to Spain and satisfactory to the United States and just to Cuba. I beg you to withhold all action until you receive my report of such conference, which I will send Thursday night, March 31.
WOODFORD.

From Mr. Woodford to the President.
[Nos. 62, 63.] *Legation of the United States*

Madrid, April 1, 1898.

Dear Mr. President: Yesterday's conference was a sorrow to me, for I have worked hard for peace. Last night I telegraphed you as follows:

Madrid, March 31, 1898.
President McKinley, Washington:
My No. 62. Have just telegraphed to the Department of State my official report of the adjourned conference held this afternoon, Thursday. It has turned, as I feared, on a question of agreements. Spanish pride will not permit the Ministry to propose and offer an armistice, which they really desire, because they know that armistice now means certain wounds next autumn. I am told confidentially that the offer of armistice by the Spanish Government would cause revolution here. Leading generals have been sounded within the last week, and the ministry

have gone as far as they dare go to-day. I believe the ministry are ready to go as far and as fast as they can and still save the dynasty here in Spain. They know that Cuba is lost.

Public opinion in Spain has moved steadily toward peace. No Spanish ministry would have dared to do one month ago what this ministry has proposed to-day.

The Spanish ministers said yesterday that their statement went as far as they could possibly go. Perhaps this is true, but they said the same some weeks ago and yesterday they yielded on two points.

First, they are willing to arbitrate the Maine matter. Some days ago they talked fight if we should even suggest that they were responsible for the loss of the Maine. **Secondly**, they will revoke the *reconcentrado* order, and place a large sum at General Blanco's disposal for the relief of the necessities. It is not long since they denied the very existence of the horrible conditions they now admit.

There is no real war spirit here among the middle and lower classes. Last September most of the people were ready for war. The war spirit has been diminishing steadily and now prevails only among the aristocracy, the political classes, and the generals and officers of the army. The army is still the controlling factor in Spanish politics, and the attitude of the army constitutes the real danger to-day.

Faithfully, yours,
STEWART L. WOODFORD.

From Mr. Polo de Bernabé to Mr. Woodford
[No. 26] *Home-Rule Government of Cuba*

Sir: I am enclosing an important letter from Cuba.

The colonial government of Cuba desires through your Excellency to make known to the President of the United States that although there are some Cubans in arms, there are an immense number who accept home rule, and are resolved to work zealously under this form of government in order to reestablish peace and prosperity in the land. The insurgents form a minority, while the autonomists represent the majority of the Cuban people decided to save the interests of civilization by means of justice and liberty. The Cuban people has a perfect right to govern itself according to its wishes and aspirations, and in no way would it be just for a foreign will to impose upon it a political regime which it seems contrary to its happiness and unsuitable to its needs.

The home-rule government of Cuba hopes that the President of the United States, faithful to the noble traditions of the great North American Republic, will consider and respect the rights of the Cuban people, not permitting violence to prevail. It also hopes that he will contribute by powerful action to the reestablishment of peace in Cuba under the sovereignty of the mother country and with a home-rule government.

The home-rule government of this island, which is a Cuban government, protests energetically against the falsehoods of a part of the American press, published with the malignant intention of firing passions, making it appear that injustice and brutal force reign in Cuba, and that home rule has failed.

There is no good faith in these stories. As was said by the immortal Washington, *"Honesty is the best policy."* The Cuban parliament is about to meet, and both the spirit of America and the principles of right demand respect for the will of the majority of this people.

JOSÉ MARÍA GÁLVEZ,
President of the Home-Rule Government of Cuba.

While begging your Excellency to be so kind as to forward to its high destination the foregoing telegram, which expresses the true facts and the will of the Cuban people as declared through the medium of the president of its government, I seize this opportunity, etc.

LUIS POLO DE BERNABÉ.

From Mr. Sherman to Mr. Woodford.
[Telegram.]
US Department of State

Washington, April 4, 1898.

Congress may very possibly take decisive action middle or end of this week. You should notify the United States Consuls in Spain and cooperate with them in notifying the United States consular officers in Spain who are American citizens to arrange to leave their offices in charge of friendly power, and, if they desire, quietly prepare for departure from Spain upon notice, either special or public, of a rupture of relations.

If rupture comes you had better proceed to Paris and await further instructions.

AN.SHERM

Images, top to bottom:
Anti-American demonstration in Madrid in 1896;
Monument to **Segismundo Moret** at the *Plaza de San Juan de Dios* in Madrid;
Don Luis Polo de Bernabé, Spanish Ambassador to Washington after the resignation of Dupuy de Lôme.

From Mr. Sherman to Mr. Woodford.
[Telegram.]
Department of State

Sir: I have thin evening written Mr. Bowen, the consul-general at Barcelona, informing him that it is possible that diplomatic relations between Spain and the United States may be severed at any time this week, and that he should at once instruct all United States consuls who are American citizens to arrange to leave the records and property of their consulates in the charge of some friendly power and, if they so desire, to quietly make preparations for departure from Spain upon either public or official notice of rupture of relations. I have sent by the same mail a copy of such letter to Julio Harmony, Coruña; Andrew F. Fay, Bilbao; Richard M. Bartleman, Málaga; Franklin C. Bevan, Almería; John Howell Carroll, Cádiz; William W. Wysor, Jerez de la Frontera; and Samuel B. Caldwell, Sevilla. I have asked Mr. Bowen to communicate such further instructions as he may deem advisable to them or to other consular officers of American citizenship whose names 1 may have omitted, and have asked him to notify me at once if I can cooperate with him further.

In case of necessity entrust the legation to the British Embassy.

I am, very respectfully, yours,
SHERMAN.

From Mr. Sherman to Mr. Woodford.
[Telegram.]
Department of State

Washington April 5, 1898.

Should the Queen proclaim her answer to the previous telegram before 12 o'clock noon of Wednesday, April 6, will you sustain the Queen, and can you prevent hostile action by Spain?

Faithfully, yours,
STEWART L. WOODFORD.

Mr. Day to Mr. Woodford.
[Telegram.]
Department of State

Washington, April 5, 1898—12 midnight.

The President highly appreciates the Queen's desire for peace. He cannot assume to influence the action of the American Congress beyond a discharge of his constitutional duty in transmitting the whole matter to them with such recommendation as he deems necessary and expedient.

The repose and welfare of the American people require restoration of peace and stable government in Cuba. If armistice is offered by the Government of Spain the President will communicate that fact to Congress.

The President's message to Congress to-morrow will recount the conditions in Cuba; the injurious effect upon our people; the character and condition of the conflict, and the apparent hopelessness of the strife. He will not advise the recognition of the independence of the insurgents, but will recommend measures looking to the cessation of hostilities, the restoration of peace and stability of government in the island in the interests of humanity, and for the safety and tranquility of our own country.

Tuesday night, 12.

DAY.

From Polo de Bernabé to Mr. Day.
US Department of State

Sir: I am enclosing a summary of a Proclamation by Mr. Blanco, Governor and Captain-General and General in chief of the army in Cuba. He has stated in force the following:

Article 1. From the publication of the present order in the *Gaceta de la Habana*, the reconcentration of the inhabitants of the rural districts is abolished throughout the entire island. ,

Article 2. The protective juntas and all the civil and military authorities shall facilitate by all the means in their reach the return of the rural inhabitants to their former places of residence.

Article 3. Under direction of the Cabinet Council and through the Secretary of Public Works the government of Cuba shall proceed the preparation and immediate establishment of all the public works necessary or useful to give employment and subsistence to the country people and their families.

Article 4. The expenses resulting from the execution of the regulations of the present order may be charged to the extraordinary war credit.

Article 5. All the orders heretofore published upon the reconcentration of the rural population, are hereby abolished.

Habana, March 30, 1898.

POLO DE BERNABÉ

From Mr. Woodford to Mr. Sherman
[No. 207] *Legation of the United States*

Madrid, April 5, 1898.

Sir: Today 1 received a note from the British Charge

d'Affaires, stating that in compliance with my request he telegraphed to his Government on the 3d instant, reporting that I had asked that in the event of my departure becoming necessary Her Majesty's embassy should take charge of American interests and property in Spain, so that they might enjoy the protection of the British flag. He also informs me that Sir Julian Pauncefote, the British ambassador at Washington, has been instructed to inform the United States Government that Her Majesty's Government will willingly undertake the protection of United States interests in Spain if this should, unfortunately, become necessary. Sir Julian Pauncefote has further been informed that it will be necessary, according to usage, to obtain consent of the Spanish Government, and it has been suggested to Sir Julian by Lord Salisbury that the United States Government may think that an application on the subject would at present be premature.

I am, etc.,

STEWART L. WOODFORD.

Joint note of the Powers.
Washington, April 6, 1898.

The undersigned representatives of Germany, Austria-Hungary, France, Great Britain, Italy, and Russia, duly authorized in that behalf, address, in the name of their respective Governments, a pressing appeal to the feelings of humanity and moderation of the President and of the American people in their existing differences with Spain. They earnestly hope that further negotiations will lead to an agreement which, while securing the maintenance of peace, will afford all necessary guaranties for the reestablishment of order in Cuba.

The Powers do not doubt that the humanitarian and purely disinterested character of this representation will be fully recognized and appreciated by the American nation.

JULIAN PAUNCEFOTE,	For Great Britain.
MR. HOLIEN,	For Germany.
JULES CARBON,	For France.
VON HENGELMULLER,	For Austria-Hungary.
DE WOLLANT,	For Russia.
G. C. VINCI,	For Italy.

From Señor Polo de Bernabé to Mr. Sherman.
[Memorandum.—Translation.]
Legation of Spain at Washington

Washington, April 10, 1898.

The minister plenipotentiary of Spain has the honor to state to the honorable Secretary of State of the United States of America that Her Majesty the Queen Regent, inspired by the sentiments of concord and peace which animate her, has given appropriate instructions to the general in chief of the army of Cuba, to the end that he shall concede an immediate suspension of hostilities for such time as he shall deem prudential, in order to prepare and facilitate people, in that island.

General Blanco has to-day published the corresponding bando, and reserves to himself to determine in another bando the duration and other details of its execution, with the sole aim that so transcendental a measure shall lead within the shortest possible time to the desired pacification of Cuba.

The Government of Her Majesty, by this most important step, has set the crown to her extraordinary efforts to obtain the pacification of Cuba through the instrumentalities of reason and of right.

As the island of Cuba is represented in the Cortes of the Kingdom, a privilege which is not enjoyed by any other foreign autonomic colony, the Cuban senators and deputies in the Cortes may there present their aspirations if they desire more.

The minister of Spain trusts that these statements, inspired by the earnest desire for peace and concord which animates the Government of Her Majesty, will be appreciated at their just worth by the Government of the United States.

POLO DE BERNABÉ

Mr. Sherman to Mr. Woodford.
[Telegram]
Department of State

The grounds for an intervention by the United States may be briefly summarized as follows:

First. In the cause of humanity and to put an end to the barbarities, bloodshed, starvation, and horrible miseries now existing there, and which the parties to the conflict are either unable or unwilling to stop or mitigate. It is no answer to say this is all in another country, belonging to another nation, and is therefore none of our business. It is specially our duty, for it is right at our door.

Second. We owe it to our citizens in Cuba to afford them that protection and indemnity for life and property which no government there can or will afford, and to that end to terminate the conditions that deprive them of legal protection.

Third. The right to intervene may be justified by the very serious injury to the commerce, trade, and business of our people, and by the wanton destruction of property and devastation of the island.

Fourth. The present condition of affairs in Cuba is a constant menace to our peace, and entails upon this Government an enormous expense. With such a conflict waged for years in an island so near us and with which our people have such trade and business relations.

John Sherman, from the State of Ohio, Republican, author of the Sherman Antitrust Act in 1890, brother of General William Tecumseh Sherman of Civil War fame, appointed by McKinley as Secretary of State in 1897;
Regent Queen María Cristina de Austria, widow of Alfonso XII of Spain, and her son, the future King Alfonso XIII.

These elements of danger and disorder already pointed out have been strikingly illustrated by a tragic event which has deeply and justly moved the American people. I have already transmitted to Congress the report of the naval court of inquiry on the destruction of the battleship Maine in the harbor of Havana during the night of the 15th of February. The destruction of that noble vessel has filled the national heart with inexpressible horror. Two hundred and fifty-eight brave sailors and marines and two officers of our Navy, reposing in the fancied security of a friendly harbor, have been hurled to death, grief and want brought to their homes, and sorrow to the nation.

When the inability of Spain to deal successfully with the insurrection has become manifest, and it is demonstrated that her sovereignty is extinct in Cuba for all purposes of its rightful existence, and when a hopeless struggle for its reestablishment has degenerated into a strife which means nothing more than the useless sacrifice of human life and the utter destruction of the very subject-matter of the conflict, a situation will be presented in which our obligations to the sovereignty of Spain will be superseded by higher obligations, which we can hardly hesitate to recognize and discharge.

Department of State,
Washington, April 12, 1898.

Mr. Sherman to Mr. Woodford.
[Telegram]
Department of State

Washington, April 17, 1898.

House of Representatives, 324 to 19, passed yesterday afternoon resolution authorizing and directing the President to intervene at once to stop the war in Cuba, with the purpose of securing peace and order there and establishing, by the free action of the people thereof, a stable and independent government of their own, and empowering him to use the land and naval forces to execute that purpose.

Senate Committee on Foreign Affairs reported yesterday resolution declaring that the people of the Island of Cuba are and of right ought to be free and independent, demanding that Spain relinquish authority and government in Cuba and withdraw land and naval forces there from, and empowering the President to use Army and Navy and militia to carry resolution into effect. It was decisively voted to-day. The Senate, Saturday evening, by 67 votes to 21, passed the resolution.

The situation is most critical.

JOHN SHERMAN.

From Mr. Woodford to Mrs. Bowen and Day
Madrid, April 20, 1898.
Bowen, Consul General, Barcelona:
Prepare for withdrawal from Spain. Notify Consuls to be ready to leave at once. If any consul believes himself in immediate danger he is authorized to quietly leave at his discretion.

I have also telegraphed Washington this morning as follows:
Madrid, April 20, 1898.
Day, Assistant Secretary, Washington:
Have received telegram of Tuesday morning. Am prepared to withdraw. Have notified consuls to be ready.
Very respectfully, yours,
STEWART L. WOODFORD.

[Enclosure.]
Mr. Sherman to Mr. Woodford.
[Telegram.]
Department of State

Washington, April 20, 1898

You have been furnished with the text of the Joint Resolution voted by the US Congress on the 19th instant in relation to the pacification of the island of Cuba. In obedience to that act, the President directs you to immediately communicate to the Government of Spain said resolution, with the formal demand of the Government of the United States that the Government of Spain at once relinquish its authority and government in the island of Cuba and Cuban waters. In taking this step the United States hereby disclaims any disposition or intention to exercise sovereignty, jurisdiction, or control over said island except for the pacification thereof, and asserts its determination when that is accomplished to leave the government and control of the island to its people under such free and independent government as they may establish.

If, by the hour of noon on Saturday next, the 23d day of April, instant, there be not communicated to this Government by that of Spain a full and satisfactory response to this demand and resolution, whereby the ends of peace in Cuba shall be assured, the President will proceed without further notice to use the power and authority enjoined and conferred upon him by the said joint resolution to such extent as may to necessary to carry the same into effect.
SHERMAN.

Top Photo:
19 April 1898 - The U.S. Congress enacts a **Joint Resolution** demanding independence for Cuba, and giving President McKinley the authorization to declare war if Spain does not yield. The resolution includes the *Teller Amendment*, which denies the U.S. the right to annex Cuba and makes it official American policy to promote Cuban democracy and independence. **20 April 1898** - U.S. President McKinley signs the congressional joint war

Lower Photo:
Eugene Thiebaut is seen signing the **Peace Protocol** to end the Spanish American War as President William McKinley and ten other men look on.

Señor Polo de Bernabé to Mr. Sherman.
[Translation.]
Legation of Spain at Washington

Washington, April 20, 1898. (Received 11.35 a. m.)

Mr. Secretary: The resolution adopted by the Congress of the United States of America, and approved to-day by the President, is of such a nature that my continuance in Washington becomes impossible and obliges me to request you the delivery of my passports.

The protection of Spanish interests will be entrusted to the French Ambassador and to the Austro-Hungarian Minister. On this occasion, very painful to me, I have, etc.

LUIS POLO DE BERNABÉ.

Mr. Sherman to Señor Polo de Bernabé.
Department of State

Washington, April 20, 1898

Mr. Minister: I have the honor to acknowledge the receipt of your note of this day's date, in which you state that the resolution adopted by the Congress of the United States of America, and to-day approved by the President, is of such a nature as to make your continuance in Washington impossible and constrains you to request that your passports be given you. You add that the protection of Spanish interests is entrusted to the ambassador of France and the minister of Austria-Hungary.

In response to your request I have the honor to hand you a passport for yourself, your family, and your staff. I beg also to inform you that arrangements have been made for a guard to attend you during your presence in the territory of the United States.

Sincerely regretting the step that you have felt constrained to take,

I avail myself, etc.,
JOHN SHERMAN.

From Mr. Woodford to Mr. Sherman
[Telegram]
Legation of the United States,

Madrid, April 21, 1898. (Received 9.02 a. m.)

Early this (Saturday) morning, immediately after the receipt of your open telegram and before I had communicated same to Spanish Government, Spanish Minister for Foreign Affairs notified me that diplomatic relations are broken between the two countries and that all official communication between their respective representatives have ceased. I accordingly asked for safe passport. Turn legation over to British embassy and leave for Paris this afternoon. Have notified consuls.

MR. WOODFORD.

Mr. Woodford to Mr. Sherman.
[Telegram.]
Legation of the United States

Madrid, April 21, 1898.

Following is text of official note received this morning at 7.30 o'clock from Spanish Minister of State:

In compliance with a painful duty, I have the honor to inform your Excellency that, the President having approved a resolution of both Chambers of the United States which, in denying the legitimate sovereignty of Spain and in threatening armed intervention in Cuba, is equivalent to an evident declaration of war, the Government of His Majesty has ordered its Minister in Washington to withdraw without loss of time from the North American territory with all the personnel of the legation.

By this act the diplomatic relations which previously existed between the two countries are broken off, all official communication between their respective representatives ceasing, and I hasten to communicate this to your Excellency in order that on your part you may make such dispositions as seem suitable.

I beg your Excellency to kindly acknowledge the receipt of this note, and

I avail myself, etc.

WOODFORD.

Blockade of Cuban ports.
By the President of the United States or America.
A PROCLAMATION

Whereas, by a joint resolution passed by the Congress and approved April 20, 1898, and communicated to the Government of Spain, it was demanded that said Government at once relinquish its authority and government in the island of Cuba, and withdraw its land and naval forces from Cuba and Cuban waters: and the President of the United States was directed and empowered to use the entire land and naval forces of the United States, and to call into the actual service of the United States the militia of the several States to such extent as might be necessary to carry said resolution into effect; and

Whereas, in carrying into effect said resolution, the President of the United States deems it necessary to set on foot and maintain a blockade of the north coast of Cuba, including all ports on said coast between Cárdenas and Bahía Honda and the port of Cienfuegos on the south coast of Cuba:

Now, therefore, I, William McKinley, President of the United States, in order to enforce the said resolution, do hereby declare and proclaim that the United States of America have instituted and will maintain a blockade of the north coast of Cuba, including ports on said coast between Cárdenas and Bahía Honda and the port of Cienfuegos on the south coast of Cuba, aforesaid, in pursuance of the laws of the United States and the law of nations applicable to such cases. An efficient force will posted so as to prevent the entrance and exit of vessels from the ports aforesaid. Any neutral vessel approaching any of said ports, or attempting to leave the same, without notice or knowledge of the establishment of such blockade, will be duly warned by the commander of the blockading forces, who will indorse on her register the fact, and the date, of such warning, where such endorsement was made; and if the same vessel shall again attempt to enter any blockaded port, she will be captured and sent to the nearest convenient port for such proceedings against her and her cargo as prize, as may be deemed advisable.

Neutral vessels lying in any of said ports at the time of the establishment of such blockade will be allowed thirty days to issue there from.

In witness whereof, I have hereunto set my hand and caused the seal of the United States to be affixed.

Done at the city of Washington, this 22d day of April, A. D. 1898, and of the independence of the United States the one hundred and twenty-second.

[seal] WILLIAM McKINLEY

John Sherman, Secretary of State
Call for Volunteers against Spain

By the President of the United States.
A PROCLAMATION.

Whereas a joint resolution of Congress was approved on the twentieth day of April, 1898, entitled **"Joint Resolution for the recognition of the independence of the people of Cuba,"** demanding that the Government of Spain relinquish its authority and government in the island of Cuba, and to withdraw its land and naval forces from Cuba and Cuban waters.

Whereas, by an act of Congress entitled "An act to provide or temporarily increasing the military establishment of the United States in time of war. and for other purposes," approved April 22, 1898, the President is authorized, in order to raise a volunteer army, to issue his proclamation calling for volunteers to serve in the Army of the United States:

In an age of partisan politics and partisan journalism, *Puck* became the nation's premier journal of graphic humor and political satire of the issues of the day. It was published from 1871 until 1918.
Images above, from top to bottom and left to right:
Uncle Sam teaching Cuba how to construct a government; **Máximo Gómez listening to the American eagle**; the **Regent Queen Maria Cristina trying to control Cuba and the Philippines at the same time**;
Cuba telling uncle Sam *"I came to buy, not to beg..."*

Now, therefore, I, William McKinley, President of the United States, by virtue of the power vested in me by the Constitution and the laws, and deeming sufficient occasion to exist, have thought fit to call forth, and hereby do call forth, volunteers to the aggregate number of 125, 000, in order to carry into effect the purpose of the said resolution; the same to be apportioned, as far as practicable, among the several States and Territories and the District of Columbia, according to population, and to serve for two years, unless sooner discharged.

In witness whereof I have hereunto set my hand and caused the seal of the United States to be affixed.

Done at the city of Washington, this twenty-third day of April, A. D. 1898, and of the independence of the United States the one hundred and twenty-second.

[seal] WILLIAM MCKINLEY

Executive Mansion,
Washington, April 25, 1898.
War with Spain—Maritime Imp.
By the President of the United States of America:
A PROCLAMATION.

Whereas by an act of Congress approved April 25, 1898, it is declared that war exists and that war has existed since the 21st day of April, A. D. 1898, including said day, between the United States of America and the Kingdom of Spain:

I, William McKinley, President of the United States of America, by virtue of the power vested in me by the Constitution and the laws, do hereby declare and proclaim:

1. The neutral flag covers enemy's goods, with the exception of contraband of war.

2. Neutral goods, not contraband of war, are not liable to confiscation under the enemy's flag.

3. Blockades in order to be binding must be effective.

4. Spanish merchant vessels, in any ports or places within the United States, shall be allowed till May 21, 1898, inclusive, for loading their cargoes and departing from such ports or places.

5. Any Spanish merchant vessel which, prior to April 21, 1898, shall have sailed from any foreign port bound for any port or place in the United States, shall be permitted to enter such port or place, and to discharge her cargo, and afterward forthwith to depart without molestation

6. The light of search is to be exercised with strict regard for the rights of neutrals, and the voyages of mail steamers are not to be interfered with except on the clearest grounds of suspicion of a violation of law in respect of contraband or blockade.

In witness whereof I have hereunto set my hand and caused the seal of the United States to be affixed.

Done at the city of Washington, on the twenty-sixth day of April, in the year of our Lord one thousand eight hundred and ninety-eight, and of the Independence of the United States the one hundred and twenty-second.
[seal] WILLIAM McKINLEY.

Blockade - Southern Cuba
By the President of the United States:
A PROCLAMATION.

Whereas for the reasons set forth in my proclamation of April 22, 1898, a blockade of the ports on the northern coast of Cuba, from Cárdenas to Bahía Honda, inclusive, and of the port of Cienfuegos, on the south coast of Cuba, was declared to have been instituted; and

Whereas it has become desirable to extend the blockade to other Spanish ports:

Now, therefore, I, William McKinley, President of the United States, do hereby declare and proclaim that, in addition to the blockade of the ports specified in my proclamation of April 22, 1898, the United States of America has instituted and will maintain an effective blockade of all the ports on the south coast of Cuba, from Cabo Francés to Cabo Cruz, inclusive.

Neutral vessels lying in any of the ports to which the blockade is by the present proclamation extended will be allowed thirty days to issue there from with cargo.

In witness whereof I nave hereunto set my hand and caused the seal of the United States to be affixed.

Done at the city of Washington, this twenty-seventh day of June, A. D. 1898, and of the Independence of the United States the one hundred and twenty-second.
WILLIAM McKINLEY.

Mr. Sherman to Mr. Fitzhugh Lee
[Telegram]
US Department of State

Washington, April 20, 1898.

In compliance with a painful duty, I have to inform you that, the President having approved a resolution of both Chambers of the United States which, in denying the legitimate sovereignty of Spain and in threatening armed intervention in Cuba, is equivalent to an evident Declaration of War, the Government of the United States has ordered its Consul General in Havana to withdraw without loss of time from the territory of Cuba with all the personnel of the legation.

Prepare and execute the withdrawal from Cuba. Notify all Consuls in the island to be ready to leave at once. If any Consul believes himself in immediate danger he is authorized to quietly leave at his discretion.

As previously agreed, in case of necessity, entrust the property, functions and pending matters of the legation to the British Embassy.

I am, very respectfully, yours,
SHERMAN.

Finally, the War started on April 25, 1898. It was an anticipated but frightening prospect.

POSTSCRIPT

The inevitable 1898 Spanish-American War would be, in many ways, unique in history. Rarely had a constitutional monarchy and a republic engaged in an armed conflict of this magnitude. How and why a very weak old and frayed power like Spain would choose to expend its resources by resisting militarily a juvenile and ambitious democracy?

Spain saw in the Autonomists in Cuba a solution for its dilemma: Cuba was dear to Spain because it became the last possession of what one had been a formidable empire. Sending Weyler to Cuba, however, was the worst strategic decision they could have made. Conceiving the notion they could fight a war with the US was an even greater mistake. Spain was a fading imperial power, and of course they wished to maintain its Cuban colony; it knew, however, that the U.S. was a far superior military power. Madrid knew of the economic interdependence between the U.S. and Cuba. They mistakenly thought the US was ready to go to war...

> *«to pursue its economic interests, which were considerable and direct in Cuba...they were acting according to their expansionist, imperialistic interests.»*

They miscalculated the extent to which the American public would support a war. It was a fact that US exporters supported the war to dismantle the colonial preferential tariffs that kept their goods out of Cuba, but a majority of US business interests in the late 1890s did oppose war with Spain over the Cuban issue... Public opinion in the US was not "bellicose." Americans knew Spain to be autocratic rather than democratic. Internally, McKinley and his Republican businessmen were dovish, not wanting to rock the boat of business with an armed conflict. The Democratic minority tried in vain to exacerbate things. It was not until the Maine incident that they succeeded in propelling the country into "*an splendid little war.*" By then, the political defection of some

Republicans to support the Democratic minority's became inevitable. It was a 12 to 1 disadvantage for Spain.

What was about to happen would confirm the words of Richard Olney, Grover Cleveland Secretary of State, in 1896:

> «Today the United States is practically sovereign on this continent, and its fiat is law upon the subjects to which it confines this interposition.»

In contrast with the "**real news**" that Fitzhugh Lee was dealing with during the years 1895 to 1898, the Yellow Press in the US was dealing with the "**fake news**" presented to the public by the likes of Pulitzer and Hearst. It was at those times that both terms became well known to the American public.

Joseph Pulitzer, under the burden of keeping the world informed. On the wall, over the door the motto: "**sensation, sensation, sensation**..."

INDEX

Year
1895, 7, 9, 10, 11, 14, 16, 17, 19, 20, 24, 31, 43, 59, 61, 108, 110, 125, 152, 153, 163, 231, 233, 277, 282
1896, 13, 18, 19, 20, 21, 25, 43, 60, 63, 108, 156, 218, 234, 235, 329
1897, 7, 18, 27, 30, 32, 33, 34, 36, 37, 38, 43, 64, 65, 81, 84, 85, 86, 90, 91, 92, 93, 94, 95, 96, 97, 98, 99, 100, 101, 102, 107, 108, 110, 125, 130, 131, 134, 135, 137, 138, 139, 141, 142, 143, 149, 152, 153, 154, 156, 159, 161, 197, 219, 230, 235, 258, 263, 264, 271, 279
1898, 8, 23, 67, 68, 105, 106, 107, 108, 109, 110, 114, 115, 119, 122, 123, 126, 127, 128, 129, 130, 134, 135, 136, 144, 147, 148, 149, 150, 151, 152, 153, 154, 155, 157, 158, 159, 169, 181, 196, 198, 213, 218, 219, 224, 225, 226, 229, 233, 248, 270, 273, 275, 279, 280, 281, 284, 287, 290, 293, 294, 295, 296, 297, 299, 300, 301, 304, 309, 311, 313, 314, 315, 318, 319, 321, 322, 325, 327
1899, 72, 73, 96
1900, 74, 75, 76, 96
1901, 78, 79

A
Autonomy, 8, 11, 15, 16, 37, 38, 39, 40, 81, 85, 91, 94, 96, 97, 98, 99, 100, 101, 109, 110, 121, 122, 131, 138, 141, 148, 159, 160, 179, 180, 263, 264, 276, 284, 285, 286, 297, 301, 304, 308

B
Bayamo, 11, 12
Bethlehem Steel, 31

C
Calixto García, 15, 17, 72, 106, 137, 138, 139, 153, 286, 292
Cánovas, 34, 35, 37, 39, 66, 92
34, 66, 92
Cárdenas, 128, 169, 170, 171, 173, 292, 323
Colony, 8, 9, 18, 22, 37, 42, 112, 113, 122, 150, 289, 290, 316, 328

D
Diario de la Marina, 15, 90, 100, 105, 106, 107, 109

E
El Siglo, 90
El Zanjón, 8, 9
Eva Canel, 249

F
Filibusters, 90, 91, 286
Fitzhugh Lee, 14, 16, 18, 26, 27, 30, 33, 34, 39, 40, 42, 86, 90, 91, 93, 95, 97, 98, 99, 100, 101, 102, 105, 107, 109, 110, 115, 119, 122, 123, 127, 128, 129, 130, 135, 150, 168, 229, 247, 248, 264, 270, 289, 292, 293, 327
Frederic Remington, 25

G
General Blanco, 14, 85, 86, 91, 92, 94, 100, 120, 122, 134, 137, 141, 150, 154, 155, 157, 165, 249, 250, 254, 257, 259, 260, 261, 268, 269, 275, 285, 310, 316
Guajiros, 22

H
Hearst, 24, 25, 27, 102, 115, 121, 212
Hotel Inglaterra, 39, 90, 106, 214, 219, 222, 254

I
Insurrectos, 27, 90

J
John Quincy Adams, 26
Juragua Iron Company, 31

L
La Discusión, 16, 90, 09
La Gaceta, 100
La Lucha, 42, 90, 91, 97
Library of Congress, 6

M
Maceo, 11, 12, 13, 14, 17, 64, 106
Maine, 16, 42, 67, 125, 126, 128, 163, 164, 165, 168, 181, 187, 190, 192, 194, 195, 196, 197, 198, 201, 202, 205, 206, 208, 209, 211, 213, 216, 218, 221, 222, 223, 226, 229, 248, 250, 251, 253, 255, 256, 268, 277, 281, 284, 292, 298, 308, 310, 318, 329
Manigua, 15, 26
Martí, 2, 19, 93
Martínez Campos, 8, 11, 225, 226, 248, 249
Masó, 11, 139, 154, 245, 265
Matanzas, 2, 10, 14, 30, 94, 105, 115, 131, 132, 134, 135, 136, 171, 172, 173, 214, 276, 279, 280, 293, 294, 296
Mayía Rodríguez, 90, 92

McKinley, 19, 27, 28, 29, 30, 32, 33, 34, 35, 36, 37, 38, 40, 41, 42, 62, 66, 74, 77, 78, 84, 91, 115, 116, 121, 123, 125, 150, 151, 163, 285, 292, 299, 300, 309, 323, 325, 326, 329

Mr. Day, 84, 86, 90, 91, 93, 94, 95, 96, 97, 99, 100, 101, 105, 107, 108, 110, 114, 115, 119, 122, 123, 127, 128, 129, 130, 131, 134, 135, 139, 141, 142, 143, 149, 150, 151, 152, 153, 154, 157, 159, 161, 287, 293, 294, 297, 305, 306, 309, 313, 314

N

New York Herald, 38, 249

New York Journal, 16, 21, 42, 102, 115, 125, 156, 212

New York World, 24, 41, 42, 212

Non-combatants, 85, 94, 98, 162

P

Polo de Bernabé, 273, 310, 311, 314, 315, 316, 321

Presentados, 15

President Cleveland, 14, 18, 26, 27, 31, 34, 60, 64, 285

PROCLAMATION, 81, 129, 322, 323, 325, 326

Pulitzer, 24, 25, 27, 41

R

Reconcentración, 22

Roosevelt, 36, 121

S

Sagasta, 37, 38, 40, 74, 81, 95, 96, 110, 121, 225, 284, 289, 290, 300, 301, 305, 306

Santiago, 10, 30, 31, 70, 71, 90, 105, 136, 137, 138, 139, 141, 142, 143, 144, 147, 148, 149, 153, 154, 155, 157, 158, 159, 246, 247, 265, 267, 295, 296, 297

Santos Guzmán, 219, 221, 224, 225, 248, 249, 253

Senator Foraker, 229, 231, 250, 254, 255, 261, 265

Senator Frye, 181, 196, 198, 248, 253, 270

Senator Gray, 213, 248, 250, 253, 256

Senator Morgan, 250, 254, 255, 260

Sherman, 76, 77, 84, 101, 273, 275, 276, 292, 293, 294, 295, 296, 311, 313, 314, 315, 316, 318, 319, 321, 322, 323, 327

Stephen Crane, 24

T

The Express, 95, 96

Thomas Jefferson, 26

Torpedo, 168, 181, 182, 183, 185, 186, 188, 189, 190, 192, 193, 194, 196, 199, 201, 205, 206, 208, 250, 256, 292

V

Voluntarios, 16

W

Washington, 5, 19, 23, 28, 31, 35, 36, 38, 40, 41, 42, 64, 69, 71, 77, 78, 81, 84, 93, 98, 99, 100, 101, 107, 109, 110, 114, 122, 125, 126, 130, 141, 150, 151, 152, 163, 165, 168, 181, 196, 198, 205, 206, 210, 230, 238, 263, 271, 273, 275, 279, 280, 285, 287, 289, 290, 292, 293, 294, 295, 296, 305, 309, 311, 313, 315, 318, 319, 321, 322, 323, 325, 326, 327

Washington Post, 38

Weyler, 12, 15, 21, 22, 23, 33, 37, 38, 39, 60, 81, 84, 85, 87, 88, 92, 94, 99, 100, 101, 102, 105, 107, 108, 109, 110, 116, 119, 125, 129, 160, 179, 206, 219, 221, 222, 223, 224, 225, 226, 248, 249, 250, 253, 254, 257, 259, 264, 267, 276, 283, 285, 291, 328

Woodford, 35, 36, 37, 273, 274, 275, 284, 286, 287, 292, 293, 294, 295, 297, 299, 300, 301, 304, 305, 306, 308, 309, 310, 311, 313, 314, 315, 316, 318, 319, 321, 322

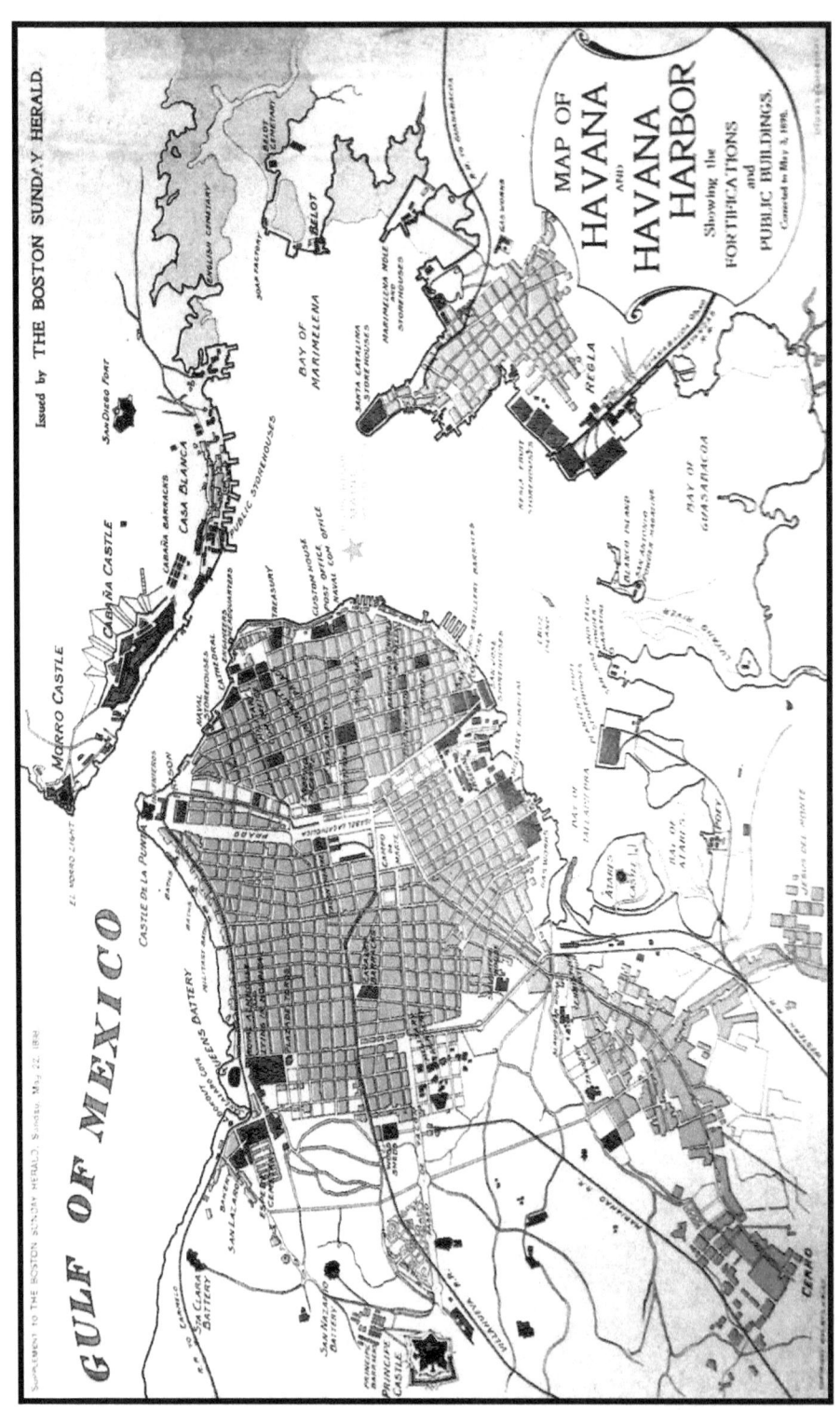

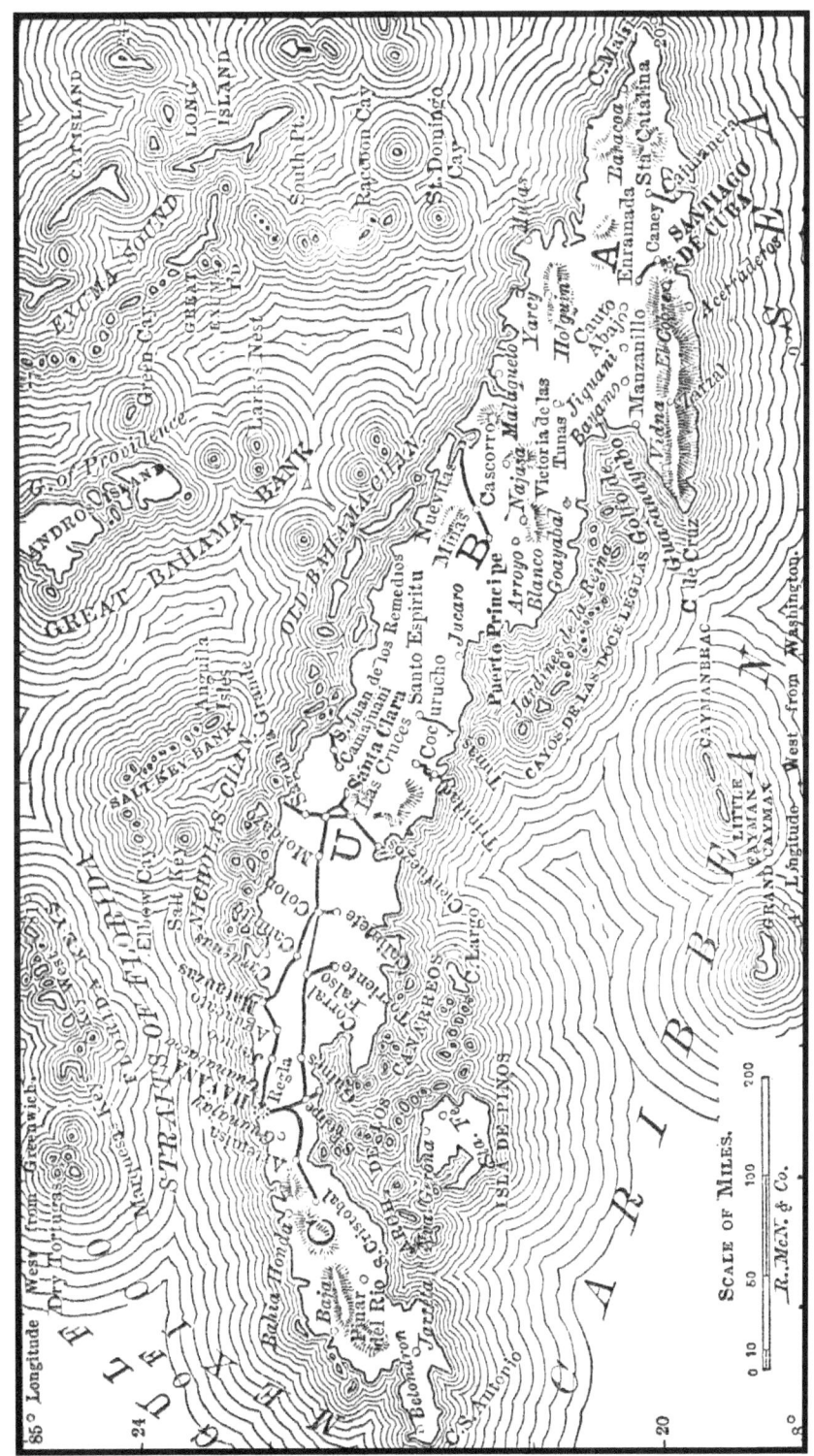

PUTTING YELLOW JOURNALISM IN ITS PLACE.

The US Army reacts to Yellow Journalism

The origin of the term **Yellow Journalism** was probably the yellow color of the Spanish flag... or perhaps a reference to the yellow fever that turned out to be a deadly weapon against American soldiers... or yellow meaning coward.

On August 17, 1898, US General Shafter expelled from Cuba all *New York Journal* and *New York World* journalists *"for their negative actions as unworthy members of an honorable craft"*... the *Washington Post* declared that the New York papers were *"predisposed causes of crime..."* the *Washington Times* urged people to call on legislators to prohibit *"these classes of news"* that the *NY Journal* and the *NY World* were offering...

 ***Raúl Eduardo Chao*** *received his PhD from Johns Hopkins University and after a brief stint in industry spent 18 years in academe, as Full Professor and Department Chairman at the* **Universities of Puerto Rico** *and* **Detroit**. *In 1986 he founded a very successful management consultancy, assisting companies and government agencies to develop positive work environments and process improvement techniques as the means to secure improvements in productivity and quality.* **The Systema Group** *had as clients many Fortune 100 companies and Federal and State organizations, both in the US and abroad. As its Chairman, Chao wrote a dozen books and numerous articles in newspapers and reviewed journals. He and his wife Olga live in Coral Gables, Florida and spend long periods of time in Paris.*

www.ingramcontent.com/pod-product-compliance
Lightning Source LLC
Chambersburg PA
CBHW060513080526
44586CB00012B/474